MW00827329

SEMIOTEXT(E) FOREIGN AGENTS SERIES

Published by Semiotext(e)
PO Box 629, South Pasadena, CA 91031
www.semiotexte.com

Special thanks to John Ebert.

Cover art by Elad Lassry, *Girl (Green/Red)*, 2011. C-print, painted frame, 14.5 x 11.5 x 1.5 inches.
Courtesy of David Kordansky Gallery, Los Angeles, CA.

Design by Hedi El Kholti

ISBN: 978-1-58435-130-6
Distributed by The MIT Press, Cambridge, Mass. and London, England
Printed in the United States of America

10 9 8 7 6 5 4 3 2

SIGNS AND MACHINES

CAPITALISM AND THE PRODUCTION OF SUBJECTIVITY

Maurizio Lazzarato

Translated by Joshua David Jordan

\<e\>

Contents

Introduction[1]

To say that desire is part of the infrastructure comes down to saying that subjectivity produces reality. Subjectivity is not an ideological superstructure.

At the time of Leninism, the government had to be overturned—the trade unions were economists, traitors—power had to go to the Soviets: in short, there was an idea, there was something. But here, really, there is no idea. There's nothing at all. There's the idea of macroeconomics, of a certain number of factors: unemployment, the market, money, all abstractions that have nothing at all to do with social reality.

—Félix Guattari, "Crise de production de subjectivité," Seminar of April 3, 1984

In a seminar in 1984, Félix Guattari argued that the crisis affecting the West since the early 1970s was, more than an economic or political crisis, a crisis of subjectivity. How are we to understand Guattari's claim?

Germany and Japan came out of the Second World War completely destroyed, under long-term occupation, both socially and psychologically decimated, with "no material assets—no raw materials, no reserve capital." What explains the economic miracle? "They rebuilt a prodigious 'capital of subjectivity' (capital in the form of knowledge, collective intelligence, the will to survive, etc.). Indeed, they invented a new type of subjectivity out of the devastation itself. The Japanese, in particular, recovered aspects of their archaic subjectivity, converting them into the most 'advanced' forms of social and material production. [...] The latter represents a kind of industrial complex for the production of subjectivity, one enabling a multiplicity of creative processes to emerge, certain of which are, however, highly alienating."[2]

Capitalism "launches (subjective) models the way the automobile industry launches a new line of cars."[3] Indeed, the central project of capitalist politics consists in the articulation of economic, technological, and social flows with the production of subjectivity in such a way that political economy is identical with "subjective economy." Guattari's working hypothesis must be revived and applied to current circumstances; and we must start by acknowledging that neoliberalism has failed to articulate the relation between these two economies.

Guattari further observes capitalism's capacity to foresee and resolve systemic crises through apparatuses and safeguards that it came to master following the Great Depression. Today, the weakness of capitalism lies in the production of subjectivity. As a consequence, systemic crisis and the crisis in the production of subjectivity are strictly interlinked. It is impossible to separate economic, political, and social processes from the processes of subjectivation occurring within them.

With neoliberal deterritorialization, no new production of subjectivity takes place. On the other hand, neoliberalism has destroyed previous social relations and their forms of subjectivation (worker, communist, or social-democrat subjectivation or national subjectivity, bourgeois subjectivity, etc.). Nor does neoliberalism's promotion of the entrepreneur—with which Foucault associates the subjective mobilization management requires in all forms of economic activity—offer any kind of solution to the problem. Quite the contrary. Capital has always required a territory beyond the market and the corporation and a subjectivity that is not that of the entrepreneur; for although the entrepreneur, the business, and the market make up the economy, they also break up society.

Hence the long-standing recourse to pre-capitalist territories and values, to long-established morals and religions, and to the formidable modern subjectivations of nationalism, racism, and fascism which aim to maintain the social ties capitalism continually undermines. Today, the ubiquity of entrepreneurial subjectivation, manifest in the drive to transform every individual into a business, has resulted in a number of paradoxes. The autonomy, initiative, and subjective commitment demanded of each of us constitute new norms of employability and, therefore, strictly speaking, a heteronomy. At the same time, the injunction imposed on the individual to act, take the initiative, and undertake risks has led to widespread depression, a *maladie du siècle*, the refusal to accept homogenization, and, finally, the impoverishment of existence brought on by the individual "success" of the entrepreneurial model.

For the majority of the population, to become an economic subject ("human capital," "entrepreneur of the self") means no more than being compelled to manage declining wages and income, precarity, unemployment, and poverty in the same way one would manage a corporate balance-sheet. As the crisis wrought by repeated "financial" debacles has worsened, capitalism has abandoned its rhetoric of the knowledge or information society along with its dazzling subjectivations (cognitive workers, "manipulators of symbols," creative self-starters and luminaries). The crisis has brought debt and its modes of subjection to the fore in the figure of the indebted man. Now that the promises of wealth for all through hard work, credit, and finance have proved empty, the class struggle has turned to the protection of creditors and owners of "securities." In the present crisis, in order for the power of private property to assert itself, the articulation of "production" and the "production of subjectivity" relies on debt and the indebted man.

Obviously, we are talking about a negative subjection, the most obvious indication that flows of knowledge, action, and mobility, although continually solicited, lead only to repressive and regressive subjectivation. The indebted man, at once guilty and responsible for his lot, must take on himself the economic, social, and political failures of the neoliberal power bloc, exactly those failures externalized by the State and business onto society.

It is no longer a matter of innovation, creativity, knowledge, or culture but of the "flight" of owners of capital whose "exodus" consists in their plundering the welfare state while refusing to pay taxes. In this way, the univocity of the concept of production (both economic and subjective) allows us to see that the financial crisis is not only about economics, it is also a crisis of neoliberal governmentality whose drive to turn every individual into an owner, a business, and a shareholder has miserably run aground with the collapse of the American real-estate market.

Japan is emblematic of the impossibility of resolving the crisis afflicting the country since the 1990s without a new model of subjectivity. Like every other country in the world, Japan is now post-Fordist, yet more than any other country it has had the greatest difficulty replacing the Fordist "capital of subjectivity" (full employment, a job for life, the ethics of work, etc.) that made it rich. It is not enough to inject astronomical sums into the economy; it is not enough to stabilize the banks, weaken and destabilize the job market, impoverish workers, and so on, in order to promote growth. To new social, economic, and political conditions, subjectivity must be made to correspond, one cognizant of those conditions and able to persist within them. It is in this sense that the Japanese financial and economic crisis is above all a crisis in the government of behavior. Economics and subjectivity go hand in hand.

The unions and political parties on the "left" provide no solutions to these problems because they too have no alternative subjectivities on offer. The people, the working class, labor, producers, and employment no longer have a hold on subjectivity, no longer function as vectors of subjectivation.

Today's critical theories similarly fail to account for the relationship between capitalism and processes of subjectivation. Cognitive capitalism, the information society, and cultural capitalism (Rifkin) capture the relationship but do so all too reductively. On the one hand, knowledge, information, and culture are far from sufficient to cover the multiplicity of economies that constitutes "production." On the other hand, their subjective avatars (cognitive workers, "manipulators of symbols," etc.) fall short of the multiple modes of subjection and political subjectivation that contribute to the "production of subjectivity." Their claim to found a hegemonic paradigm for production and the production of subjectivity is belied by the fact that the fate of the class struggle, as the crisis has shown, is not being played out in the domains of knowledge, information, or culture.

While these theories make short shrift of the relationship between production and the production of subjectivity, Jacques Rancière and Alain Badiou neglect it completely. For them, one simply has nothing to do with the other. Instead, they assert the need to conceive a radical separation between "economics" and "subjectivity," thereby developing an economistic conception of the economy and an utterly "political" or "idealist" conception of subjectivity.

Despite the rise of public and private apparatuses for the production, adaptation, and control of subjectivity, apparatuses whose authoritarianism has only intensified during the crisis, we must insist with Guattari that subjectivity still has no ground or means for subjectivation. "This is a major crisis. A crisis of what? In my opinion, it is a major crisis because the problem that's at the tip of everyone's tongue is the following: Shit, we've got to at least have a religion, an idea! [...] we can't leave everything up in the air like this!"[4]

But what does the concept of the production of subjectivity entail? What is meant by subjectivation and, in particular, political subjectivation?

In capitalism, the production of subjectivity works in two ways through what Deleuze and Guattari call apparatuses [*dispositifs*] of social subjection and machinic enslavement.

Social subjection equips us with a subjectivity, assigning us an identity, a sex, a body, a profession, a nationality, and so on. In response to the needs of the social division of labor, it in this way manufactures individuated subjects, their consciousness, representations, and behavior.

But the production of the individuated subject is coupled with a completely different process and a completely different hold on subjectivity that proceeds through desubjectivation. Machinic enslavement dismantles the individuated subject, consciousness, and representations, acting on both the pre-individual and supra-individual levels.

Among contemporary critical theories (those of Badiou, cognitive capitalism, Judith Butler, Slajov Žižek, Rancière, etc.), it is largely a question of subjectivity, the subject, subjectivation, and the distribution of the sensible. But what they neglect is how capitalism specifically functions—that is, through "machinic enslavements." These critical theories seem to have lost sight of what Marx had to say about the essentially machinic nature of capitalism: "machinery appears as the most adequate form of fixed capital; and the latter, in so far as capital can be considered as being related to itself, is the most adequate form of capital in general."[5]

Such is even more the case today given that, unlike in Marx's time, machinisms have invaded our daily lives; they now "assist" our ways of speaking, hearing, seeing, writing, and feeling by constituting what one might call "constant social capital."

Nowhere in their analyses do we encounter these technical and social machines in which "humans" and "non-humans" function together as component parts in corporate, welfare-state, and media assemblages. Rancière and Badiou have radically elided them altogether. Thus machines and machinic assemblages can be found everywhere except in contemporary critical theory.

Now, capitalism reveals a twofold cynicism: the "humanist" cynicism of assigning us individuality and pre-established roles (worker, consumer, unemployed, man/woman, artist, etc.) in which individuals are necessarily alienated; and the "dehumanizing" cynicism of including us in an assemblage that no longer distinguishes between human and non-human, subject and object, or words and things.

Throughout this book, we will examine the difference and complementarity between apparatuses of "social subjection" and those of "machinic enslavement," for it is at their point of intersection that the production of subjectivity occurs. We will trace a cartography of the modalities of subjection and enslavement, those with which we will have to break in order to begin a process of subjectivation independent and autonomous of capitalism's hold on subjectivity, its modalities of production and forms of life.

It is therefore essential to understand that the subjectivity and subjectivations capitalism produces are meant for the "machine." Not primarily for the "technical machine" but for the "social machine," for the "megamachine," as Lewis Mumford calls it, which includes the technical machine as one of its products.

What are the conditions for a political and existential rupture at a time when the production of subjectivity constitutes the most fundamental of capitalist concerns? What are the instruments specific to the production of subjectivity such that its industrial and serial production by the State and the corporation might be thwarted? What model and what modalities of organization must be constructed for a subjectivation process that joins micro- and macropolitics?

In the 1980s, Michel Foucault and Guattari each followed different paths to arrive at the conclusion that the production of subjectivity and the constitution of the "relation to the self" were the sole contemporary political questions capable of pointing the way out of the impasse in which we still continue to founder. Each in their own way they revealed a new dimension irreducible to power and knowledge relations. As the power of self-positioning and existential affirmation (Guattari), the "relation to the self" (Foucault) derives—in its double sense of *originating in* and *drawing off*—from these relations. The subjective is not, however, dependent on them. For Foucault, taking the "care of the self" as one's starting point does not mean pursuing the ideal splendor of a "beautiful life" but rather inquiring into the overlap of "an aesthetics of existence" and a politics that corresponds to it. The problems of "an other world" and "an other life" arise together in a politically engaged life whose precondition is a break with established conventions, habits, and values. Nor does Guattari's aesthetic paradigm call for an aestheticization of the social and political but rather for making the production of subjectivity the central practice and concern of a new way of political action and organizing.

Subjectivation processes and their forms of organization have always given rise to crucial debates within the labor movement and have occasioned political ruptures and divisions between "reformists" and "revolutionaries."

The history of the labor movement remains incomprehensible if we refuse to see the "wars of subjectivity" (Guattari) in which the movement has engaged. "A certain type of worker during the Paris Commune became such a 'mutant' that the bourgeoisie had no choice but to exterminate him. They liquidated the Paris Commune just as they did, in a different time, the Protestants on Saint-Bartholomew's."[6]

The Bolsheviks did not explicitly think of inventing a new kind of militant subjectivity which would, among other things, respond to the Commune's defeat.[7]

Examining processes of political subjectivation by foregrounding the "micro-political" (Guattari) and the "micro-physical" (Foucault) dimensions of power does not dispense with the need to address and reconfigure the macro-political sphere.

It's an either/or: either someone, whoever it is, comes up with new methods for the production of subjectivity, whether Bolshevik, Maoist, or whatever; or the crisis will just keep on getting worse.[8]

In his way, Guattari not only remained faithful to Marx but to Lenin as well. Of course, the methods for the production of subjectivity that came out of Leninism (the party, the conception of the working class as vanguard, the "professional revolutionary," etc.) are no longer relevant to current class compositions. What Guattari retains from the Leninist experiment is the methodology: the need to break with "social-democracy," to construct tools for political innovation extending to the organizational modalities of subjectivity.

Just as the production of subjectivity cannot be separated from "economics," it cannot be separated from "politics." How must we conceive of political subjectivation? All political subjectivation entails a mutation and a reconversion of subjectivity that affects existence. It cannot only be political in the sense that both Rancière and Badiou give the term.

Subjective mutation is not primarily discursive; it does not primarily have to do with knowledge, information, or culture since it affects the nucleus of non-discursivity, non-knowledge, and non-acculturation lying at the heart of subjectivity. Subjective mutation is fundamentally an existential affirmation and apprehension of the self, others, and the world. And it is on the basis of this non-discursive, existential, and affective crystallization that new languages, new discourses, new knowledge, and a new politics can proliferate.

We will first examine this question from a specific perspective: the paradoxical relationship that the discursive—that is, what is actualized in language but also within the spatiotemporal coordinates of knowledge, culture, institutions, and the economy—maintains with the non-discursive, as the focal point of self-production, self-positioning, and existential affirmation.

The same critical theories that neglect the machinic specificity of capitalism also fail to problematize the relationship between the discursive and the existential. Indeed, they assign a central role to the former, that is, to language in the realm of politics (Rancière), "production" (cognitive capitalism, Paolo Virno), and the constitution of the subject (Žižek and Butler).

Structuralism may be dead, but language, which founds the structuralist paradigm, is still alive and well in these theories. To grasp the limits of the new "logocentrism," we will have to take a step backwards, returning to the critiques of structuralism and linguistics advanced in the 1960s and 70s by Guattari, Deleuze, and Foucault. In different ways, their critiques demoted language from the central role it was made to play in politics and subjectivation processes following the "linguistic turn" in analytic philosophy and Lacanian psychoanalysis. They set forth a new semiotic theory and a new theory of enunciation better able to register how signs function in these processes and in the economy. In particular, we will return to Guattari's semiotic theory. While affirming that each subjectivation process implies the operations of mixed, signifying, symbolic, and asignifying semiotics, Guattari considers the latter, as they operate in the economy, science, art, and machines, the specificity of capitalism.

What role and function do different signifying, symbolic, and asignifying semiotics have in *running* and *controlling* capitalist deterritorialization and reterritorialization? And what is their relationship with the subjectivation process?

Guattari and Foucault do not stop at deposing the "imperialism" of language over other modes of expression and other formations of subjectivity. While emphasizing the strategic importance of different semiotics for steering and controlling capitalist flows and subjectivity production, they argue that in order to bring together the conditions for rupture and subjective reconversion, *we must move beyond both language and semiotics*.

Further, they enact "a radical divorce" (Guattari) between pragmatic linguistics and existential pragmatics, between the semiotic logic that produces meaning and the pragmatics that produces existence and political rupture.

In the act of enunciation (in the same way as in every act of creation), a power of self-positioning, self-production, and a capacity to secrete one's own referent emerges, a power which has little to do with Saussurean "speech," the Lacanian "signifier," or the performatives and speech acts of analytic philosophy.

A force of self-affectation, self-affirmation, and self-positioning doubles power and knowledge relations, defying the powers and knowledge in place. It provides the conditions for rupture as well as for processes of political subjectivation—indeed, for processes of subjectivation *tout court*. The rules governing the production of the self are those "optional" and processual ones invented by constructing "sensible territories" and by a singularization of subjectivity (Guattari), by creating the alterity of "an other life" and "an other world" (Foucault). Hence the recourse, not to cognitive, linguistic, and informational methods and paradigms, but to political, ethical-aesthetic approaches and paradigms—the "aesthetic paradigm" of Guattari and the "aesthetics of existence" of Foucault.

Only as a mutation of subjectivity, as the crystallization of a new existence (Guattari), gains consistency can one attempt a new relationship to economic, linguistic, technical, social, and communicational flows.

To produce a new discourse, new knowledge, a new politics, one must traverse an unnamable point, a point of absolute non-narrative, non-culture, and non-knowledge. Thus the (tautological) absurdity of conceiving production as the production of knowledge *by way of* knowledge. Theories of cognitive and cultural capitalism and the information society, which are supposed to be theories of innovation and creativity, fail precisely to conceive the process through which "creation" and "innovation" occur, for language, knowledge, information, and culture are largely insufficient to these ends.

In order for political subjectivation to occur, it must necessarily traverse moments in which dominant significations are suspended and the hold of machinic enslavements is thrown off. Strikes, struggles, revolts, and riots constitute moments of rupture with and suspension of chronological time, of the neutralization of subjections and dominant significations. Immaculate, virginal subjectivities do not then appear but rather focal points, emergences, the beginnings of subjectivation whose actualization and proliferation depend on a constructive process that must articulate the relation between "production" and "subjectivation" in a new way.

But are the struggles, revolts, riots, and strikes that have spread around the globe in response to the violence of the crisis sufficient for instituting a political rupture with capitalism?

The analysis of the Soviet Revolution, which returns like a refrain in Deleuze and Guattari's work, offers certain, even if only formal, insights which help to understand the limits of the current political situation. In their work, the modes of subjectivity production are translated into politics. Under capitalism, processes of political subjectivation must both enter and break from economic, social, and political flows. The two operations are indispensable: start from the hold machinic enslavements and social subjections maintain over subjectivity and produce a rupture, which is always at the same time an invention and constitution of the self.[9]

"Revolution" erupts from history, that is, from economic, political, and social conditions while it simultaneously leaves these causes and conditions behind by creating new possibilities. It derives and, paradoxically, does not derive from history.

Viewed through the lens of post-May '68 struggles rather than as a historical reconstruction, the "Leninist rupture" is characterized by the coexistence of different orders: the order of causes and the order of desire (the existential, non-discursive dimension), the order of "preconscious investments" governed by causes and aims and the order of "unconscious revolutionary investments" which have as their cause a rupture in causality, the condition for opening new possibilitiess.

Such an opening, "prepared by the subterranean work of causes, aims, and interests," only becomes real through something of another order, by "a desire without aim or cause."[10]

Revolutionary possibility can always be identified by the impossibility it makes real, and by the fact that a *process* erupts secreting other systems of reference at the very place where the world was once closed. As in all creation (whether artistic, scientific, or social), the suspension of the ordinary course of things first of all affects subjectivity and its forms of expression by creating the conditions for new subjectivation. This process must be problematized.[11]

Although the forms of Leninist organization are today neither possible nor desirable, the "break with causality," the turn from the expected course of things, the impossible that becomes real, the organization and metamorphosis of subjectivity—these remain the burning questions of all revolutionary movements.

> And even though one can and must assign the objective factors […] within causal series that made such a rupture possible, the Bolshevik group […] becomes aware of the immediate possibility of a proletarian revolution that would not follow the anticipated causal order of the relations of forces.[12]

Today it is easy to identify the chain of causes, aims, and interests at work in the present crisis. The choices are endless. What is lacking are precisely the characteristics of revolutionary action: the "rupture with causality," the possibility of inventing a politics, like that of the "Leninist rupture," that does more than follow the chain of causes, aims, and interests already in play. In order to take on consistency, in order to install its modes of organization and metamorphose subjectivity, the revolutionary event, in its break with causality, must transform the social, economic, and political conditions from which it arises and ward off the action of the State, the medias, reactionary forces, and so on. It is the complexity of this process that seems, for the moment, to escape political movements. We have in fact a proliferation of political experimentations that appear then just as quickly fade because they are unable to initiate the modes of macropolitical, reproducible, and generalizable subjectivation.

For its part, capital is also in a "subjective" impasse which forces it to suspend democracy and adopt forms of authoritarian governance.

The current crisis now produces only negative and regressive subjections (the indebted man), and capitalism is unable to articulate production and the production of subjectivity other than by reasserting the need to protect the owners of capital. The crisis is nowhere near the end. Given this, the theoretical tools we intend to develop here will hopefully prove useful for conceiving the conditions of political subjectivation, one which is at the same time an existential mutation antithetical to capitalism, whose crisis is already of historic proportions.

The problem in the 1960s was overturning the two behemoths of the party and the union, which prevented all political innovation and blocked the emergence of new subjects and new ways of conceiving and practicing politics (micropolitics: young workers, minorities, the women's movement, etc.). Today, with the party gone and unions completely integrated into capitalist logic, macropolitical action and its forms of organization, based on an irreducible multiplicity of subjectivation processes, are at the heart of our urgent underlying question: "What is to be done?"

1

Production and the Production of Subjectivity:

Between Social Subjection and Machinic Enslavement

> Of the two definitions of a manufacture given by Ure, and cited
> by Marx, the first relates machines to the men who tend them,
> while the second relates the machines and the men, "mechanical
> and intellectual organs," to the manufacture as the full body
> that engineers them. In fact, the second definition is literal and
> concrete.
>
> —Félix Guattari, *Chaosophy*

> It is not machines that have created capitalism, but capitalism that
> creates machines, and that is constantly introducing breaks and
> cleavages through which it revolutionizes its technical modes of
> production.
>
> —Gilles Deleuze and Félix Guattari, *Anti-Oedipus*

1. Social Subjection and Machinic Enslavement

Guattari and Deleuze bring to fulfillment the discoveries of
Marx and classical political economy: the production of wealth
depends on abstract, unqualified, subjective activity irreducible
to the domain of either political or linguistic representation. The

production of wealth (and production, period) operates at the intersection of two heterogeneous power apparatuses—social subjection and machinic enslavement. What is called economy is the assemblage of this dual investment of subjectivity such that, as Guattari puts it, "one must enter the field of subjective economy and stop concentrating only on political economy," which was incapable of realizing the full ramifications of its discoveries.

By assigning us an individual subjectivity, an identity, sex, profession, nationality, and so forth, social subjection produces and distributes places and roles within and for the social division of labor. Through language it creates a signifying and representational web from which no one escapes. Social subjection produces an "individuated subject" whose paradigmatic form in neoliberalism has been that of "human capital" and the "entrepreneur of the self." The last avatar of individualism, which has made the person the center and source of action, emerged with the financial crisis during which the injunction to become "human capital" has been transformed into the negative and regressive figure of the indebted man. The individual is still guilty and responsible for his fate except that today he is fated to debt.

Foucault describes the mode of governmentality of "subjects" who must think of and produce themselves as actors in their own assignations such that domination issues from the subjects themselves (self-exploitation, self-domination). The user's, worker's, and consumer's actions and the divisions man/woman, parent/child, teacher/student, and so on, are invested with knowledge, practices, and norms—whether sociological, psychological, managerial, or disciplinary—which solicit, encourage, and motivate the production of individuals consequently alienated within the social and gendered division of labor.

As Marx had already argued, social subjection is a process by which capital relations become personified; the "capitalist" acts as "personified capital," that is, as a function derived from capital flows. Thus the factory worker is "personified labor," a function derived from variable capital flows, and individual "persons" are social persons derived from abstract quantities.

But this is only one of the ways in which capitalism acts on subjectivity. An entirely different process and an entirely different capture of subjectivity—"machinic enslavement"—come to be superimposed on the production of the individuated subject or person. Unlike social subjection, machinic enslavement occurs via desubjectivation by mobilizing functional and operational, non-representational and asignifying, rather than linguistic and representational, semiotics.

In machinic enslavement, the individual is no longer instituted as an "individuated subject," "economic subject" (human capital, entrepreneur of the self), or "citizen." He is instead considered a gear, a cog, a component part in the "business" and "financial system" assemblages, in the media assemblage, and the "welfare-state" assemblage and its collective institutions (schools, hospitals, museums, theaters, television, Internet, etc.). Enslavement is a concept that Deleuze and Guattari borrowed explicitly from cybernetics and the science of automation. It means the "management" or "government" of the components of a system. A technological system enslaves ("governs" or "manages") variables (temperature, pressure, force, speed, output, etc.), ensuring the cohesion and equilibrium of the functioning of the whole. Enslavement is the mode of control and regulation ("government") of a technical or social machine such as a factory, business, or communications system. It replaces the "human slavery" of ancient imperial systems

(Egyptian, Chinese, etc.) and is thus a mode of command, regulation, and government "assisted" by technology and, as such, represents a feature specific to capitalism.

Deleuze describes precisely the types of subjectivity over which this dual power apparatus exercises control. Subjection produces and subjects individuals, whereas in enslavement "[i]ndividuals becomes '*dividuals*,' and masses become samples, data, markets, or '*banks*.'"[1]

The dividual "functions" in enslavement in the same way as the "non-human" component parts of technical machines, as organizational procedures, semiotics, and so on.

Subjection manufactures a subject in relation to an external object (a machine, a communications apparatus, money, public services, etc.) of which the subject *makes use* and with which he acts. In subjection the individual works or communicates with another individuated subject by way of an object-machine, which functions as the "means" or mediation of his actions or use. The "subject-object" logic according to which social subjection functions is a "human, all too human" logic.

Machinic enslavement, on the other hand, does not bother with subject/object, words/things, or nature/culture dualisms. The dividual does not stand opposite machines or make use of an external object; the dividual is contiguous with machines. Together they constitute a "humans-machines" apparatus in which humans and machines are but recurrent and interchangeable parts of a production, communications, consumption, etc., process well exceeds them.

We no longer act nor even *make use*[2] of something, if by act and use we understand functions of the subject. Instead, we constitute mere inputs and outputs, *a point of conjunction or disjunction* in the economic, social, or communicational processes run and governed by enslavement.

The subject/object, human/machine, or agent/instrument relationship gives way to a total configuration in which there is a convergence/assemblage of forces that do not split into "living" and "dead," subjective and objective, but are all variously "animated" (physical and sub-physical forces of matter, human and subhuman forces of "body and mind," machine forces, the power of signs, etc.). In enslavement, relations among agents and signs indeed exist, but they are not intersubjective, the agents are not people, and the semiotics are not representational. Human agents, like non-human agents, function as points of "connection, junction, and disjunction" of flows and as the networks making up the corporate, collective assemblage, the communications system, and so on.

Not only is the dividual *of a piece with* the machinic assemblage but he is also *torn to pieces* by it: the component parts of subjectivity (intelligence, affects, sensations, cognition, memory, physical force) are no longer unified in an "I," they no longer have an individuated subject as referent. Intelligence, affects, sensations, cognition, memory, and physical force are now components whose synthesis no longer lies in the person but in the assemblage or process (corporations, media, public services, education, etc.).

Enslavement does not work with "subjects" and "objects," it works on their deterritorialization (or their decodification), that is, with the molecular components, the non-individuated intensive, subhuman potentialities of subjectivity, and the non-individuated, intensive, molecular component parts and potentialities of matter and machines. Science transforms matter into decoded flows; by going from processing "forces" to molecules and atoms and continuously intensifying deterritorialization, it mobilizes even their chemical and nuclear elements. Money and finance are perfectly capable of deterritorializing (or decodifying) social "matter," as the last thirty years of neoliberalism have shown. They undermine and circumvent laws (in particular those dealing with labor) as well as the codes of social, economic, and political subjects established with Fordism. Employees and their institutions, employers and their factories, and the State and its welfare apparatus have been subjected to deterritorialization processes that have radically transformed them.

Enslavement works with decoded flows (abstract work flows, monetary flows, sign flows, etc.) which are not centered on the individual and human subjectivity but on enormous social machinisms (corporations, the collective infrastructures of the welfare state, communications systems, etc.).

Capital is not a mere relationship among "people," nor is it reducible to an intersubjective relationship as Hannah Arendt suggests, for whom there is not an ounce of matter in human action. A power relation exists but one constituted by social machines and "assisted" by technical machines.

Foucault's analysis of power is concerned with machinism as well. The panopticon "is an important mechanism, for it automatizes and deindividualizes power. Power has its principle not so much in a person as in a certain concerted distribution of bodies, surfaces, lights, gazes; in an arrangement whose internal mechanisms produce the relation in which they are caught up. [...] There is a machinery that assures dissymmetry, disequilibrium, difference. Consequently, it does not matter who exercises power. Any individual, taken almost at random, can operate the machine."[3]

As in Guattari and Deleuze, the panopticon functions in a diagrammatic, that is, non-representational way. It is a "diagram of a mechanism of power," "a figure of political technology that may and must be detached from any specific use" (an "abstract machine," as Deleuze and Guattari put it), which is "destined to spread throughout the social body."[4]

To say that the neoliberal economy is a subjective economy does not mean that it promises a new "humanization" of the alienated subject through industrial capitalism, but only that subjectivity exists for the machine, that subjective components are functions of enslavement.

Subjections and subjectivations serve these social and technical machines and every person's functions and roles are assigned through them. In capitalism, power relations are not personal as in feudal societies (or in Rancière's "distribution of the sensible"), they issue from the organization of machinisms.[5]

The fact that in the current economy one speaks, communicates, and expresses oneself does not bring us back to the linguistic turn, to its logocentrism, and the intersubjectivity of speakers; it is indicative rather of a machine-centric world in which one speaks, communicates, and acts "assisted" by all kinds of mechanical, thermodynamic, cybernetic, and computer machines.

2. Human/Machine Versus Humans/Machines

We find the dual presence of subjection and enslavement in ergonomics.

"Humans-machines" (in the plural) systems must not be considered a mere collection of "human-machine" (in the singular) workplaces since they differ in nature from the subject/object, human/machine "dyad." In humans-machines systems, where "numerous human and non-human elements interact [...] the component parts of all work can be expressed in terms of information." But here the "anthropocentric aspect of the notion of information disappears."[6] In ergonomics, one no longer speaks of "signal-organism-response," nor does one employ the model of communication theory, in which exchanges are realized between individuated subjects and allow for "appropriate, although limited, emitter-receptor analogies."[7] In ergonomics, one speaks of "input and output," which have nothing to do with anthropomorphism.

To move from ergonomic terms to the philosophical concepts articulated by Guattari, enslavement involves neither subjects nor objects as such but "ontologically ambiguous" entities, hybrids, "objectivities/subjectivities," in other words, "subject-object biface" entities.

"Objects," machines, protocols, diagrams, graphs, and software lose their "objectivity" and become capable of constituting vectors of "proto-subjectivation" or focal points of "proto-enunciation." That machines, objects (and signs), do so means that they *suggest, enable, solicit, prompt, encourage, and prohibit certain actions, thoughts, and affects or promote others*. Very significantly, Foucault uses the same verbs to describe how power relations function. Machines, objects (and signs), act in precisely the same way as an "action upon an action" (Foucault). This must not be understood merely as a relation of one human being with another. Non-humans contribute just as humans do to defining the framework and conditions of action. One always acts within an assemblage, a collective, where machines, objects, and signs are at the same time "agents."

If subjection calls on consciousness and the representations of the subject, machinic enslavement activates both much more and much less than consciousness and representation, in other words, much more and much less than the person, the individual, and intersubjectivity.

Machinic enslavement activates *pre-personal, pre-cognitive*, and *preverbal* forces (perception, sense, affects, desire) as well as *supra-personal* forces (machinic, linguistic, social, media, economic systems, etc.), which, beyond the subject and individuated relations (intersubjectivity), multiply "possibilities."[8]

Here it is not a matter of civil society or political institutions, dependent on "individuated subjects," the person, the "rights of man," and citizens. Rather, enslavement is the mode in which science, economics, communications networks, and the welfare state function. Guattari calls this domain, whose ("diagrammatic") activities involve neither representation nor consciousness, machinic (or molecular) in order to distinguish it from the world of individuated subjects. The forms of diagrammatic (non-representational) activity specific to machinic enslavement are heterogeneous to the representational activities of the political system as well as to the representational functions of language.

Molecular or machinic—the terms are synonymous—indicate a difference in kind and not in scale with the molar dimension of individuated subjects, representation, and consciousness.

The two domains differ in other ways as well. Subjection refers to the transcendence of models into which subjectivities must fit and to which they must conform (man/woman, capitalist/worker, teacher/student, consumer, user, etc.), whereas enslavement instead refers to the immanence of the process as it unfolds, to the becoming that involves the molecular, machinic, and supra-individual dimension of subjectivity.

Capitalism owes its efficacy and power to the fact that it joins two heterogeneous dimensions of subjectivity—the molar and molecular, individual and pre-individual, representational and pre-representational (or post-representational).

3. The Egyptian Megamachine: The First Form of Enslavement

In machinic enslavement lie the novelty, the secret, and the power specific to capitalism, which exploits the molecular, pre-personal, and supra-personal activities of subjectivity. The enormous productivity and potentiality of science, and of the capitalist economy, have to do with the nature of these machinic assemblages. Indeed, capitalist machinic enslavement is a "resurrection" of what Lewis Mumford calls the "myth of the machine," the archaic megamachine—the Egypt of the pyramids. For Deleuze and Guattari, the latter marks the first emergence of enslavement, in which "human beings themselves are constituent pieces of a machine they compose among themselves and with other things (animals, tools) under the control and direction of a higher unity."[9]

The archaic megamachine is not primarily technological but social since it is composed of "a multitude of uniform, specialized, interchangeable" parts "rigorously marshaled together and coordinated in a process centrally organized and centrally directed"[10] and of very simple technical machines: the ramp and the lever (the wheel, pulley, and screw had not yet been invented). Mumford's megamachine is, along with Simondon's technical objects and the celibate machines of the avant-gardes (Duchamp), one of the theories Deleuze and Guattari appropriate in their own thought. One finds in Mumford's work many of the elements that determine the complex conditions for their concept of the machine: human flows whose "mechanization" long preceded the mechanization of human tools; the machinic phylum of the "'simple machines' of classical mechanics" (the result of previous inventions and practices); sign flows ("translating speech into graphic record not merely made it possible to transmit impulses and messages throughout the system, but to fix accountability when written orders were not carried out").[11]

And then there is the incorporeal dimension of this universe of values: the myth of divine-right royalty, the sun cult, and "cosmic fantasies" alone can guarantee the transformation of "men into mechanical objects [...] assembling these objects in a machine." The megamachine also requires the "production of subjectivity," a subjectivity for the machine, a subjectivity for enslavement. Workers had "minds of a new order: mechanically conditioned, executing each task in strict obedience to instructions, infinitely patient, limiting their response to the word of command."[12] But the megamachine in addition necessitates subjectivations (the priesthood and bureaucracy) that ensure, respectively, "a reliable organization of knowledge, natural and supernatural; and an elaborate structure for giving orders, carrying them out, and following them through."[13] The bureaucracy and caste system are part of an administration defined as a machinism rather than a structure.

Beginning in the sixteenth century, capitalism, by reviving the megamachine, profoundly changed the forms of enslavement. It progressively reduced the number of "recalcitrant and unreliable" human operators and multiplied the more reliable "mechanical, electronic, and chemical" ones.[14]

The history of neoliberalism is marked by a "generalized enslavement" that is today's megamachine. Its apparatuses go well beyond the factory, which is but one site of their initial actualization. New social and technical machines have taken hold over behavior and attitudes not only in the workplace and in labor generally, but also in daily life. In our most "human" actions (speaking, communicating, writing, thinking, etc.), we are "assisted" by a new generation of machines. "If motorized machines constituted the second age of the technical machine, cybernetic and informational machines form a third age that reconstructs a generalized regime of enslavement: recurrent and reversible 'humans-machines systems' replace the old nonrecurrent and nonreversible relations of subjection between the two elements. In the organic composition of capital, variable capital defines a regime of subjection of the worker (human surplus value), the principal framework of which is the business or factory. But with automation comes a progressive increase in the proportion of constant capital; we then see a new kind of enslavement: at the same time the work regime changes, surplus value becomes machinic, and the framework expands to all of society."[15]

4. The Functions of Subjection

Capitalism is characterized by a dual regime of subjectivity, subjection—centered on the subjectivity of the individual subject—and enslavement, involving a multiplicity of human and non-human subjectivities and proto-subjectivities. Although heterogeneous, these two regimes or processes of subjectivity are complementary, interdependent, and contribute to the functioning of capitalism.

Capitalism is essentially a series of machinisms, although the latter's subjectivations and personifications can never be reduced to mere copies mechanically derived from the conditions of these apparatuses. On the contrary, machinisms imply social instruments for decision-making, management, reaction, technocracy, and bureaucracy which cannot be deduced simply from the functions of technical machines.

Subjections not only generate the "persons" of capitalist and worker but also those that make the social machine run (man/woman, teacher/student, the bureaucrat and functionary, etc.).

The social sciences arose in order to facilitate the production of individuated subjects. Linguistics makes the person the origin of enunciation, psychoanalysis constructs a familial unconscious for him (one "structured like a language"), which serve to equip the individual subject with a representational and personological unconscious. In turn, economics endows the individual with a rationality that establishes him as a person free to choose and decide, while political science makes him the agent of individual rights, which it is imperative he transfer to representatives in order to avoid a war of all against all. But it is perhaps property rights that form the most successful individualizing apparatuses of subjectivation. By dividing the assemblage into subjects and objects, they empty the latter (nature, animal, machines, objects, signs, etc.) of all creativity, of the capacity to act and produce, which they assign only to individual subjects whose principal characteristic is being an "owner" (an owner or non-owner).

Property is not only an apparatus for economic appropriation but also for the capture and exploitation of non-human subjectivities and machinic proto-subjectivities. By ensuring that creation and production are uniquely the feats of "man," it uses the "world," emptied of all "soul," as its own "object," as the instrument of its activities, as the means to its ends.

Subjection plays an essential role, because it allows capitalism to establish different molar hierarchies: a first hierarchy between man (as a species) and nature and a second hierarchy within culture between man (gender, white, adult, etc.) and woman, child, and so on. These two hierarchies are the antecedents fundamental to the more specifically economic hierarchies.[16]

Subjection imposes these hierarchies by operating at the intersection of the machinic molecular and the social molar, by converting and reducing multiplicity to a series of dualisms (subject/object, nature/culture, individual/society, owner/non-owner). This translation of machinic multiplicity into dualisms not only enables hierarchization but also totalization, of which holistic Durkheimian theory constitutes the theoretical prototype.

Revolutionary political action must also position itself between the molecular and the molar, although with a completely different end in view. First, that of converting the machinic dimension into forms of subjectivation that critique, reconfigure, and redistribute these molar dualisms and the roles and functions to which we are assigned within the division of labor.

Second, that of taking enslavement's desubjectivation as an opportunity for producing something other than paranoid, productivist, consumerist individualism. This is how we avoid the false choice between being condemned to function like one component part among others in the social machinery and being condemned to become an individual subject, human capital (worker, consumer, user, debtor), "man."

Subjection works against this possibility by assuring the reterritorialization and recomposition of subjective components "freed" by the machinic enslavement of the individuated "subject." The latter is burdened with guilt, fear, and personal responsibility.

The concept of subjection, although with important variations, is a common thread in the philosophy and sociology of the last fifty years. However, "machinic enslavement" is Deleuze and Guattari's original contribution to our understanding of how capitalism works.

Theories that only account for "social subjection" while totally neglecting machinic enslavement (Rancière's and Badiou's, for example) end up distorting capitalism so much that they can hardly explain the processes of "political" subjectivation that are supposed to take place. If one considers capitalism only from the point of view of "subjection" or the distribution of the sensible, one loses the specificity of the forms of machinic desubjectivation and their diagrammatic functioning. Without accounting for enslavements, one risks confusing, as Rancière and Badiou do, Greek democracy with capitalism, the work of artisans and slaves with the machinic work of the "workers," Marx with Plato.[17]

Even Foucault's concept of governmentality can be improved and developed by combining social subjection and machinic enslavement. To the pastoral power exercised on individuals, one must add another, different type of power and control acting on "dividuals," exercised not by the State but by private enterprise. In reality, since the early twentieth century, governmentality has increasingly meant the "government of dividuals."

With the rise of advertising in the 1920s and later the advent of television, an ever well-organized machine has developed of which Google and Facebook can be considered the crowning achievements. The latter make up immense "databanks" which function as marketing apparatuses. They gather, select, and sell millions of data on our behavior, purchases, reading habits, favorite films, tastes, clothes, and food preferences as well as the way we spend our "free time." The information concerns "dividuals," whose profiles, composed of the convergence of data, are mere relays of inputs and outputs in production-consumption machines.

"Dividuals" have a statistical existence controlled by apparatuses whose operations differ from the individualization carried out by pastoral power, which is exercised on "real" individuals. The governmentality of dividuals, managed by flows, networks, and machines, not only plays a part in the individual's representations and conscious behavior but in the desires, beliefs, and sub-representational reality of subjectivity. Governmentality is practiced at the junction of the individual and the dividual, the individual as the dividual's subjectivation.

Enslavement does not operate through repression or ideology. It employs modeling and modulating techniques that bear on the "very spirit of life and human activity." It takes over human beings "from the inside," on the *pre-personal* (pre-cognitive and preverbal) level, as well as "from the outside," on the *supra-personal* level, by assigning them certain modes of perception and sensibility and manufacturing an unconscious. Machinic enslavement formats the basic functioning of perceptive, sensory, affective, cognitive, and linguistic behavior.

We are thus subject to a dual regime. We are, on the one hand, enslaved to the machinic apparatuses of business, communications, the welfare state, and finance; on the other hand, we are subjected to a stratification of power that assigns us roles and social and productive functions as users, producers, television viewers, and so on.

Subjection and enslavement are functions that can be assured by a single person or distributed among different people. Take the example of a corporation: salaried employees are enslaved to the automatization of procedures, machines, and the division of labor, functioning as the "inputs" and "outputs" of the process. But when a breakdown, an accident, or a malfunction occurs, the subject-function, consciousness, and representations must be mobilized in order to "recover" from the incident, explain it, and mitigate its effects with a view to returning the automatic functions and enslavement procedures to their normal state.

Political action must therefore be understood in a new way, since it must operate against both subjection and enslavement, refusing the former's injunction to inhabit certain places and roles in the social distribution of labor while constructing, problematizing, and reconfiguring the machinic assemblage, in other words, a world and its possibilities. Do machinisms open possibilities and potentialities for emancipation or do they ineluctably lead to catastrophe? Can one build new existential territories by combating enslavements and the currently deterritorialized, technologized present?

CAPITAL AS A SEMIOTIC OPERATOR: SIGNIFYING SEMIOTICS AND ASIGNIFYING SEMIOTICS

Capital is not only a linguistic but also a "semiotic operator." The distinction is fundamental because it establishes that flows of signs, as much as labor and money flows, are the conditions of "production."

From a semiotic perspective, machinic enslavement and social subjection entail distinct regimes of signs. Social subjection mobilizes signifying semiotics, in particular language, aimed at consciousness and mobilizes representations with a view to constituting an individuated subject ("human capital"). On the other hand, machinic enslavement functions based on asignifying semiotics (stock market indices, currency, mathematical equations, diagrams, computer languages, national and corporate accounting, etc.) which do not involve consciousness and representations and do not have the subject as referent.[18]

Signs and semiotics operate according to two heterogeneous and complementary logics. On the one hand, as in machinic enslavement, they produce operations, induce action, and constitute *input and output, junction and disjunction*, components of a social or technological machine. On the other hand, as in social subjection, they produce meaning, significations, interpretations, discourse, and representations through language. Linguistic but also critical theories (Rancière,

Virno, cognitive capitalism, etc.) recognize only the second logic while neglecting the first, which is specific to capitalism.

Asignifying semiotics act on things. They connect an organ, a system of perception, an intellectual activity, and so on, directly to a machine, procedures, and signs, bypassing the representations of a subject (diagrammatic functioning). They play a very specific role in capitalism since "essentially, capitalism depends on asignifying machines."[19]

Stock market indices, unemployment statistics, scientific diagrams and functions, and computer languages produce neither discourses nor narratives (these obviously have their place but among enslavements). They operate by putting to work and multiplying the power of the "productive" assemblage. Asignifying semiotics remain more or less dependent on signifying semiotics; yet at the level of their intrinsic functions they circumvent language and dominant social significations. The European Central Bank raises the discount rate by one percent and tens of thousands of "plans" go up in smoke for lack of credit. Real estate prices collapse, as in the case of American subprimes, and thousands of households are no longer able to pay their mortgages. Social Security posts a deficit and measures to reduce "social spending" are put in place.

Flows of asignifying signs act directly on material flows—beyond the divide between production and representation—and function whether they signify something for someone or not. Mathematical equations, computer programs, and diagrams "directly participate in the process of generating their object, whereas an advertising image only provides an extrinsic representation of it (although then it is productive of subjectivity)."[20] Instead of referring to other signs, asignifying signs act directly on the real, for example, in the way that the signs of computer language make a technical machine like the computer function, that monetary signs activate the economic machine, that the signs of a mathematical equation enter into the construction of a bridge or an apartment building, and so on.

Sign machines not only and not primarily work at the level of social representations or in order to produce meaning. They involve modes of more abstract (deterritorialized) semiotization than that of the signifying semiotics in the economic, scientific, and technical spheres. Considered in this way, sign machines operate "prior" and "next" to signification, producing a "sense without meaning," an "operational sense." Their operations are diagrammatic insofar as the subject, consciousness, and representation remain in the background.

The asignifying semiotics of the economy, of money, easily circumvent laws, conventions, and institutions. The most deterritorialized, like money and finance, are the most formidably efficient.

What matters to capitalism is controlling the asignifying semiotic apparatuses (economic, scientific, technical, stock-market, etc.) through which it aims to depoliticize and depersonalize power relations. The strength of asignifying semiotics lies in the fact that, on the one hand, they are forms of "automatic" evaluation and measurement and, on the other hand, they unite and make "formally" equivalent heterogeneous spheres of asymmetrical force and power by integrating them into and rationalizing them for economic accumulation. In the economic crisis, asignifying financial ratings and stock market indices have dominated, deciding the life and death of governments, imposing economic and social programs that oppress the governed. The signifying semiotics of the media, politicians, and experts are mobilized in order to legitimate, support, and justify in the eyes of individuated subjects, their consciousness and representations, the fact that "there is no alternative."

Modern-day financialization is simply an intensification of indexing and symbolizing systems that enable the evaluation and control of differentials in value in and between different domains. Mass consumption and the mass media constitute other semiotic systems of evaluation[21] and management that enable the integration and "rationalization" of differences in behavior, opinion, and meaning in accordance with economic logic.

Signifying semiologies (language, stories, discourses), on the other hand, are used and exploited as techniques for control and management of the deterritorialization undermining established communities, social relations, politics, and their former modes of subjectivation. They are meant to model, format, adjust, and reconfigure the subjectivation process according to the "individual subject," whose systematic failure has always lead and continues to lead to the opposite of individualism, namely, to the "collectivism" of nationalism, racism, fascism, Nazism, machinism, and so on.

The machinism of language is one of the most important apparatuses for reterritorializing the decoded flows of individuals, persons, and individuated subjects. Through its "rudimentary psychology," language leads us to believe in "the 'I,' in the 'I' as being, in the 'I' as substance, and it *projects* this belief in the I-substance onto all things—this is how it *creates* the concept of 'thing' in the first place."[22] Language, Nietzsche argues, entails a metaphysics of the subject and the object, a metaphysics at once anthropomorphic and "crudely fetishistic."

If our societies are no longer based on individuals, they are not based on language either. Whatever one might say about the "linguistic turn," it is but one semiotics among others and by no means the most important for ensuring the deterritorialized operations of these megamachines.

The Concept of "Production"

In Deleuze and Guattari's return to and renewal of the Marxian concept of "production" subjection and enslavement define, together and through their difference and complementarity, the "economic" functioning of capitalism. By buying the labor force, capital pays for subjection: hours at work (at a given task), availability (of the unemployed, or the "free time" of the television viewer), and so on. But in reality what capital buys is not only the presence of the labor force at the business, in the institution or social function, nor the availability, the free time, of the unemployed or television viewer. What it buys is first of all the right to exploit a "complex" assemblage that includes, through enslavement, "modes of transportation, urban models, the media, the entertainment industries, ways of perceiving and feeling, every semiotic system."[23] Enslavement frees powers of production incommensurate with those of employment and human labor.

In the law of value presented in *Capital*, Marx still has an "anthropomorphic" and "anthropocentric" view of production,[24] since surplus value, like labor time, is human. Only the worker's labor is productive of surplus value, whereas machines do nothing more than transmit the value that results from the labor time necessary for their manufacture. Attentive to the tremendous increase in "constant fixed capital" (of machinery), Deleuze and Guattari introduce the concept of machinic surplus value and machinic time.[25]

These temporalities are those of enslavement in which subject and object, human and non-human, natural and artificial become indistinguishable. Machinic temporalities make up the factors essential to capitalist production. Unlike human time and surplus value, machinic temporalities and surplus value have the striking attribute of being neither quantifiable nor assignable.[26]

Anti-Oedipus enumerates different forms of surplus-value production (human surplus value, financial surplus value, machinic surplus value, or innovation/knowledge surplus value) in the same way as *A Thousand Plateaus* describes a multiplicity of capture mechanisms of the same surplus value (rent, profit, taxes). The three forms of its production coexist and converge, notably in the economic sphere (which also encompasses forms of production that are not specifically those of capitalist surplus value). This attempt to account for the nature of capitalist exploitation does not seem to me any more promising than the move to attach this multiplicity to the unity of "knowledge" and "innovation," as cognitive capitalist theories endeavor to do.[27]

Multiplicity can be found everywhere in capitalism, in economic production, social production (of the unemployed, the student, the user, etc.), in the production of mass-communications, and in finance. Indeed, it is never an individual or even a group of individuals (intersubjectivity) who work, communicate, or produce. In capitalism, one always works or produces in and through a collective assemblage. But the collective does not only consist of individuals and elements of human subjectivity. It also includes "objects," machines, protocols, human and non-human semiotics, affects, micro-social and pre-individual relations, supra-individual relations, and so forth.

In the same way, it is never an individual who thinks, never an individual who creates. An individual who thinks and creates does so within a network of institutions (schools, theaters, museums, libraries, etc.), technologies (books, electronic networks, computers, etc.), and sources of public and private financing; an individual immersed in traditions of thought and aesthetic practices—engulfed in a circulation of signs, ideas, and tasks—that force him or her to think and create.

In private enterprise, the employee must act and identify himself as a producer, subjugated to machines that remain external to him but of which he makes use. Yet it is never the employee (individuated subjectivity) or the simple cooperative actions of employees (intersubjectivity) that produce. The productivity of capital depends, on the one hand, on the mobilization and assemblage of organs (the brain, hands, muscles, etc.) and human faculties (memory, perception, cognition, etc.) and, on the other hand, on the "intellectual" and physical performance of machines, protocols, organizations, software, or systems of signs, science, and so on. That is to say that productivity depends in large part on enslavement (and its diagrammatic functioning, which circumvents representation, consciousness, and language), in which, it must be emphasized, relations are not intersubjective, agents are not persons, and semiotics are not by any stretch solely signifying.

Capital, therefore, does not simply extort an extension of labor time (the difference between paid human time and human time spent at the workplace), it initiates a process that exploits the difference between subjection and enslavement. For if subjective subjection—the social alienation inherent to a particular job or any social function (worker, unemployed, teacher, etc.)—is always assignable and measurable (the wage appropriate to one's position, the salary appropriate to a social function), the part of machinic enslavement constituting actual production is never assignable nor quantifiable as such.

In machinic enslavement, individual labor and production are not proportional. Production is not the amount of time spent doing individual work. We must distinguish between labor (the activity actually carried out) and employment (a merely juridical status), because the former exceeds the latter. But we must also distinguish labor as a real activity and production, which mobilizes a series of human and non-human elements.

Production and productivity only partially have to do with employment (or even labor); they are above all a matter of the machinic assemblage, that is, the mobilization of the powers of machinism, communications, science, and the social, just as Marx foresaw in the *Grundrisse*.[28]

However, in modern-day capitalism one must go further still, since it is never a corporation that produces, even if considered from the perspective of machinic enslavement. In its current configuration, capitalist production is nothing other than an assemblage of assemblages, a process of processes, that is, a network of assemblages or processes (the corporation, the social, the cultural, the technological, the political spheres, gender, public relations, science, consumption) each one traversing the other.

Capital appropriates this unassignable, unmeasurable value by way of three principal apparatuses of capture: profit, rent, and taxes.

The "business" assemblage extends, combines with, and presupposes other assemblages (national and para-national collective institutions of the welfare state, mass media systems, cultural institutions, educational systems, finance, consumption, etc.), all of which function by uniting and pushing to the extreme individualization (subjection) and deindividualization (enslavement).

We are subjugated to the television machine as a user and consumer, identifying with programs, images, and narratives as a subject, with a subject's consciousness and representations. On the other hand, we are enslaved "insofar as television viewers are no longer consumers or users, nor even subjects who supposedly 'make' it, but intrinsic component pieces that are no longer connected to the machine in such a way as to produce or use it."[29]

With enslavement, the component parts of subjectivity function as inputs and outputs of the "television" assemblage, as so much *feedback in the immense network of synchronized dividuals constituted by enslaved viewers*. The relation between human and non-human elements "is based on internal, mutual communication, and no longer on usage or action."[30]

Pollsters can measure the "available brain time" spent in front of the television but not what occurs during this time. The production of information that results from the combination of the assemblage of image, sound, and representational flows of the individual and the component parts of subjectivity of the dividual can neither be assigned nor measured from the economic point of view. This, while subjectivity is subjected to a semiotic machining which transforms and formats it.

The welfare-state institutions that govern unemployment compel the unemployed to act and to identify themselves as "beneficiaries" of unemployment insurance, that is, as human capital responsible for their employability. But at the same time the unemployed are forced to function as a simple adjustment variable of the labor market, as a flexible and adaptable part of the "automatic" functions of job supply and demand.

On the one hand, "pastoral" control and coercion apparatuses, meticulously attending to the education, projects, qualifications, and behavior of the unemployed, force them to institute themselves as subjects. On the other hand, the market considers them deindividualized component parts assuring its automatic self-regulation. Thus, if unemployment insurance is the measure of what the unemployed person's availability costs (the measure of subjection), then what the unemployed produces with his mobility and flexibility on the job market, what he produces as a consumer or insofar as he makes the unemployment-insurance machine run (as part of the feedback of the "social machine": the information he provides, even despite himself, the subjective and objective index he represents, even despite himself) is unassignable and unmeasurable.

The individual is a subject (human capital) in the financial system in yet another way. As an "investor/debtor," he can be viewed as the very model of subjectivation: the promise he makes to reimburse his debt means that memory and affects (such as guilt, responsibility, loyalty, trust, etc.) must be created to ensure the fulfillment of the promise. But once credit has entered the finance machine, he becomes something else entirely, a mere input of the financial assemblage. Indeed, the credit/debt incorporated into the assemblage loses all reference to the subject who contracted the debt. Credit/debt is literally torn to pieces (in the same way the assemblage tears the subject to pieces) by the financial machine, which the subprime crisis has shown all too well. It is no longer a matter of this or that investment, of this or that debt: the financial assemblage has transformed the subject into a currency that acts as "capital," into money that generates money.

The unemployed, the worker, the television viewer, the saver, and so on, are subject not only to "pastoral" techniques of individualization (Foucault) but to veritable machines of subjectivation and desubjectivation. Under capitalism, the processes of subjectivation and desubjectivation are just as machinic as the production of any other kind of industrial commodity.

The hypotheses Deleuze and Guattari advanced in the 1970s are in large part still relevant today. Subjection still concerns labor even if its meaning has imperceptibly but undoubtedly shifted from the "labor" of the worker to the "labor" of the entrepreneur. Since the 1980s, we have moved from the "productive" force of the working class to that of private enterprise, in particular because of social democracy. One everywhere praises "the value of work," wittingly maintaining the ambiguity, for by work we now mean not only the activity one performs for a boss, but also the "work on the self" one must carry out in order to transform oneself into "human capital."

With enslavement, on the other hand, labor is split in two directions: that of "intensive" surplus labor, which no longer has anything to do with labor but rather with "a generalized machinic enslavement," such that one may provide surplus value without doing any work (children, the retired, the unemployed, television viewers, etc.); and that of extensive labor which "has become erratic and floating."[31]

In these circumstances, users (of unemployment insurance, television, public and private services, etc.), like all consumers, tend to become "employees." "Consumer labor"[32] epitomizes a productivity that no longer adheres to the "physico-social definition of labor."

Desire and Production

From the economic point of view, subjection determines wages and revenues which have only an indirect relationship with "real production," in other words, with machinic enslavement. Subjection divides the population between those who are employed and those who are not, between those who have social rights and those who do not, between "active" and "inactive" populations, with no basis in economic necessity, because a person's contribution to "production" (to machinic enslavement) is neither assignable nor measurable.

Subjection functions according to binary segmantarities (employment/unemployment, producer/consumer, men/women, artist/non-artist, productive/non-productive, etc.), whereas enslavement functions according to a flexible segmentarity, which traverses subjections and their binaries. In machinic enslavement, the split between employed/unemployed, insurance/welfare, productive/non-productive, no longer pertains. From the point of view of "real production," from the point of view of the assemblage or process, everyone "works," everyone is "productive" (or "available," like the unemployed), in various forms.

"In a certain way, the housewife holds a job at home, the child at school, the consumer at the supermarket, the viewer in front of the television screen." On the side of machinic enslavement, children "work in front of the television; they work at the day-care center with toys created to improve their productive performance. In a sense, this work is comparable to that of apprentices at professional schools."[33]

For Guattari, the notion of the workplace must be expanded to most non-salaried activities and the notion of private enterprise to the collective apparatuses of the welfare state, the media, and so on. Modern-day capitalism requires a new perspective in order to account for its socialization, its hold on the (supra-individual) "social"[34] as well as on that which is infra-individual in subjectivity.

Since the postwar years, unions and the Left have shifted emphasis from "labor to work." This has left to business leaders and the State the fundamental political problem of integrating the "social" (Foucault) and "society" (Italian Operaism) and capitalist valorization.

Recognizing the consequences of capital's socialization, Deleuze and Guattari argue for the univocity of the concept of production. If production and the social overlap, then the "field of desire" and the "field of labor," the "economy" and the production of subjectivity, infrastructure and superstructure, can no longer be taken separately. The question of production is inseparable from that of desire (Guattari) such that political economy is no more than a "subjective economy."

The production of subjectivity does not refer, then, to an ideological superstructure; it produces reality and, specifically, economic reality. It is in fact what defines modern-day capitalism, in which *"work on the self" (praxis) and "labor" (production) combine.*

Contrary to Rancière's and Badiou's thinking, "production" is not a matter of "economics." Nor is it limited to the cultivation of knowledge, culture, etc., as cognitive capitalism claims. Rather, it captures and exploits something more profound and transversal to society on the whole: the process of singularization and the production of new modes of subjectivation whose basis is desire.

The subjective essence of production described by classical economists (Smith, Ricardo) and Marx can no longer be confined solely to "labor" since today's capitalism includes the ethico-political dimension of "work on the self." In *Anti-Oedipus*, Deleuze and Guattari advance a fundamentally new concept of desire appropriate to the new nature of "economy" wherein "labor" and "work on the self," production and subjectivation, coalesce and desire serves to define economy as the "production of the possible."

Capitalist deterritorialization acts on desire such that it is no longer human, properly speaking, but machinic. Desire is not the expression of human subjectivity; it emerges from the assemblage of human and non-human flows, from a multiplicity of social and technical machines. Deterritorialized desire has nothing to do with "drives" or "conatus." It is a question instead of the possible, of the creation of new potentialities, of the emergence of what appears possible within the framework of capitalist domination.[35]

Deterritorialized desire breaks with conceptions of capitalism as mere rationalization and calculation, with the image of its actions as aimed solely at the accomplishment of an objective. Its subjective ("anthropological") model does not follow that of the Calvinist/Weberian deferral of desires nor the Freudian model of their repression.

Another dimension must be brought into play, one which was always already present but which only today's "economy" makes salient. Deterritorialized desire, machinic desire, bears with it an "economy of possibilities" and an autopoietic (self-productive) subjectivity which explains the nature of modern-day capitalism and above all its crisis. Capitalism can no longer contain them within the limits of private property or the subjective figure of the entrepreneur of the self.

The Failure of "Human Capital"

The strength of capitalism lies in its ability to integrate desire as an "economy of possibilities" into its own functioning in order to promote and solicit a new subjective figure: the economic subject as "human capital" or entrepreneur of the self.

Looking to account for the change, cognitive capitalist theory reduces the production of subjectivity or the "subjective" economy to the knowledge economy, to the information economy, and to the innovation economy. Cognitive capitalism concedes too much to economic "science" and, in particular, to the theory of "endogenous growth," which make knowledge the driver of the economy. Knowledge is less the basis of modern-day capitalism than the production process of subjectivity centered on desire—desire on which even knowledge, information, and cultural production depend. It is not a matter of cognitive subjectivity but of techniques of power (subjection and enslavement) operating transversely to a multiplicity of forms of activity.

The current crisis stems from the fact that the production of this subjective figure has failed. Neoliberalism has been unable to articulate "production" and the "production of subjectivity." Neoliberalism aims indiscriminately at the economy and subjectivity, at "labor" and the ethico-political work on the self. It reduces the latter to an injunction to become "a kind of permanent and multi-faceted enterprise," whether that of an IT specialist, a maid, or a supermarket clerk. But with the crisis liberalism has created, the promise that "work on the self" was supposed to offer "labor" in terms of emancipation (pleasure, a sense of accomplishment, recognition, experimentation with new forms of life, upward mobility, etc.) has been transformed into the imperative to take upon oneself the risks and costs for which neither business nor the State are willing to pay.

In the current crisis, for the majority of the population "work on the self" means no more than the "entrepreneurial" management of unemployment, debt, wage and revenue cuts, reductions in social services, and rising taxes.

Following the financial debacle of 2007, which exposed the impossibility of creating an economy of possibilities within the limits of private property, capitalism has gradually rid itself of its epic narratives based on freedom, innovation, creativity, the knowledge society, and so on. The population must now concern itself solely with everything finance, business, and the welfare state "externalize" onto society and leave it at that.

It is now clear that the autonomy and freedom that entrepreneurial initiative was supposed to bring to "work" instead mean a much greater dependency not only on institutions (business, State, finance) but also on a despotic superego ("I" am my own boss, therefore I am to blame for everything that happens to me!).

Modern-day capitalism finds the surplus it seeks less in knowledge than in the subjective implication to which the "immaterial worker" must yield in the same way as migrant and factory workers, users of social services, and consumers, all of whom provide an enormous quantity of free labor.

The semiotic and disciplinary machining to which subjectivities are subjected is not primarily cognitive (capitalism does not need as many educated people, as many cognitive workers, as cognitive capitalism believes). The aim of the capitalist machine is to furnish individuals with patterns of conscious or "unconscious" behaviors that compel them to submit to the "rites of passage" and "initiation" of the business, the welfare state, the consumer and media society, and so on. Capitalism obliges individuals to assume the "superegos" necessary for filling hierarchical roles and functions, whether those of the unemployed, factory workers, retirees, consumers, or cognitive workers.

With the crisis, the semiotic and disciplinary formatting operated by subjections and enslavements converge in the production and reproduction of the creditor/debtor relationship. Filling these roles and functions requires debt and its subjective iteration, the indebted man.

2

Signifying Semiologies and Asignifying Semiotics in Production and in the Production of Subjectivity

Mass production and the mass exportation of the white, conscious, adult, male subject always have as their correlate the reining in of intensive multiplicities, which elude all types of centralization, every signifying arborescence.

    —Félix Guattari, *Lignes de fuite*

To transform the unconscious into discourse is to bypass the dynamics, to become complicit with the whole of Western *ratio*, which kills art at the same time as the dream. One does not in the least break with metaphysics by placing language everywhere.

    —Jean-François Lyotard, *Discourse, Figure*

In modern-day capitalism subjectivity is the product of a world-wide mass industry. For Guattari, it is even the primary and most important of capitalist effects since subjectivity conditions and participates in the production of all other commodities.[1] Subjectivity is a "key commodity" whose "nature" is conceived, developed, and manufactured in the same way as an automobile, electricity, or a washing machine. More than an economic or political crisis, the crisis in which we have been stuck since the 1970s represents a crisis in the production of subjectivity, which can hardly be explained by technical, economic, or political processes.

Subjectivity, subjectivation, processes of subjectivation, and subjection are all concepts that consistently appear in critical thought since the 1960s (Foucault, Rancière, etc.), covering different and often contradictory ideas. In this regard Félix Guattari, who went further in the conceptual problematization and cartography of the features and modalities of the production of subjectivity, points to several pitfalls it is best to avoid.

First of all, the structuralist impasse, which reduces subjectivity to the mere result of signifying operations: "What the structuralists say isn't true; it isn't the facts of language or even communication that generate subjectivity. At a certain level, it is collectively manufactured in the same way as energy, electricity, or aluminum."[2]

The production of subjectivity puts into play something very different from linguistic performance: ethological, fantasmic dimensions, economic, aesthetic, and physical semiotic systems, existential territories, and incorporeal universes, all of which are irreducible to a semiology of language. The concept of the substance of expression must be pluralized in order to bring to the fore the extralinguistic, non-human, biological, technological, aesthetic, and machinic substances of expression.

The second pitfall comes from phenomenology and psychoanalysis, whose concepts reduce "the facts of subjectivity to drives, affects, intra-subjective apparatuses and relations," which Guattari also defines as "intersubjective drivel."[3] Technical (digital, communicational, media) and social machines modulate and format subjectivity by acting not only within memory and sense but also within the unconscious. This non-human, machinic part of subjectivity is irreducible to intra- and inter-subjective relations.

To avoid the third, sociological pitfall, we must move away from methodological individualism and holism. Processes of subjectivation or semiotization are not centered on individual agents or on collective (intersubjective) agents. The production of subjectivity is indeed a "collective" process, yet the collective both goes beyond the individual, in an extra-personal dimension (machinic, economic, social, technological systems), and precedes the person (preverbal intensities within a system of affects and intensities).

Finally, there is the last difficulty, which Guattari calls the "complex of infrastructures": a material infrastructure that generates an ideological superstructure (Marxism), an instinctual infrastructure that generates the psyche (Freud), or deep syntactic and linguistic structures that produce linguistic (signified) content.

We will look to avert these three stumbling blocks while at the same time avoiding the pitfalls of structuralism.

1. The Remnants of Structuralism: Language Without Structure

Structuralism is dead, but what founded its paradigm—language—is still very much alive. Surprisingly, it is doing quite well, even after the critical theories that came out of the major theoretical innovations of the 1960s and 70s cleared a way out of structuralism.

Here, however, language does not have the systemic and combinatory neutrality of structuralism. Critical thought has radically politicized language yet without ever fully giving up on the logic according to which language is unique to man and thus the cornerstone of politics. For Paolo Virno, politics must not be sought in the uses the speaker makes of it; language is intrinsically political insofar as its activity or praxis is realized in the public sphere. Politics and the possession of language are literally one and the same. For Rancière, the logos constitutes the measure and verification of politics' sole principle—equality. Even a command, for one to be given, presupposes a minimum of equality, the equality of logos. In order for subordinates to understand and execute an order, they must share the same language as the person who issues it. Equality is in this way verified in language.

Judith Butler considers all her work an extension of Hannah Arendt's affirmation that "men become political beings as beings of language." In the same vein, Giorgio Agamben establishes a strict relationship between language and human nature, because man, "uniquely among living things, [...] *has put* [...] *his very nature at stake in language.*"[4]

The more or less critical, more or less problematic, references are first of all Aristotle and his twofold definition of man ("Man is the only animal to possess language" and "man is a political animal"), Hannah Arendt, and analytic philosophy. For Virno and Butler, the latter provides the starting point for a repoliticization of language through an analysis of the relationship between "words and power."

According to Pascal Michon, who instead draws on the German tradition, we have undergone a "forgetting of the specificity of language." The critique of capitalism and a truly subversive politics of art must be founded on "humanity's sole creative force, the sole utopian force: the force of language."[5]

Today, Lacan's psychoanalysis, an apogee of structuralist thought, seems to be attracting new disciples. With Freudian themes interpreted in terms of Saussurean linguistics (the Hegelian master-slave dialectic), the subject becomes an effect of language and language the source of the subject; the unconscious is structured like a language and, like a language, it functions through metaphor and metonymy.[6] The "chain of signifiers," their combinatory, their "autonomy," their exteriority, their existence prior to all experience, produces both the signified and the subject. The Hegelian-Lacanian formation of the subject is faithfully taken up by Žižek and, albeit with certain revisions, by Butler. Although she refuses the "structuring role of the law of the father," Butler has the signifier act as a performative within Lacanian theory— leading to the same results. Language functions as a molar constraint, as a transcendental, as an "original and radical servitude" that "precedes and exceeds" the subject.

In an attempt to move beyond the reductive hypotheses inherited from Marxism, which made language a superstructure or ideological artifact, Rancière transforms language along with affects into the very origin of society: "the 'social' [...] is in fact constituted by a series of discursive acts and reconfigurations of a perceptive field."[7]

Language and affects not only define the object of the distribution of the sensible, according to Rancière (with the bourgeoisie controlling speech and "educated meaning" while the proletariat emits only animal noise, expressing itself through "brute sense"), they also constitute new productive forces. For my friends in cognitive capitalism, the nature of labor and capital is given through language and affects as well. Cognitive labor mobilizes the latter and cognitive capitalism captures and exploits them.

This way of understanding language, even if defined according to its political or productive function, seems to me a sharp discrepancy with the nature and functioning of subjectivity, enunciation, and production in modern-day capitalism. In all these theories, and despite their critical aims, we remain in a "logocentric" world, whereas with capitalism we have for some time entered a "machine-centric" world that configures the functions of language in a different way.

In the machine-centric universe, one moves from the question of the subject to that of subjectivity such that enunciation does not primarily refer to speakers and listeners—the communicational version of individualism—but to "complex assemblages of individuals, bodies, material and social machines, semiotic, mathematical, and scientific machines, etc., which are the true sources of enunciation."[8] The sign machines of money, economics, science, technology, art, and so on, function in parallel or independently because they produce or convey meaning and in this way bypass language, significations, and representation.

In the mid-1960s, Pier Paolo Pasolini described the hold capital's modes of semiotization have over language as the beginning of a "post-human world" in which the sites of linguistic creation shift to "production" and machinisms. Given Italy's linguistic "backwardness," this process appeared in a particularly striking way. In the linguistic sphere, the second industrial revolution brought about *the substitution of languages of infrastructures* [...] *for the languages of superstructures.*" It had always been the case, from Egyptian civilization to the first industrial revolution, that "the linguistic models that dominate a society and make it linguistically unitary are the models of the cultural superstructures" and of the intellectual elites in law, literature, education, and religion. Then suddenly, with the turn from capitalism to neo-capitalism, which coincided with the transformation of the "scientific spirit" into the integral "application of science" to production, "the languages of the infrastructures, let us say simply the languages of production, are guiding society linguistically. It had never happened before."[9]

The languages of "production-consumption" produce "a kind of downgrading of the word, tied to the deterioration of the humanistic languages of the elites, which have been, until now, the guiding languages."[10] The centers that create, develop, and unify language "*are no longer the universities, but the factories.*"[11] The "interregional and international" language of the future will be a "signing" language of "a world unified by industry and technocracy," that is, "a communication of men no longer men."[12]

This is exactly the opposite of what one finds asserted by the exponents of the linguistic turn: analysis is supposed only to examine the "language of infrastructures" and the subordination of "humanist" languages, language, and signifying semiotics to the semiotics of production and consumption.

Even Hannah Arendt in *The Modern Condition* warns us that although the "ability to act," to "start new unprecedented processes," is still present,[13] it has become the privilege of the sciences which "have been forced to adopt a 'language' of mathematical symbols […] that in no way can be translated back into speech." If we "adjust our cultural attitudes to the present status of scientific achievement, we would in all earnest adopt a way of life in which speech is no longer meaningful," for scientists "move in a world where speech has lost its power."[14] Arendt subtly remarks something her commentators have failed to notice, namely that the close relationship between action and speech, which occurs "without the intermediary of things or matter,"[15] belongs to a "human condition" which has not been our condition since at least the first industrial revolution.

Pasolini's analyses, which show that it is not only in the sciences that "language has lost its power," are carried still further in the work of Guattari. The latter specifies the nature and function of the "languages of infrastructures" in his most important contribution to the question: asignifying semiotics.

To map the "languages of infrastructures" and the modes of machine-centric subjectivation/enunciation, one must follow Guattari's advice to "exit language" by doing two things: dissociate subjectivity from the subject, from the individual, and even from the human, and cease considering the power of enunciation exclusive to man and subjectivity.

Guattari sees no reason to deny the equivalent of a subjectivity—the equivalent of a "non-human for-itself [*pour soi*]" (which he calls proto-subjectivity) and of a power of enunciation (which he calls proto-enunciation)—with living and material assemblages. He asks rather that we consider the possibility of forces other than those of the individuated subject's consciousness, sense, and language that might function as vectors of subjectivation or as focal points of enunciation.

Guattari extends the autopoietic power, the potential of self-production, to all machines. It is a power capable of developing its own rules and modes of expression, a power which Francisco Varela reserves solely for living machines. "[A]ll machinic systems, whatever domain they belong to—technical, biological, semiotic, logical, abstract—are, by themselves, the support for proto-subjective processes, which I will characterize in terms of modular subjectivity" or "partial subjectivity."[16]

Modes of subjectivation, assemblages of semiotization and enunciation of all kinds—human and non-human, collective or individual—coexist within biological, economic, aesthetic, scientific, and social processes.

Guattari's theory captures the fate of the creative function in capitalism. Languages as such have no privilege in creation. On the contrary, their functioning "can even slow down or prohibit any semiotic proliferation, and it often remains for nonlinguistic components to catalyze mutations and break […] the dominant linguistic significations" and to serve as heterogeneous vectors of subjectivation. "Genetic codes throughout the history of life and iconic systems, like art, throughout the history of humanity, have been at least as rich […] as linguistic systems."[17]

If one considers all human and non-human reality as "expressive," that is, as source, emergence, and detonator of processes of subjectivation and enunciation, then reality is present in our actions as multiple possibilities, as "optional matter." Thought and choices are exercised on the "economy of possibles"; they do not start with man and do not rely exclusively on "a signifying discourse produced between speakers and listeners." The history of evolution teaches us that if the "freedom" of possible choices exists at "higher" anthropological stages, they must be presupposed and found equally at the most "elementary" levels of the living being and matter. Subjectivity, creation, and enunciation are the results of an assemblage of human, infra-human, and extra-human factors in which signifying, cognitive semiotics constitute but one of the constituent parts.

Guattari is not alone in approaching subjectivity and enunciation from "the point of view of things themselves" rather than that of the subject, human consciousness, and representation. We can find the same theme, though in very different terms, in Benjamin, Pasolini, or Klemperer. But well before their theoretical formulation, the new machines of industrial production, cinema, and art revealed a metamorphosis of the subject, object, and their modes of expression.

The cinema's invention disclosed a reality expressed without representation or linguistic mediation. It was no longer necessary to trace signs and symbols in order to show an object, beings, or relations. Reality signified all by itself. In art, a radical rupture occurred at the beginning of the century when ready-made, following cinema's example, signified by way of the object itself, unassisted by the sign or language. Properly speaking, ready-mades are no longer representations but "presentations."

Duchamp's *Bottle Rack* or *Fountain* are objects mass-produced by industrial machinisms, produced by a new power—rather than that of *homo faber*, the power of a machinic assemblage, which assembles sign, material, and labor flows. Addressing this form of capitalist production, Marx evoked a global, non-qualified subjectivity manifesting itself in any object whatsoever. Guattari explodes "Marxist" anthropomorphism and its modes of expression by pushing the deterritorialization of subjectivity to the extreme.

That objects might start "speaking," start "expressing themselves" (or start dancing, as they do in the celebrated passage from the first book of *Capital*), is not capitalist fetishism, the proof of man's alienation, but rather marks a new regime of expression which requires a new semiotics. This is not simply a reversal of the subject's activity manifesting itself as the *animation* of the object, a reversal one need only stand back on its head. This is an irreversible process that shifts the question of the subject to that of subjectivity and from human subjectivity to machinic, biological, social, aesthetic, etc., proto-subjectivities. The return to "humanism," whatever it may mean, is in any case neither possible nor desirable.

Guattari deploys the philosophical program of *Capitalism and Schizophrenia* in the realm of semiotics and the production of subjectivity. The point is to leave behind the subject/object dualism imposed on multiplicities, which are neither subjects nor objects, by inscribing nature and culture along an indeterminate continuum.

From this point of view, the linguist Louis Hjelmslev's work of the late 1960s and early 1970s on categories of expression and content proved fundamental. In Hjelmslev, however, the pair expression/content remains prisoner to the Saussurean opposition between signifier and signified, whereas for Guattari expression does not refer to the signifier or language but to a collective semiotic machine preexisting both (a collective assemblage of enunciation encompassing diverse and heterogeneous substances of human and non-human expression). Likewise, content does not refer to the signified but to a social machine that preexists it (a machinic assemblage of action and passion we can by no means reduce to the economic, social, or political spheres). The double articulation of expression and content is not a specific property of language; the latter represents only one functional modality of the organic, biological, social, aesthetic, etc., strata of reality.

The enlarged conception of this twofold relationship allows us to avoid the pitfalls of Marxism and structuralism, because expression and content, one presupposing and reversing the other reciprocally, maintain no causal relationship. Expression does not depend on content (Marxism), nor is content the product of expression (linguistic structuralism). Subjectivity is neither the result of linguistic or communicational expression nor the product of deeper socioeconomic contents.

In a fundamental methodological shift, Guattari asks us to grasp the subject/object relation and the expression/content relation "by the middle," to foreground and problematize the "expressive instance," that is, the enunciation. In this way, he lays the basis for a new pragmatics, a new theory of enunciation, in which, paradoxically, the ground of enunciation is existential, not discursive.[18]

2. Signifying Semiologies

> In the beginning of assemblages of enunciation, we find neither
> verb, nor subject, system, nor syntax…: instead, there are compo-
> nents of semiotization, subjectivation, conscientization,
> diagrammatism, and abstract machinisms.
> —Félix Guattari, *The Machinic Unconscious*

> A sign, in terms of its expressiveness, is the equivalent of another sign
> (any other sign); every hierarchy among signs is unjust, unjustifiable.
> —Pier Paolo Pasolini, *Heretical Empiricism*

The strength of capitalism lies in its articulation of processes of
social subjection and machinic enslavement as well as in the effects
of their respective signifying and asignifying semiotics. Both apparatuses play a fundamental role in controlling processes of capitalist
deterritorialization and reterritorialization, for they enable the
adjustment, modification, solicitation, assemblage, and stabilization
of processes of desubjectivation and subjectivation. The fundamental
distinction between signifying semiologies and asignifying semiotics
has to do with the different ways in which they function and their
very different effects on subjectivity. We will examine them separately in order to elucidate the distinction, one which no less always
involves mixed semiotics.

Instead of making language the site for the verification of equality,
instead of considering it implicitly political because a manifestation
of the publicity of action or, even, of making it a new productive
force, Guattari proposes to "exit language" and develop a semiotic
theory beyond human semiotics. In a capitalism organized
around and founded on asignifying semiotics (Pasolini's "languages of

infrastructures"), language is only "one particular but in no way privileged example of the functioning of a general semiotics." This general semiotics must account for both signifying speech and the machines of aesthetic, technical-scientific, biological, and social signs.

Guattari distinguishes among different types of semiotics situated beyond the measures and hierarchizations of human language: "natural" a-semiotic encodings (crystalline systems and DNA, for example), *signifying semiologies* including symbolic (or pre-signifying, gestural, ritual, productive, corporeal, musical, etc.) semiologies and semiologies of signification, and, finally, *asignifying* (or post-signifying) *semiotics*. This represents Guattari's most important contribution to our understanding of capitalism and the production of subjectivity.

In "natural" a-semiotic encodings, expression is not an autonomous stratum with regard to content. In a rock, in a crystalline structure, the "form" is conveyed by the "material" itself, such that expression and content are inherent to each other. There is no differentiating between a mineral, chemical, or nuclear stratum and a semiotic stratum organized into an autonomous syntax.

The separation, the autonomization, of expression begins to develop with the emergence of life. With plants and animals "form" is transmitted through codes that create complex molecules and reproductive systems of species which begin to autonomize and to separate from "substance."

With human behavior, signifying semiologies, and asignifying semiotics, transmission no longer depends on genetic codes but on learning, memories, languages, symbols, diagrams, graphs, equations, and so on, in other words, on semiotics functioning according to an autonomous syntax and strata of expression. In semiologies of signification, unlike natural encodings, expression and content maintain a relationship of interpretation, reference, and signification.

1. The Political Functions of Semiologies of Signification

Despite the specific attention paid to symbolic and asignifying semiotics which lie outside of language, Guattari has left us with a very precise picture of how language functions within capitalism.

The establishment of a language and of a system of dominant significations is always first of all a political operation before it is a linguistic or semantic one. A certain type of language and certain modes of individuated semiotization and subjectivation are necessary in order to stabilize the social field disrupted by capitalist deterritorialization, a deterritorialization which undermines previous subjectivities, forms of life, and institutions. Stabilization entails the predominance of a national language, carrying with it the laws and modes of functioning of incipient capitalism over dialects, exceptional languages, and modes of infantile, "pathological," and artistic expression. The national language reduces them to marginality by bringing them "before the court of dominant syntaxes, semantics, and pragmatics."

The constitution of linguistic exchange and of distinct and individuated speakers is, on the one hand, coextensive with the constitution of economic exchange, of its rational agents, and of the juridical contract and its contracting parties. On the other hand, it is coextensive with psychic instances of the "self" (id/superego) and the "other."

Capitalist formations have recourse to a particular type of signifying semiotic machine which, overcoding all the other semiotics, allows "economic" production as well as the production of subjectivity to be administered, guided, adjusted, and controlled. By exercising power over symbolic semiotics, the semiotics of signification function as both a general equivalent of expression and a vector of subjectivation centered on the individual.

Throughout Guattari's work we encounter the comparison with symbolic (pre-signifying) semiotics such as they function in primitive societies. This allows us to grasp the sudden change as well as the novelty the "imperialism and despotism" of language represents.

First of all, capitalism requires that symbolic semiotics (whether gestural, ritual, productive, corporeal, musical, etc.) be hierarchized and subordinated to language. Unlike language, they "do not involve a distinguishable speaker and hearer. Words do not play a major part, since the message is carried not via linguistic chains, but via bodies, sounds, mimicry, posture and so on."[19] Since symbolic semiotics are "transitional, polyvocal, animistic, and transindividual," they are not easily assigned to individuated subjects, to persons ("I," "you").

In our capitalist societies there is still this transindividual mode of functioning but it is confined to marginal forms of expression: madness, infancy, artistic creation, and creation period, as well as amorous or political passion.

Symbolic semiologies and the semiology of signification cannot be distinguished by the strata of expression they put in play. Symbolic semiologies function according to a multiplicity ("n") of strata or substances of expression (gestural, ritual, productive, corporeal, musical, etc.), whereas semiologies of signification bring together only two strata (signifier/signified).

In primitive societies, different semiotic strata (artistic, religious, linguistic, economic, corporeal, musical, and so on) do not enter into dependent or hierarchized relation with each other. Speech interacts directly with other forms of expression (ritual, gestural, musical, productive, etc.) instead of constituting a higher modality of it.

Each stratum of expression conserves its specific consistency and autonomy. The translatability of different semiotic strata is not accomplished through a formalization of expression (the signifier) that overpowers other semiotics, but through a social assemblage (tribe, community) which, on the contrary, precludes the emergence of a single signifying substance, of a signifying synthesis, of a system that hierarchizes and subordinates other forms of expression to language. In capitalism, on the other hand, these nonverbal forms of expression depend on language.

"The signs of society can be interpreted integrally by those of language, but the reverse is not so. Language is therefore interpreting society."[20] In this way, Émile Benveniste concludes the superiority of language over other semiotic systems. It leads Guattari to remark: "One sought to make symbolic semiotics dependent on linguistic semiologies on the pretense that they could not be deciphered, understood, or translated without recourse to language. But what does that prove? We wouldn't say that because we take a plane to go from the US to Europe that the two continents depend on aviation."[21]

Generalized exchange is not part of the economic sphere alone. The comparison, quantification, and exchange of economic values necessitate, first of all, significations that remain invariant in time and space, enabling a general translatability of semiotics into a linguistic "standard." Determining "value" requires the institution of a national language that operates the comparison and internal translatability of languages and local dialects.

In reality, words and sentences have no sense except within a particular enunciation, a specific syntax, and a local micro-political situation. Every day every one of us passes through a multiplicity of heterogeneous languages: a language we speak to our families, at work, with friends, with God, with our superiors, and so on. Language has to function as an equivalent to these different semiotics, which express power relations and local heterogeneous desire.

Unlike the territorialized assemblages of primitive societies, capitalism must realize the homogenization, uniformization, and centralization of different human and non-human expressive economies: language, icons, gestures, the language of things (urbanism, commodities, prices, etc.). All semiotics must be compatible with and adapt to the semiotics of capital, especially those having to do with the labor force.

Individuals are from birth subjected to semiotic processing; initiation into semiotics is the very first "labor" accomplished. Guattari compares it to the work of trainees in industry.

> The child not only learns to speak a native language; he also learns the codes for walking down the street, a certain kind of complex relationship to machines, electricity, etc. [...] and these different codes have to be made part of the social codes of power. This aspect of general exchange among semiotics is essential to the capitalist economy. [...] The initiation to capital above all entails this semiotic initiation to various codes of translatability and to the corresponding invariant systems.[22]

The semiotic assembly line not only produces knowledge and information but also attitudes, stereotypes of behavior, and submission to hierarchies. One must never dissociate "the work of semiotization going into professional development from the work of modeling and adapting workers" to power relations.[23] The unconscious, "superegoistic" investment in professional roles, the acceptance—as "active" as possible—of subordination, is as important as obtaining "knowledge" and learning skills. One never exists without the other; the latter is, moreover, activated only once the former is assured.

2. Reference, Signification, Representation

The establishment of invariant significations, of relations of equivalence and stable translatability among semiotics, which serve as bases to the production of subjectivity, is accomplished by a formalized sign-machine coordinating what Guattari calls the semiotic triangle: "reference, signification, representation." Denotation institutes a biunivocal relationship between the sign and the thing designated (the referential function), whereas in symbolic semiotics this relation is floating, vague, uncertain, "unsure of itself." In certain "uncivilized languages," a mere shift in accent is all that is needed to change not only the meaning but also the word. The signifying expression loses the polyvocality and multi-referentiality it possesses in symbolic semiologies in order to designate in an exclusive and univocal way.

By joining the sign to its referent, reference denotes a reality that becomes the "sole" and "unique" reality, the dominant reality, whereas in primitive societies "realities" are multiple. Each semiotic system (religious, social, magic, animal, animistic) expresses a heterogeneous world whose composition is maintained by the social assemblage of the group.

The reduction of polyvalence and multi-referentiality, the neutralization of the "heterogeneous, mixed, vague, dissymmetric" specific to symbolic semiotics, and the primacy of the "pure," the invariant, and the specialized—all this is epitomized in the mathematical theory of information. The invariance of the information to be transmitted is precisely *the* concern. The standardization of language eliminates as much as possible the intensities and affects not univocally assignable, which, being unable to ensure stable denotation and meanings, threaten to function on their own.

In "neocapitalism" (Pasolini), this process of rationalization and impoverishment of expression subsequently develops still further. The "technological principle of clearness, of communicative exactness, of mechanical scientificity, of efficiency,"[24] works on language from the inside. For Pasolini, these principles constitute a stratum that is not simply added to other strata historically registered in language (the Latin stratum, the humanist stratum, etc.). The last signifying stratum to evolve toward the "signaletic" efficiency of applied science has come to overpower the others, rendering them homologous with the ends and necessities of languages of "production/consumption."

In order to neutralize all polyvocality and multidimensionality of expression, to reduce all vagueness and uncertainty, significations are directly encoded by a linguistic machine that intersects the syntagmatic axis of *selection* of the signifying unities of language, in conformity with a grammatical order, and a paradigmatic axis of *composition of sentences* and *significance*, according to a semantic order, such that meaning becomes "automatic." The intersection of these two axes does not constitute a universal mode of expression but rather a veritable machine for structuring, mapping, and establishing meanings.

In primitive societies, "One symbol interprets another symbol which is itself interpreted by a third and so on, without the process ending in a final signifier whose sense would be sedimented, for example, in a dictionary and without the sequence compelling us to respect a grammaticality that determines rigorous rules of syntagmatic concatenation."[25]

It is only with the definitive installation of capitalism in the nineteenth century that one sees firmly imposed the "'absolute stability of the signified, under the proliferation of the relations of designation [...] in order to ground the comparison of forms.'"[26]

In capitalism, grammar and syntax function as the police of language. "A rule of grammar is a power marker before it is a syntactical marker."[27]

Modern government of behavior entails that the significations defining the functions and limits of our actions (man, woman, worker, boss, etc.), determining our roles within the social division of labor, are solidly established and leave as little room as possible for interpretation and dispute.

With the third term of the semiotic triangle—representation— the world is split into a mental or symbolic world (a world of images, representational icons, symbols) and a "real, denoted" world. The sign does not directly refer to reality; it is no longer directly connected to a referent. Now, in order to be semiotically efficient, the sign must pass through the mediation of the symbolic order, it must pass through the signifying machine.

In this way, representation makes signs "powerless" insofar as they do not act directly and pragmatically on the "real." To be transformed, they must pass through the mediation of consciousness, representation, and the subject.[28] The comparison with primitive societies highlights the separation effected in capitalism between production and representation, between the signifier and the real. For "primitive peoples," flows of signs constitute a reality in the same way as material flows. There is no separation between semiotic production and material production because signs continue in the real and vice versa.

Primitives are *realists*, not mystics. The imaginary and symbolic are real. There is no otherworld. Everything extends into everything else. There is no separation-break. The Bambara does not imitate, metaphorize, index. Its dance and its mask are full signs, a total sign that is simultaneously representation and production. [...] It doesn't watch representation impotently. It is itself, collectively, the spectacle, the spectator, the scene, the dog, etc. It is transformed through expression. [...] This is a sign in touch with reality. Or a sign such that there is no break between reality and imaginary... mediated by a symbolic "*order*." No break between gesture, speech, writing, music, dance, war, men, the gods, the sexes, etc.[29]

In the semiotic triangle, everything becomes logical and formal. Significations seem to have been secreted immanently through the syntactical structures of language itself.

The dominant significations (identity, sex, profession, nationality, etc.) from which it is difficult to escape (individually through madness, infancy, alcohol, drugs, creation, love, or collectively through political action) are produced at the intersection of a twofold formalization process: that of the linguistic machine which automates those expressions, interpretations, and responses imposed by the system, and that of the formation of powers producing signifieds.

Suppose I come into the room wearing a long gown: in itself it means nothing, but if I am doing it to show that I am a transvestite, there is no problem; but if, say, a conference of clergy wearing cassocks is taking place, then it will have quite a different meaning. In a mental hospital, it could be interpreted differently again: "He's not too well today—wearing a dress again." In other words for a man to wear a gown means one thing if he is a judge or a priest, another if he is a lunatic, yet another if he is a transvestite. Signification is inseparable from taking power.[30]

Structuralism confers unity and autonomy on signifying semiotics as if there were such a thing as language in itself, capable of secreting meaning according to deep syntactical structures and signification, whereas "Language is everywhere, but it does not have any domain of its own. *There is no language in itself.* What specifies human language is precisely that it never refers back to itself, that it always remains open to all the other modes of semiotization."[31]

The closure and formalization of language are political mechanisms, because "anything that fails to be caught in the neutralization of non-linguistic components conserves the possibility of the system of intensity's going out of control."[32] The closure of semiotics of signification within a world of "pure significance," what Guattari defines as the "impotentization" of the sign, is what makes it very difficult for structuralism and analytic philosophy to problematize the pragmatics and "existential function" of expression.

In our societies, expression must always be accomplished via denotations that establish and recognize only one reality, the dominant reality—through meaning that bi-univocally establishes the relationship between the sign and its referent and through the mental and impotentized world of representation separating the sign from the real. Expression thus circumscribed and formalized contributes to the production of a new subjectivity. In primitive societies, the referent of symbolic semiotics is the group, the collective assemblage, the community. With semiologies of signification, the referent is the individuated subject (and its double, the transcendental subject), the empty subject withdrawn into himself, cut off from the assemblages and connections that constitute him, living as the autonomous, free source of his actions and enunciations.

Individualization is established and rooted in language through what Guattari calls "personologization." The normalizing power of language lies in "linguistic Oedipalization," whose objective "consists in formalizing the subjectivation of statements according to an abstract encoding of the I-you-he type, which 'provides the speakers with a shared system of personal references.'"[33]

The subject of enunciation (a composite subjectivity "in flesh and blood" rich in a multiplicity of semiotics, in modes of perception and knowledge) who says "I" tears himself away from the global, lived, existential dimension of the assemblage, merges with the subject of utterance ("I"), with the "social" linguistic form that precedes and defines him. By molding itself to the subject of the utterance ("I"), the collective assemblage of enunciation submits to the individualizing linguistic machine. The latter, in turn, overcodes semiotic systems and the different expressive modalities of subjectivity in accordance with the modalities of the "semiotic triangle." The multiplicity of semiotics, the plurality of enunciative focal points, the veritable sources of enunciation, are reduced to the individual subject.

Personologization of psychic apparatuses (the ego, the superego, the id) corresponds to linguistic personologization (I-you-he).[34] The normalizing power of psychoanalysis converges with the normalizing power of signifying semiotics in the creation of the individual as both guilty and responsible for his guilt.

Infrapersonal intensities (relational, affective, emotive, existential intensities, intensities of desire, "where you do not know if you are a man, woman, dog, plant, or anything at all, where you no longer know who is who, no longer know who is speaking to whom") and extrapersonal intensities, those of massive economic, linguistic, social, etc., machines, are confined to this twofold—linguistic and psychic—personologization.

The inclusive-disjunctive syntheses of primitive societies ("I am jaguar") are no longer found only among the mad, children, artists, and poets ("I is an other"). The linguistic signifying machine operates and imposes "exclusive disjunctions" (you are a man, you are a woman, etc.) which prevent becomings, heterogeneous processes of subjectivation; it recognizes only identities defined by these significations (man, child, animal, etc.) and by specialized functions (worker, boss, student, etc.). The structure of the modern signification machine opposes inclusive-disjunctive syntheses, concentrating all subjectivity and expressivity in man by reducing the other (nature, things, the cosmos) to an object.

The subjectivity of capitalist societies is not only an autonomous and independent subjectivity confined to the individual, it is also a subjectivity fragmented into compartmentalized and "interiorized faculties" (Reason, Understanding, Sense, etc.) each in opposition to the other according to the dualisms of the sensible and the intelligible, the real and the imaginary, thought and extension.

In primitive societies "an individual's psychism was not organized into interiorized faculties but was connected to a range of expressive and practical registers in direct contact with social life and the outside world."[35]

The individuated subject of capitalist societies is endowed with an "individuated body," with a "naked body," a "shameful body," which must be made part of domestic and social economies. The naked body, the shameful body closed in on itself like language, autonomous and independent, detached from the multiplicity of the assemblages that constitute it, is a construction of industrialized societies which make it a "natural" body. It is not at all clear, according to Guattari, that we have "a body, for we are assigned a body, a body is produced for us." Other collective assemblages of enunciation and action "machine" other bodies, other ways of behaving, and other relationships with the community.

> The primitive body is never a naked body, but always a subset of the social body, traversed by markers of the socius, by tattoos, by initiations, etc. This body does not contain individuated organs: it is itself traversed by souls, by spirits, which belong to the set of collective assemblages.[36]

Guattari seems to be taken by the same "fanatical Marxism" to which Pasolini lays claim when he underscores the political function of linguistics. The "linguistic machine" and its theories are pressed into the service of the law, morality, Capital, and religion. They systematize, structure, consolidate, and enable power formations. The constitution of national languages (meta-languages originating in an internal colonization of dialects and local ways of speaking) and the institution of the Nation State are processes that mutually sustain one other. Linguistic unification is above all political unification. It is only "with the installation of a State machine [that] signifying power really acquires its autonomy."[37]

Pasolini reminds us that beneath the nineteenth century's extensive research in linguistics which constructed the semiotic conditions of capitalism there is at once expansion and colonialism within European countries and imperialist expansion and colonialism outside of them. Every linguist in industrialized Europe concentrated on "purely oral language" (a category distinct from "language" and "speech") and on the "pure speakers" who "belonged to a historical world anterior to theirs [...] like colonialists with peoples of color. It is the fatal racism of the bourgeoisie." After the Second World War, European bourgeoisies changed their relationship with these "pure speakers," using them "as immigrants, to keep salaries low. Lille and Cologne, Paris and London, are full of Italian, Greek, Spanish, Algerian, Moroccan, Negro 'speakers'—who increase in number immensely every year." In this light, Pasolini gives Lévi-Strauss—and his brand of structuralism—special attention, calling him "the poet of low wages."[38]

3. Asignifying Semiotics

Whereas with social subjection and the semiologies of signification we are in a molar world inhabited by distinct and individuated subjects and objects, machinic enslavement and asignifying semiotics operate beyond the subject/object, sign/thing, production/representation divide.

Asignifying semiotics (stock listings, currencies, corporate accounting, national budgets, computer languages, mathematics, scientific functions and equations as well as the asignifying semiotics of music, art, etc.) are not beholden to significations and the individuated subjects who convey them. They slip past rather than produce significations or representations.

They involve more abstract modes of semiotization than language. They manifest themselves in the sciences, industrial corporations, the service industry, stock market, military, artistic, and communicational machines rather than in the world of civil society, political representation, or democracy.

A worthwhile approach to analyzing asignifying semiotics is by way of the "concept of the machine." Since the extraordinary expansion of machinism to every aspect of life—that is, not only to "production" as was the case in Marx's time—no adequate theorization of the machine has been advanced except in a handful of authors' work, among which Guattari's.[39]

To understand the concept of the "machine," one must set aside the subject/object, nature/culture opposition, for that is the only way one can separate "human nature" and the machine. The machine is not a subset of technique but partakes of the essence of man; indeed, the machine is a prerequisite to technique.

We must move beyond the classical model centered on the tool, which makes the machine an extension and projection of the living being. Such a model remains founded on the "humanistic and abstract" model in which the machine serves as an organ or prosthesis. Guattari's machinism does not oppose man and machine "in order to evaluate the correspondences, the extensions, and possible or impossible substitutions of one for the other," but instead brings them into "communication in order to show how man *is a component part* of the machine, or combines with something else to constitute a machine. The other thing can be a tool, or even an animal, or other men."[40]

The concept of machine *stricto sensu* must therefore be expanded to the functional whole which connects it not only to man but also to a multiplicity of other material, semiotic, incorporeal, etc., elements.

It is utterly insufficient to conceive of the machine solely in terms of technique. The machine is at once a material and semiotic, actual and virtual, assemblage. On the one hand, before being a technique, the machine is diagrammatic, that is, inhabited by diagrams, plans, and equations. On the other hand, in the machine there are "visible, synchronic" dimensions (the assemblage of component parts, plans, equations), but also virtual, diachronic dimensions, since it is situated at the intersection of a series of past machines and the infinity of machines to come. The factory, for example, is a machine of which men and technical machines are but factors, component parts. It makes up an assemblage that surpasses them. Public institutions, the media, the welfare state, and so on, must also be considered—non-metaphorically—machines, because they assemble (machine) multiplicities (people, procedures, semiotics, techniques, rules, etc.). Art too is a machine, an assemblage whose terms—the artist and the artwork—can be extracted from the assemblage only via abstraction: "There is not one operator or one material that is the object of the operation, but a collective assemblage that involves the artist individually and his public, and all the institutions around him—critics, galleries, museums."[41]

The distinction Francisco Varela makes between "allopoietic machines," which produce something other than themselves, and autopoietic machines, which generate and determine their own organization through an "incessant process of replacing their component parts," reduces technological machines to instrumental apparatuses incapable of self-generation. Such is true only if one separates man and his indiscoverable nature from machines and their no less indiscoverable essence. If, on the other hand, we consider the machinic assemblage they constitute with human beings, "they become ipso facto autopoietic."[42]

To understand the humans-machines functional whole, one must rid oneself both of the mechanistic thesis of "the structural unity of the machine," which makes it appear as a "single object," and of the vitalist thesis of "the specific, personal unity of the living organism," which makes it appear as a "single subject," whereas both the subject and the object are multiplicities. Once the *structural* and *vitalist* unity is undone, once we have recognized the multiplicities of elements, functions, expressions, and contents that constitute man as well as machine, a "domain of nondifference [is established] between the microphysical and the biological, there being as many living beings in the machine as there are machines in the living."[44]

Industrial psychologists have reluctantly begun to admit that the relation between man and machine is not primarily instrumental but rather affective, that the object is "animated," that it is constituted of networks of forces, that to work means to exercise an occupation on these forces.[45]

Unlike a thinker like Heidegger, for Guattari, the machine does not turn us away from Being, the machine does not veil its existence from us. On the contrary, the machinic assemblage and the technical machine, considered as one of its components, are "productive of Being." Ontological mutations are always machinic. They are never the simple result of the actions or choices of the "man" who, leaving the assemblage, removes himself from the non-human, technical, or incorporeal elements that constitute him—all that is pure abstraction.

The recurrence and communication among the human and non-human within the assemblage, their extraordinary creativity and productivity, is not primarily due to language. Language is not sufficiently deterritorialized to fulfill this function in capitalist machinic assemblages; it is still too "human." In machinic enslavements, the ontological barrier between subject and object established by social subjections is continually blurred not because of language but because of asignifying semiotics.

Guattari makes the distinction "between semiologies that produce significations, [...] like the 'human' enunciation of people who work with machines—and [...] asignifying semiotics, which, regardless of the quantity of significations they convey, handle figures of expression that might be qualified as 'non-human' (such as equations or plans which enunciate the machine and make it act in a diagrammatic capacity on technical and experimental apparatuses)."[46]

With asignifying semiotics, we are no longer in the pre-signifying regime of the polyvocal expression of primitive societies which mix and transversalize the semiotics of dance, song, speech, and so on, nor are we in the signifying regime in which the sign refers to another sign by way of representation, consciousness, and the subject. Asignifying semiotics are a matter of assemblages where man, language, and consciousness no longer have priority.

In asignifying semiotics "we even move beyond the semiotic register." Strictly speaking, it is no longer a matter of the sign, because the distinction between the sign and the referent such as linguistics has maintained tends to lose all relevance. In theoretical physics, "No one today demands positive proof of the existence of a particle so long as it can be made to function without any contradiction in the totality of theoretical semiotics as a whole. Only when an extrinsic, experimental effect brings the semiotic system into operation does hindsight question the existence of the particle."[47] Between the sign and the referent a new kind of relationship emerges.

Guattari distinguishes between the impotentized signs of semiologies of signification, which owe their semiotic efficiency to their passage through representation and consciousness, and the "power signs," "sign-points," of asignifying semiotics, which act on material flows. "Power signs," "sign-points," have a long history, since art and religion were the first to produce them: "The Shamanic invocation, the sign-writing of the geomancer, are in themselves direct signs of power. They mark the importation into nature of signs of power."[48]

It is easy to see the difference between these signs by examining how they function within capitalism's most important institution: money. Money is an impotentized sign when it functions as exchange value, a means of payment, in other words, as a simple mediation between equivalents. In this case, it does no more than represent purchasing power[49] by establishing a bi-univocal relationship between money-signs and a given quantity of goods and services. Power signs, on the other hand, express money as capital and the role of money as credit. They represent nothing, they have no equivalents, except in the future exploitation of the labor force, nature, and society. They are power signs because instead of representing something they anticipate it, create it, and mold it. Power signs constitute the semiotics of an economy of possibles.[50]

Sign-points act in two ways. On the one hand, they are capable of operating semiotically, even if the functions of denotation and signification deteriorate; on the other hand, they are capable of intervening directly in material processes in which the functions of denotation and signification break down.

The simplest example of direct intervention is that of the microchip, where sign flows act directly on the material components. The polarities of iron oxide particles are converted into binary numbers when a magnetic strip is passed through a reader equipped with the appropriate computer program. The signs function as the input and output of the machine, bypassing denotation, representation, and signification. Sign flows engage real flows, giving orders and producing a change in conditions.

The expressive function meshes directly with material flows, and becomes capable of catalyzing machinic "choices," such as feedback, and bringing about changes of state [...]. [T]he diagrammatic formula inscribed on my parking permit sets off the mechanism of the entrance barrier: it allows me to go from an "outside" to an "inside" state.[51]

But in a more general way, we can think of monetary signs which act directly on production flows, or of a computer language which makes technical machines run. By acting on things outside of representation, signs and things "engage one another independently of the subjective 'controls' that individuated agents of enunciation claim to have over them."[52]

The semiotic functions of "power signs" do not represent, do not refer to an already constituted "dominant" reality, but simulate and pre-produce a reality that does not yet exist, a reality that is only virtually present, multiplying possibles, by creating "optional matter." Rather than given in advance, existence constitutes the very stakes of theoretical-experimental assemblages in physics and the artistic-experimental and political-experimental in other domains.

Guattari calls the operations of asignifying semiotics "diagrammatic." The diagram is a semiotic system and a mode of writing that fulfill the conditions of power signs. The concept is taken from Peirce's categories, in which diagrammatic semiotics encompass images and diagrams (also called "icons of relation"). Guattari classifies images with symbolic semiotics and makes diagrams a separate category whose functions are operational, rather than representational; they have the capacity to reproduce with great exactitude the functional articulations of a system. Diagrammatic signs, by acting in place of things themselves, produce machinic rather than significant redundancy.

Within a different theoretical framework, Bruno Latour has shown the capacity of diagrams to break through what Guattari calls the "ontological iron curtain," separating words and things, subjects and objects. Unlike language, the diagram operates a machinic, and non-signifying, translatability of phenomena by reducing optional matter: "In modeling the situation, the diagram allows for the imagining of new scenarios," new possibilities for action and creation.[53]

"Diagram" is also the name Foucault gives to the panopticon, a "machine" or "machinery" that "automatizes and disindividualizes power."[54] "Dissymmetry, disequilibrium, difference," are not assured by people but rather by machines of which individuals are component parts.[55] To understand how diagrams and asignifying semiotics function, one fundamental element is missing. Regardless of the kind of assemblage (economic, social, atomic, chemical, aesthetic, etc.), expression and content are continually subjected to processes of deterritorialization which asignifying semiotics and machines allow to be harnessed, controlled, as well as produced.

Diagrams (like equations, designs, graphs, apparatuses, machines, etc.) come to accelerate or slow down, destruct or stabilize, processes of deterritorialization which language has difficulty grasping.[56] Without diagrammatic machines and signs, without the simulation and pre-production they enable, without the capture of non-human phenomena and relations by asignifying semiotic systems, our picture of deterritorialization would be "extremely myopic and limited."

Through asignifying semiotics machines "speak," "express themselves," and "communicate" with man, other machines, and "real" phenomena. Through "power signs" they interact with the expression and content of the atomic and chemical strata of matter, the biological strata of the living being, and the cosmic strata of the universe. Like machines, atomic, biological, chemical, economic, and aesthetic strata are therefore agents "productive of Being," speakers and agents of partial "discursivity." Machines and asignifying semiotics are able to "see" these strata, "hear" them, "smell" them, record them, order them, and transcribe them, something that is impossible for human senses and language. Infinitely small and infinitely large, infinitely fast and infinitely slow, they escape our systems of perception and language.

Asignifying semiotics and machines operate in the same way in the preverbal world of human subjectivity, inhabited by nonverbal semiotics, affects, temporalities, intensities, movements, speeds, impersonal relations, non-assignable to a self, to an individuated subject, and thus, again, difficult for language to grasp.

In a machine-centric world, action on the real requires artificiality, an increasingly abstract artificiality. Man without machines, without apparatuses, without diagrams, without equations, without asignifying semiotics, would be "aphasic," incapable of "speaking" these worlds, of apprehending and intervening in processes of deterritorialization. *In a machine-centric world, in order to speak, see, smell, and act, we are of a piece with machines and asignifying semiotics.* It is in this sense that asignifying semiotics constitute focal points of enunciation and vectors of subjectivation.

The strength of capitalism lies in the exploitation of machines and semiotic systems that conjoin functions of expression and functions of content of every kind, human and non-human, microphysical and cosmic, material and incorporeal.

The asignifying semiotics and machines (economic, scientific, etc.) these functions put to "work" are connected with subjectivity and consciousness. But it is not solely nor mainly a matter of reflexive consciousness or human subjectivity. Above all, they mobilize partial and modular subjectivities, non-reflexive consciousnesses, and modes of enunciation that do not originate in the individuated subject. Guattari always uses the same example of driving a car in order to describe how subjectivity and consciousness function in machinic assemblages.

When we drive, we activate subjectivity and a multiplicity of partial consciousnesses connected to the car's technological mechanisms. There is no "individuated subject" that says "you must push this button, you must press this pedal." If one knows how to drive, one acts without thinking about it, without engaging reflexive consciousness, without speaking or representing what one does. We are guided by the car's machinic assemblage. Our actions and subjective components (memory, attention, perception, etc.) are "automatized," a part of the machinic, hydraulic, electronic, etc., apparatuses, constituting, like mechanical (non-human) components, parts of the assemblage. Driving mobilizes different processes of conscientization, one succeeding the next, superimposing one onto the other, connecting or disconnecting according to events. Often as we drive we enter "a state of wakeful dreaming," a "pseudo-sleep," "which allows several systems of consciousness to function in parallel, some of which are like running lights, while others shift to the foreground."[57]

The thought and consciousness of the individuated subject come into play when there is an obstacle, a disturbance, or an "event." Then the subject, consciousness, and representation are used in order to modify the feedback relations among the human and non-human components of the automobile "machine," in order to reestablish the automatic mechanisms and machinic operations.

Needless to say that it is in this work apparatus that we first experience the dual processing of subjectivity (desubjectivation and subjectivation, automatic functioning and individuated subjects' actions, routine and innovation). But Guattari suggests that in modern-day capitalism this is how every apparatus and institution operates.

Whereas the formalization of signifier and signified allows for only one subject, one consciousness, one unconscious, one reality, and one existence, machinic enslavement takes in a multiplicity of modes of subjectivation, a multiplicity of states of consciousness, a multiplicity of unconsciousnesses, a multiplicity of realities and modes of existence, a multiplicity of languages and semiotic systems.

If, as in the theories of Badiou and Rancière, you find no trace of "machines," machinic enslavement, asignifying or diagrammatic semiotics, you can be sure that, however interesting they might otherwise be, these theories have nothing relevant to say about the nature of capitalism—quite simply because without "machines," without asignifying semiotics, without diagrams, there is no capitalism. There are indeed relations of domination, power, and subjections, but these are not the relations of capitalist domination, power, and subjections. Still more troubling: the "distribution of the sensible," the "subject," and "political subjectivation" without the machinic assemblage, without its molecular and microphysical operations, without their non-human dimensions, amount to an idealism of the "subject" and to a politics as "pure" as it is unlikely.

My friends in cognitive capitalism present a different set of shortcomings, for they seem to have returned to the anthropomorphic limits of a certain brand of Marxism. Cognitive "labor" is supposed to mean the incorporation of the tool by the brain, a way for man to appropriate the knowledge of machines (an implausible, backwards expropriation of the machine).

If the machine is not, as the tool-inspired model has it, a prosthesis or an organ, then the humans-machines relation can be reduced neither to an *incorporation* nor to an *exteriorization*. Humans-machines relations are always on the order of a coupling, an assemblage, an encounter, a connection, a capture. Generations of Italian activists grew up reading Marx's *Grundrisse*, whose Italian translation is: "Frammento sulle macchine" (Fragment on Machines). Yet today machines seem to have disappeared from critical theory.

In Marx's time, there was only the inside of the factory (with a concentration and intensity incomparably lower to that of today's corporations) and the outside, the latter among a handful of apparatuses such as the railroads. Today, they are everywhere except in critical theory. They are everywhere and especially in our daily lives.

I wake up in the morning, turn on the lamp, and I provide the catalyst that "activates" a network. If one follows the electric flows passing through an infinity of networks, one will trace things all the way back to the nuclear power plant. As I make breakfast, I put machines to work (the stove, the refrigerator, etc.), which, depending on the case, free up domestic work or increase its productivity. Still half-asleep, I turn on the radio, which subjects speech and voice to profound "machinic" transformations. The usual spatial and temporal dimensions of the sound world are suspended. The human sensory-motor schemas on which sound perception is based are neutralized. The voice, speech, and sound are deterritorialized because they lose every kind of relationship with a body, a place, a situation, or a territory.[58]

Before going out, I make a phone call. In what time and space does the conversation take place? Once outside, I take out money from an ATM that gives me orders (enter your password, take your card, and take your money!). If I make a mistake, the machine refuses to give me the money and "eats" my card. To take the subway I have to submit to the orders of another automaton, the ticket machine, which fills the emptiness left by the humans at the ticket counters.

If I have not had the time to read the newspaper on the Internet, I buy it and experience "speech" and, in particular, political speech, which, unlike Arendt's theory, does not express itself through the voice but rather through "objects and matter," in other words, speech that, as with the radio, is no longer logocentric but machine-centric.[59]

If I have a problem with unemployment or my welfare check, I contact a call center which each time asks me to press 1 or 2 or 3. The same thing happens when making an appointment with the electric company, subscribing to an Internet service, obtaining information about my bank account, and so on. I have to figure things out for myself even if I lose time doing it, since it is impossible to find a human being within these networks. Moreover, the time that I lose is time gained by the company or institution, time that I have graciously made available to them.

I make a call from my cell phone connected to a satellite or I send an SMS. I take a taxi guided by the non-human voice and intelligence of GPS—"in one-half mile go left, then turn right," etc.

In the afternoon I order books online, I Skype with a Brazilian friend, and I respond to my e-mails; I plug into different information networks—political, cultural, etc. I send an instant message on my computer.

At the supermarket, I fight with the automatic check-out that is supposed to save me time, while I do the work, for free, of a clerk usually employed part-time. If I buy a plane or train ticket online, I avoid going to the station, but I must, however reluctantly, carry out unpaid "work" that increases the productivity of the train company or airline. My perception of the world is filtered through the images on television (3 hours 30 minutes per day on average), movies, the Internet, etc., etc. 99.9% of the music that we listen to is recorded and distributed by every kind of machine. Even at the local library the "loans and returns" are no longer handled by human beings but by machines. Humans are left to deal with the breakdowns and ensure that humans function correctly as component parts of the assemblage.

We could all continue the list of our relationships, whether problematic, indifferent, or pleasurable, with the machines that "assist" us daily in even our smallest everyday activities. In modern-day capitalism, we are surely not confronted with an economic, social, and political model of production of "man by man," as cognitive capitalist theory maintains. We are faced with an immense machinic phylum that, in one way or another, affects us and forces us beyond logocentrism.

We must rise to a challenge beyond the limits of central or hege-monic "knowledge," cognitive work, or the "distribution of the sensible." We must free the human and non-human forces that the first industrial revolution imprisoned in *labor*, *language*, and *life*, and do so not in order to find an "original" subjectivity, but to open and activate other processes of its production by seizing on the deterritorialization of work, language, and life as an opportunity. The particular interest that Guattari takes in machines and asignifying semiotics stems from the possibility they offer to collective action of moving beyond the ways of life and subjectivation based on work, language, and (biopolitical) life. Asignifying semiotics and technical, scientific, artistic, and revolutionary processes of deterritorialization constitute the propitious conditions for doing away with the humanist, familialist, and personological modes of representation, the nationalist, racist, and classist modes of subjectivation, according to which capital is territorialized and in which individuated subjects become alienated. The suspicions analytic philosophy and psychoanalysis provoke have to do with their role in stabilizing and maintaining capitalist deterritorialization by providing the categories and methodologies for reterritorializing the desubjectivation carried out through the machinic enslavement of the individual, the person, and the "ego." Language acts as the raw material for the semiotic engineering responsible for manufacturing an individuated subject adapted to the dominant significations that assign him a role, an identity, and a function within the social division of labor.

3

Mixed Semiotics

> A subjective fact is always the product of an assemblage of hetero-
> geneous semiotic levels.
> —Félix Guattari, "Agencements. Transistances. Persistances,"
> Seminar of December 12, 1981

Although we can distinguish different semiotics for the needs of analysis, modes of expression are always the result of "mixed semiotics" which are at once signifying, symbolic, and asignifying. We will here describe how the stock market functions, how a medium such as the cinema, the infant's "subjectivity," and the organization of service sector labor function as mixed semiotic assemblages. We must underscore that, in each of these cases, linguistic, cognitive, and communicational semiotics do not always play the principal role. Accounting for mixed semiotics will profoundly alter our understanding of enunciation since all these semiotics—and not only language—constitute sources of enunciation and focal points of subjectivation. Analyzing these different cases, we will focus closely on the shift from the individuated subject to subjectivation carried out by capitalist machinisms as well as Guattarian theory.

1. The Trader's Machinic Subjectivity

A caricatural yet widespread version of the "subject" is *homo economicus*, a subject capable of exercising sovereign rational control over his choices and actions. The financial trader represents its fully realized paradigm, although his subjectivity has nothing sovereign or rational about it.

Finance is the prime example of diagrammatic semiotics in which signs function in place of the "objects" to which they refer. The sign flows circulating from computer to computer in real time constitute a reality that is as objective as material flows; they influence subjectivity and the functional links in the system which set share prices and act directly on the "real" economy.

In the trading room there are only diagrams, only curves traced by a worldwide computer network, which indicate the upward and downward movements of share prices. Several semiotics are already mobilized here: "impotentized signs" limited to representing price history, but also "power signs," "particle-signs," "sign-points," which stimulate, anticipate, make prices happen—in short, these are diagrammatic signs that transform the "real." Unlike the referential function, there is not one reality but a multiplicity of heterogeneous realities: the reality of the "real" economy, the reality of forecasts about the economy, as well as the reality of share prices and the reality of expectations of these prices rising or falling. The "stock market" does not refer to a single reality.

The trader's "human" subjectivity establishes focal points of proto-enunciation both in the (higher and lower) price differentials of assets and in the productivity differentials of the "real" economy forecast by the calculations of machines. These differentials represent nodes of proto-subjectivation in which human subjectivity (or, rather, components of subjectivity—understanding, memory, attention, perception, etc.) come to fit and combine with machinic proto-subjectivity.

Diagrams, curves, and data "speak," "express" themselves, and "communicate," for, by making visible, comparable, and manipulable the most diverse flows of information (machinic translatability), they forcefully contribute to decision-making and price-setting. Diagrams provide the thresholds of proto-subjectivity from which human subjectivity determines its choices. With each threshold it crosses to make a decision, to express an evaluation, and to indicate a price, subjectivity has no choice but to rely on machines, asignifying writing systems, and information codified and produced by mathematical instruments.

Enunciation would be completely different without these a-semiotic modes of writing and without machines. Given the current conditions of deterritorialization and the phenomenal accumulation of information to process, enunciation would be quite simply impossible. Curves, diagrams, and machines are indispensable components of enunciation, of "non-human" sites of partial subjectivation.

That signs (machines, objects, diagrams, etc.) constitute the focal points of proto-enunciation and proto-subjectivity means that they *suggest, enable, solicit, instigate, encourage, and prevent certain actions, thoughts, affects or promote others*. Machines, objects, and signs do more than influence certain actions, thoughts, or affects; through asignifying semiotics, machines communicate directly with other machines,, entailing often unforeseeable and incalculable diagrammatic effects on the real.[1]

The freedom, independence, and autonomy of the individual economic subject are undermined by still other forces influencing him, making him act and decide without necessarily accessing consciousness. What type of subjectivity and what semiotics are mobilized by these sites of proto-subjectivation determined by diagrams, computers, and so on? Foremost, as with primitive peoples, the insane, and children, the subjectivity is transitivist, transindividual, and the semiotics symbolic.

In order to account for the subjective behavior involved in asset pricing, convention theory and cognitive capitalist theory presuppose agents' mimetic behavior. The intersubjectivity, language, and communication of the mimetic relationship are supposed to supplant the methodological individualism of *homo economicus*, founded on rationality and sovereignty. Unfortunately, mimetic behavior is irreducible to linguistic, cognitive, or communicational intersubjectivity.

Without in the least partaking of the philosophical theory that underpins the notion of financial behavior *as* mimetic behavior, we must emphasize that for its creator, René Girard, mimetic emulation is above all the emulation of desire. One does not imitate ways of being, one does not imitate ideas or the "cognitive basis" of the "other"; one imitates desire. If mimesis implies the emulation of desire, its constitution and dissemination/circulation cannot, however, be explained by communication, language, or cognition, because affects undermine precisely the communicational, informational, linguistic, and cognitive models.

"Mimetic rationality" is not linguistic-cognitive—far from it. For affect suspends the speaker/hearer enunciative dichotomy. "Affect sticks to subjectivity," but as much to the enunciator's subjectivity as to that of his addressee. Spinoza, Guattari suggests, perfectly understood this transitivist feature of affect: "('from the fact of conceiving a thing like ourselves to be affected with any emotion, we are ourselves to be affected with a like emotion') [...]. Affect is thus essentially a pre-personal category, installed 'before' the circumscription of identities, and manifested by unlocatable transferences, unlocatable with regard to their origin as well as with regard to their destination."[2]

Affect remains "vague, atmospheric," Guattari says, in other words, it is not founded on systems of distinct oppositions as in the linguistic, communicational, or cognitive models. It is therefore quite reductive to explain mimetic behavior via linguistic, communicative, or cognitive rationality. Somewhere there are downward trends and there are upward trends in the same way as "mana" circulates in animist societies. Mimetic communication occurs through *contagion* and not through *cognition*.

When it is a matter of choosing, deciding, and exercising "freedom," the trader's human subjectivity, language, signifying semiotics, and cognitive power do not rise above but instead act, are of a piece, with machines, power signs, symbolic semiotics, and affects. Machines and power signs, no less than the individual's "freedom," are constitutive of his decision-making, choices, and *pour-soi*.

The trader's subjectivity is undoubtedly a "machinic subjectivity" whose operations can only be determined by way of the functional whole of humans-machines. Mathematical systems, data banks, interconnected computer networks, telephone networks, and so on, are part of the financier's subjectivity. Through him, groups, lobbies, interested economic and political parties, and schools of thought act and express themselves. His enunciation also depends on mimetic action and, furthermore, on the laws and rules that permit certain operations and not others, or the loosening of both laws and rules as the State has endeavored to do for the last forty years. Instead of a rational subject who controls information and his choices, *homo economicus* is a mere terminal of asignifying, symbolic, and signifying semiotics and of non-linguistic constituents which for the most part escape his awareness. We are not only well beyond the individualism and rationality of *homo economicus*, we have moved beyond "cognitive capitalism."

In this context, signifying semiologies, discourses, cognitive activities, fulfill a specific function: controlling the deterritorialization and desubjectivation the diagrammatic semiotics and symbolic semiologies define. The individual subject, his sovereignty and rational behavior, ruined by the real workings of the stock market, must literally be reconstructed, refabricated, by signifying semiologies, communication, and cognition. The discourse of economists, media, experts, and judges[3] create the belief that it is indeed the individual subject who acts and who thus must be compensated as a result. Through the semiotics of signification, stories, information, and commentary are produced which construct and legitimate the function and the role of these "individuated subjects" (traders) in public opinion.

Signifying semiologies cannot be reduced to "ideology."[4] Narratives and discourses that speak of *homo economicus*, the freedom of the entrepreneur, the self-regulating power of the markets, and so on, have no superstructural function, since it is sign machines that produce a specific and fundamental commodity: the individuated subject. The "ideological force" of signifying semiologies does not lie in the fact that it prevents us from thinking or in mere manipulation (although it can do both as well), but rather in its ability to effect a mutation in subjectivity. The refrains of neoliberalism (be an asset, be a self-starter, get rich, etc.) are there to ensure this happens. The latter do not hide a reality from us; instead, they endow us with a relationship to time, space, and others by making us exist somewhere in a world that refers every subjectivity which capitalist deterritorialization produces to the entrepreneur, individual success, competition, social Darwinism, and so on.

2. The Mixed Semiotics of the "Human"

> This opposition—on the one side, desire-drive, desire-disorder, desire-death, desire-aggression, and, on the other, interaction […]—seems to me an utterly reactionary reference.
> —Félix Guattari, *Molecular Revolution in Brazil*

In the last years of his life, Guattari often drew on Daniel Stern's book *The Interpersonal World of the Infant*[5] in order to map a cartography of the semiotic, affective, and existential components that contribute to the production of subjectivity. In Stern's work, preverbal subjectivity, expressed through asignifying symbolic semiotics, is described in its problematic relationship to the linguistic "social machine." According to Guattari, linguistic theory and analytic philosophy systematically ignore or gloss over this pre-individual subjectivity, which is at the root of all modes of subjectivation.

Stern's book undermines the unity of the subject by enumerating the multiplicity of "selves," semiotics, relations, and affects, especially preverbal ones, constituting him. The approach proves particularly enlightening when trying to apprehend the existential and self-referential dimension at the heart of Guattari's theory of subjectivity. Far from passing solely through language, cognition, or communication, the relation to the self presupposes a self-positioning that is existential, pathic, and affective prior to being linguistic or cognitive. Subjective mutation is not primarily discursive, because it is situated at the focal point of (existential) non-discursivity at the core of subjectivity. It is starting from this existential dimension that there is an emergence, a processuality, a taking on of consistency, of subjectivity. Only from this asignifying, unnamable, and incommunicable core can there be signification, language, and narrative. The point has important political implications since this same preindividual subjectivity is brought to bear by capitalist machinic enslavements to exploit affects, rhythms, movements, durations, intensities, and asignifying semiotics.

1. The Emergent Self and Asignifying Semiotics

Before acquiring language, infants actively construct forms of perceiving, communicating, and experiencing the self and the world through very rich and differentiated nonverbal semiotization. Stern's work underscores what is from the outset the trans-subjective nature of the earliest experiences of the infant, who is yet unable to distinguish between a sense of self and other.

Stern describes three "senses of self" (the sense of an emergent self, the sense of a core self, and the sense of a subjective self) that precede the "sense of verbal self." "Sense of self" does not mean, in the first three cases, "concept of," "knowledge of" or "awareness of,"[6] as these experiences do not pass through language, consciousness, or representation.

According to Guattari, the different senses of self preceding the linguistic sense of self are in no way stages in the Freudian sense but "levels of subjectivation," nonverbal focal points and vectors of subjectivation that manifest themselves throughout life in parallel with speech and consciousness. The three first senses of self are expressed through mixed, asignifying and symbolic semiotics.

Between the infant's birth and the first two months of life, he experiences the "genesis" of an "emergent interpersonal link," the genesis of what Stern calls the "sense of emergent self." There are three principal ways in which the infant experiences this: amodal perception, categorical affects, and vitality affects. The infant has a great ability to select from and organize the general and abstract features of what happens to him. Intensities, temporal figures, rhythms, and movements are features common to every sensorial form and the infant can easily identify and, from there, transpose them from one sense to another, from sight to touch, for example, or from touch to hearing.

The abstract and amodal features of what happens are apprehended through two different affective processes: categorical affects, which express anger, surprise, joy, sadness, and so on, and vitality affects, which express changes in mental states and intensity thresholds in his way of feeling. Vitality affects are "captured by dynamic, kinetic terms, such as 'surging,' 'fading away,' 'fleeting,' 'explosive,' 'crescendo,' 'decrescendo,' 'bursting,' 'drawn out,' and so on."[7] Dance, music, as well as the duration of video-cinematographic images are, according to Stern, realities that best capture these intensities, these "ways of feeling."

This global, subjective world in which there is not yet a division between subject and object, in which the self and others are indistinguishable, in which communication occurs by contagion, "is and remains," according to Stern and Guattari, the "fundamental domain of human subjectivity." It operates outside of consciousness and represents the "matrix" (Stern), the "existential core" (Guattari), of experiences from which "thoughts and perceived forms and identifiable acts and verbalized feelings will later arise. [...] Finally, it is the ultimate reservoir that can be dipped into for all creative experience."[8] All learning and all creative acts depend on this sense of emergent self. "This domain of experience remains active during the formative period of each of the subsequent domains of sense of self" as well as during later learning and creative processes.

We have access to these modes of semiotization in childhood, through psychosis, drug use, and certain altered states of consciousness, but also through artistic creation, falling in love, political passions, existential crises, and, even discursively, through philosophy.[9]

2. The Sense of a "Core Self," the Sense of a "Subjective Self," and Symbolic Semiotics

The sense of a "core self" (the self as opposed to the other and the self with the other) constitutes the experience of self and other as "entities" with "a physical presence, action, affect, and continuity." The sense of core self depends on "numerous interpersonal capacities."[10] This is still not a cognitive construction (for it occurs outside consciousness) but rather an integration of experience and a "memory without words" which provide the bases for all the more complex senses of self.

According to Stern, the period spanning two to six months is perhaps the most exclusively and intensely social period of the infant's life (the social smile, vocalizations directed at others, the mutual gaze, etc.).[11]

The sense of a subjective self occurs when the infant discovers that he has a "mind" and that others do too, that experiences, content, affects, and emotions are shareable (or not shareable) and can be communicated without words because language is yet unavailable. Self and other are no longer only core entities with a certain physical presence, action, affect, and continuity; they are entities with "internal and subjective states."

How does one relate with the subjective experience of others, share their affects, without the use of words? As Guattari and Simondon (or Spinoza) might put it, one does so through "transitivist, transindividual" subjectivity.

Between the ages of nine and twelve months, the infant is able to coordinate his "mental states," such as "joint attention," "intentions," and "affective states." Vitality (dynamic and kinetic) affects and categorical affects (joy, sadness) constitute the material enabling the infant's "attunement" and sharing, which presuppose the existence of a "shared framework" of signification and the means for "preverbal" communication (gesture, posture, facial expression and vocal expression, etc.).[12] Affects remain the "predominant mode and substance of communications with [the] mother"; other people—affects coupled with gestures, posture, nonverbal action, and vocalizations—are the "most immediate origins" of and the protolinguistic conditions for the emergence and acquisition of language.[13] As Guattari remarks, "It is at the heart of this protosocial and still preverbal Universe that familial, ethnic, urban, etc. traits are transmitted (let's call it the Cultural Unconscious).[14]

3. The Sense of a "Verbal Self" and Signifying Semiotics

The fourth sense of self, the sense of a verbal self, has to do with the *junction* and *disjunction*, the *complementarity* and *gap*, between the verbal and nonverbal parts of subjectivity, between asignifying symbolic semiotics and signifying semiologies. This is because the emergence of language is the source of a cleavage between experience as it is "lived" and as it is "represented."

If linguistic significations make our experiences with others more easily shareable, they can also make certain parts of these same experiences inaccessible to others as well as to ourselves. The nonverbal and "global" part of experience and that part of experience converted into words can very well coexist, the verbal part harmoniously enriching and expanding lived (affective) experience. But the latter may also be fractured, rendered poorly by language, consequently forcing experience underground (repression). The adult's words, "Oh, look at the yellow sunlight," specify, separate, and fracture the amodal experience of the sunray the infant has.

"The paradox that language can evoke experience that transcends words is perhaps the highest tribute to the power of language. But those are words in poetic use. The words in our daily lives more often do the opposite and either fracture amodal global experience or send it underground."[15] The three preverbal senses of self are not steps in the formation of the verbal self. They remain independent centers of semiotic and subjective "production" and continue to function in parallel with their own "autonomy" and their own semiotics.

According to Guattari, the way in which linguistics and psychoanalysis conceive of the relationship between verbal and nonverbal semiotics raises the same political problem. The theories are informed by a model founded on the opposition between a raw world of desire, drives, instinct, animality, and spontaneity, on the one hand, and, on the other, a universe of social order, the symbolic, law, and prohibition expressed by language and signifying semiotics. The semiotic-linguistic model is in reality a political model. In the same way as a supposedly undifferentiated economy of desire necessitates signifying, symbolic semiotics, the law, and taboos to provide its structure, in the process of political subjectivation we need the political party and its "democratic centralism" in order to structure and discipline the spontaneity of subjectivities.

Butler considers the model of "symbolic castration" and the "law" at once necessary and inevitable in the formation of both speech and society. The idea of a "prediscursive libidinal multiplicity that effectively presupposes a sexuality 'before the law'"[16] is part of a "romantic vision" of subjectivity even for Foucault, since we can say nothing about and do nothing with a reality prior to language, the law, the symbolic, and the taboo, contrary to what Stern demonstrates. Access to the "real" of the undifferentiated can only be assured through the "mediation" of the symbolic, the law, taboo, and the signifier.

Since desire partakes of dream, fantasy, and representation, there will always be a choice to make between a "pleasure principle" and a "reality principle." For Bernard Stiegler, the "drive" closest to animality must undergo a symbolic "sublimation" in order to reestablish the necessary functions of the "super ego" and the "law" destroyed by capitalism. Virno, for his part, follows to the letter Wittgenstein's aphorism according to which "speech" replaces "drive." Language completely reconfigures the world of drives "by shaping them from top to bottom," for it teaches us to express, with words and grammar, what is of the order of affect. In Badiou's party-less Marxist-Leninism, the opposition between the animal and the subject turns on the opposition between "desiring spontaneity" and "organization." Guattari challenges the model on the grounds that, as we have just seen, the nonverbal semiotics of subjectivity have "absolutely nothing undifferentiated about them"; they on the contrary "involve highly elaborate operations of assemblage, syntax, and modes of semiotization that do not necessarily imply the existence of metalanguage and overcoding in order to interpret, direct, normalize, and order them."[17] They are neither poorer nor richer in language; they are different.

The point is not to devalue language and signifying semiotics, but rather, as opposed to what linguistics and analytic philosophy do, to place ourselves between the discursive and the non-discursive in order to make enunciation and subjectivation "grow from the middle."

3. Cinema's Mixed Semiotics

> We go to the cinema in order to suspend for a moment our usual modes of communication.
> —Félix Guattari, "Le divan du pauvre"

A political battle has unfolded and continues to unfold around cinema for control of the effects of subjectivation and desubjectivation that the "non-human" semiotics of the cinematographic image produce on the individuated subject. The three preverbal senses of self, the sense of a verbal self, and semiotics (at once asignifying, symbolic, and signifying) are mobilized by cinematographic machinism which by deterritorializing the image and perception (the "film-eye") risks undoing, in its way, the unity of the subject.

With the cinema, we have a textbook case of how the signifying machine comes to neutralize, order, and normalize the action of symbolic and asignifying semiotics which exceed dominant significations. By hierarchizing the latter through signifying semiotics, the film industry functions like group psychoanalysis (Guattari), powerfully aiding in the construction of the roles and functions and, especially, in the fabrication of the individuated subject and his unconscious.

Guattari lists precisely the semiotics at work in the cinema:

—the phonic fabric of expression that refers to spoken language (signifying semiology);

—the sonorous but nonphonic fabric that refers to instrumental music (asignifying semiotics);

—the visual fabric that refers to painting (both symbolic and asignifying semiotics);

—the gestures and movements of the human body, etc. (symbolic semiologies);

—the duration, movements, breaks in space and time, gaps, sequences, etc., that make up asignifying "intensities."[18]

The cinema, whose effects derive above all from its use of asignifying symbolic semiotics ("linkages, internal movements of visual images, colors, sounds, rhythms, gestures, speech, etc."[19]), represented for a brief moment the possibility of moving beyond signifying semiologies, of bypassing personological individuations, and opening up possibilities that were not already inscribed in dominant subjectivations.

Film images cannot be directly encoded, marked out, and framed by the syntagmatic and paradigmatic axes that ensure the relative stability and invariance of meanings as in language. With cinema, it becomes possible to rediscover the features of pre-signifying semiotics in a post-signifying world. The cinema does not put two components of expression (signifier/signified) into play, but rather, as in primitive societies, "n": the images, sounds, and words spoken and written (texts), movements, positions, colors, rhythms, and so on. Depending on the component that prevails, there are different modalities of reading and seeing a film. "It can be seen through its colors or rhythms, through its images, through the chain of affects it creates, and there is absolutely no univocal, necessary, or unmotivated relationship between a signifying chain and the contents signified."[20]

As in primitive societies, images (symbolic semiotics) and intensities, movements, intervals, temporalities, and velocities (asignifying semiotics) reintroduce ambiguity, uncertainty, and instability into denotation and signification. Expression once again becomes polyvocal, multidimensional, and multireferential. "The semiotic components of film glide by each other without ever fixing or stabilizing themselves in a deep syntax of latent contents or in transformational systems that would lead, superficially, to manifest contents."[21]

The same impossibility of formalizing filmic language is analyzed by Pasolini. For the Italian poet, the cinema as well as an important part of human reality and of things themselves are expressed through systems of signs, in other words, by nonverbal (images or "im-signs") and non-human "languages." Images from memory and dream all have the features of film sequences, they are "almost prehuman events, or on the border of what is human. In any case, they are pregrammatical and even premorphological (dreams take place on the level of the unconscious, as do mnemonic processes)."[22]

The cinema is at once "fundamentally oneiric" and a "hypnotic monstrum." The "irrational" elements of the language of film, "barbarous, irregular, aggressive, visionary," cannot be eliminated; thus the difficulty in establishing an "institutional film language."[23] Indeed, these features, which Pasolini terms "irrational," make up the modalities of expression of affects, intensities, velocities, etc., whose functioning depends on a logic other than that of the individuated subject's rationality.

The cinema is thus capable, if for only an instant, of making us "orphans: single, amnesiac, unconscious, and eternal," and removing us from the social divisions of labor that assign us a role, a function, and a meaning.[24]

The intensities, movements, and duration of film images can produce effects of desubjectivation and disindividuation in the same way that childhood, drugs, dreams, passion, creation, or madness can strip the subject of his identity and social functions. Cinema suspends perception and the habitual coordinates of vision, making the sensorimotor system malfunction. Images and movements no longer depend on the movement of the object nor on the brain; instead, they are the automatic products of a machinic apparatus. In turn, montage disrupts the links between ordinary situations, images, and movements by compelling us to enter into different space-time blocs.

But instead of eluding dominant subjectivations, film images can, conversely, chain us to them. They are only focal points of subjectivation. As vectors of subjectivation, they can only trigger, initiate, or open processes of heterogenesis (both the production of heterogeneity and processual genesis). The consistency of subjective heterogeneity depends on the interplay of a multiplicity of forces, apparatuses, and techniques. It depends, in the final analysis, on a politics and an aesthetics. The ethico-political battle, which the American cultural industry has resoundingly won, has been fought over this focal point of heterogeneity. The industry has worked to neutralize and stifle heterogeneity by exploiting, like psychoanalysis, personological and familialist signifiers.

The shift of cinema's multireferential and polysemic semiotics toward dominant values and the domestication of the "oneiric monster" and its "irrational elements" have occurred through the reduction of symbolic semiologies and asignifying semiotics to the models of capitalist subjectivity.

The commercial cinema is "undeniably familialist, Oedipian, and reactionary. [...] Its 'mission' is to adapt people to the models required by mass consumption."[25] If it is incapable of establishing as invariable and stable significations as language, it can still produce models of subjectivity that have the force of examples, the obviousness of physical presence. Cinema acts on the depths of subjectivity because it provides subjectivity with identities and models of behavior by exploiting asignifying and symbolic semiotics. In this way, it functions like "group psychoanalysis," normalizing intensities, hierarchizing semiotics, and confining them within the individuated subject.

Commercial cinema's effect on the unconscious is even more powerful than that of psychoanalysis, since its unconscious, "populated by cowboys and Indians, cops and robbers" (in other words, a non-Oedipal consciousness, an unconscious equal to the world around us), and the range of semiotic mechanisms it mobilizes "directly connect with the spectator's processes of semiotization."[26]

The effect produced by commercial cinema and in turn by television has nothing to do with ideology, for it does not involve reflexive consciousness and representation.

"All its irrational, elementary, oneiric, and barbaric elements were forced below the level of consciousness; that is, they were exploited as subconscious instruments of shock and persuasion"[27] by the cultural industry and industry in general.

Consciousness-raising is not a sufficient response because images affect us and organize themselves in direct relation with the three "selves" preceding the linguistic self. Asignifying, symbolic semiotics do not act on consciousness but rather directly on "the continuous variation and force of existing and potential action."

Here, subjectivity has nothing to do with Althusser's ideological apparatuses, because it, and especially its components, are produced as a whole, bringing to bear what I call asignifying elements, which provide the basis for relations to time, rhythms, space, the body, colors, and sexuality.[28]

4. Signifying and Asignifying Semiotics in the Division of Labor

As a matter of fact, two axioms seem to have guided the advance of Western civilization from the outset: the first maintains that true societies unfold in the protective shadow of the State; the second states a categorical imperative: man must work.

—Pierre Clastres, *Society Against the State*

All the semiotics and modalities of subjective implication we have described come to bear in every division of labor. But whereas signifying semiotics and social subjection are recognized and analyzed as such, the processes of asignifying symbolic semiotics and those of machinic enslavement are ignored in the sociology of work (and "industrial psychology"). This is all the more surprising given that they are what constitute the specificity of the capitalist division of labor.

The same "logocentric" limit detracts from Marie-Anne Dujarier's otherwise remarkable analysis of the organization of production in "mass services" (a geriatrics clinic and a restaurant chain), wherein language is understood as a component of the division of labor and a "productive force."[29]

"Because service work is relational," the author argues, "it mobilizes *language*, to such an extent that one could even say that most often working means speaking."[30] At the same time, she enumerates a great variety and intensive use of asignifying semiotics irreducible to speech. Up and down the hierarchy, asignifying symbolic semiotics operate with signifying semiotics, but the relative weight of one with respect to the other changes according to the hierarchical level in which they function.

The board of directors does "political work when it sets the organization's goals and strategies by providing the necessary resources" ("capital, operating budget, and their allocation").[31] The board's "orders" are transmitted along the hierarchy, mobilizing the most varied asignifying transactions. Speech would be insufficient to organize the production "process" and powerless to command and activate subjectivities.

"CEOs" give preliminary form to the generic objectives handed down from the board of directors "in the form of 'development plans,' 'ethical commitments,' 'quality policies,' 'cost-saving measures,' 'authorization' 'management control,' 'digitalization,' 'marketing strategies,' 'IT systems,' 'advertising campaigns.'"[32] "Budget constraints" are also transformed into asignifying organizational elements: "budgets," "HR policies," "investment plans."

Under the CEOs, the work of "manager experts," to whom upper management has entrusted the work of turning out instructions and ensuring they are followed, "consists primarily in transforming the abstract demands for 'total quality,' 'comfort,' 'attractiveness,' 'versatility,' or 'ethics' into 'specific organizational requirements.'" The translation of CEOs' choices is non-discursive. Employees are not summoned the way Menenius Agrippa did the plebeians in an attempt to convince them with his rhetorical arsenal to put an end to their insubordination (Rancière treats the episode as a model of the egalitarian function special to language). In the capitalist organization of work this is not how orders are transmitted.

They do not function solely (and we could say principally) "inter-subjectively." Orders are not first issued through discourse but through apparatuses using asignifying semiotics. If we hold to the description given by the author herself, signifying semiotics are limited to accompanying discourse or to being completely absent from it: "Orders take the form of the organizational chart, plan, project, manual, protocol, charter, indicators, procedures, processes, and production and management software."[33]

The organization of work is first of all a question of diagrammatic pragmatics. Linguistic imperatives[34] ("you must") or exhortations ("you should"), meetings, "ideological" speeches, and so on, would have little hold on subjectivity were they not supported by asignifying semiotics (diagrams, programs, budgets, management indicators, accounting figures, etc.) which do not speak but function. They do not first address the "I" of the "salaried" individual. They set off operations while bypassing consciousness and representation. Asignifying semiotics work like a "material" cog in humans-machines, humans-organizations, humans-processes systems. They establish a reader, an interpreter, a facilitator; and yet this reader, who may very well be a human being as a machine, software, procedure, etc., is without representations.

The corporation, in certain cases (call centers), diagrammatically exploits even language, by reducing signifying semiotics to a means of signaling that simply triggers prefabricated address and response procedures. There is nothing of the dialogical event in the verbal exchange between employee and consumer. Words and propositions are the "input" and "output" of the machinic enslavement specific to service relations. Only idiots like Alain Finkielkraut still think that responsibility for the "degradation" of language lies with poor schoolchildren, immigrants' sons, the youth, etc., whereas, as Pasolini already had it in the 1960s, private enterprise and marketing are the ones responsible.

> The conversation with a consumer must be quickly referred back to a 'script' which the operator will then read word for word. He can be penalized if he "goes off" script, even for offering an intelligent or empathetic response to the customer. Thus the "prompts," replies to questions, and other forms of civility are planned out prior to the conversation. Dialogue is "triggered" according to the customer's attitude and questions. Finally, the scripts are a way of "taylorizing" conversation; the latter is split into basic units and each task performed. Conversational scripts are made up of pre-fabricated phrases thought up by those who do not speak them and spoken by those whose self-interest is not to think.[35]

The affects, intensities, and "emotions" that animate every verbal exchange are submitted to the same semiotic training, whose aim is to program and control behavior. "Emotion itself is conceived to be a task and is planned for prior to its occurrence. It can be prescribed to the employee or to the consumer independently of what they feel. Labor management institutes plans such that the employee, whether a ticket-taker, youth leader, cashier, flight attendant, hairdresser, bus driver, or museum guide, is compelled to adopt cheerful, assuring, calm, happy, or funny behavior."[36]

Analyzing the use of semiotics in the customer service relationship—from below rather than from the board of directors' perspective—Dujarier notes that "language is growing increasingly abstract." When a service is carried out, whether at the elderly person's bedside or the customer's table, "language" is "that which is constructed according to each speaker's linguistic references in the interaction between employee and consumer."[37] This "language of professionals" marks out a community of peers (employees) and allows us "to speak and, therefore, to examine what real work is."

"Higher up, in the idiom of orders and control, 'managerial' language is employed." In "the procedures, plans, and management or economic indicators used by hierarchical superiors, the semantic references are essentially taken from the language of action ('do this') and measurement ('in order to obtain a result').[38]

"Above managerial language we find the language that addresses methods and processes," the language of "experts," which produces "*discourse about discourse*" because its object is managerial discourse itself. At a still higher level, "political dis-course" concerns the evaluation of results and methods and represents what the author calls "*a discourse about discourse about discourse*," that is, a discourse about experts.

The move to ever-greater abstraction in capitalist command is always interpreted in terms of language (a "discourse about dis-course" and a "discourse about discourse about discourse"), whereas, as one moves up the hierarchy, rather than speak of abstraction, we would do better to analyze the way in which asignifying semiotics are increasingly used. The hold superior hierarchical levels have over inferior ones does not occur because of the use of metalanguage but through the exploitation of asignifying semiotics.

In monitoring, the second function devolving on those higher up the ladder, the same mechanisms and semiotics are at work as in order-giving. Monitoring consists in the activation "of major indicators, of overall rankings"; it "is exercised through tracking mechanisms" and prioritizes the automatic mechanisms and "impersonality" of asignifying ratings. Functional control wins out over disciplinary and discursive control even as it employs them both.[39]

Even "self-control," which measures the "subjective" investment of the employee's "I"—one form of social subjection—is "maintained by managerial tools (rankings, performance summaries, etc.)." Within the service industry a large part of the employee's work consists in rating, ranking, classifying ("We have to follow procedures, jot down, draw up the indicators, validate, track [...]. Personnel rate everything and rate themselves on everything").[40] Ratings make tracking possible, which machines in turn process via asignifying semiotics. The management tools mobilized through "self-control" are still machinic apparatuses, a kind of hypomnemata of labor structure.[41] The "I" of social subjection can only be separated from technical machines, from organizational machines, from processes, through abstraction.

Symbolic semiotics play an overwhelming role in the service relationship by arranging the essential aspects of business communication with customers. Through advertising, symbolic semiotics are fully part of the management techniques of labor organization. The (dreadful) business and marketing culture which they instill while molding public/customer subjectivity also directly acts on the subjectivity of employees, for whom "advertising communication is 'really' what must be produced [...]. [Employees] behave at work as if they believed, on the one hand, that the people they serve believe the promises made to them, and, on the other hand, that it is essential to fulfill them. In this interplay, the ideal promised to the consumer becomes the norm of what must be produced."[42]

Dujarier differentiates in her work among semiotics, cleverly called "mille feuilles semantics": "body language" (symbolic semiotics), "technical language" (asignifying semiotics), and "social languages" (signifying semiotics) all converge in the service relationship.[43] What is lacking in this is an appreciation of machinic enslavement. It is not an empirical but a conceptual shortcoming, since machinic enslavement is very much present in the text and clearly mentioned by those interviewed who exercise command functions in the company under the term "process."

At higher levels, the "language of experts, theoretical language, often colored with Anglicisms [...], no longer deals with work" but with "process." "Managers" are not interested in whether one belongs to a particular trade or in its legitimacy; the focus is the organization and control of "processes" essentially consisting of the application of methods, monitoring of indicators, verification of the uniformity of procedures, and the organization of meetings.

CEOs and experts "represent themselves and are considered as specialists, not in 'labor,' but in 'processes,' 'techniques,' and 'tools.' The central role played by process also emerges in monitoring procedures."[44] What first of all must be monitored and evaluated are the humans-machines systems, the mixed semiotics (signifying, asignifying, symbolic) which together make up "processes."

Sociology and industrial psychology seem to be incapable of grasping conceptually the qualitative leap that has occurred in the move from "work" to "process," from subjection to enslavement. Those high on the hierarchy no longer deal with work but with "process" which integrates labor as "one" of its parts. They organize machinic enslavement (process), in which work appears no different from machines, semiotics, procedures, advertising, and communications. Within these person-based services, whose machines do not bear down with the same crushing weight as in other industrial sectors, diagrams, schemas, indicators, budget entries, etc., take machines' place in the organization of the process.

The sociology (and the psychology) of work is imprisoned, along with the rest of sociology, in anthropomorphic thought whose "actors" are the "I" of the employee and the intersubjectivity of the "collective" of workers. Deleuze and Guattari's anti-sociology frees us from the political limits imposed by the reduction of labor organization to the personology of social subjection.

Although the Marxist and Marxian theory of value has directly or indirectly inspired the "progressive" part of sociology and industrial psychology, it in no way helps to escape this anthropomorphic paradigm, for by distinguishing "living labor" from "dead labor," it assigns all creativity and productivity to the former and relegates to the latter a mere reproductive function. The distinction between living labor and dead labor is appropriate only from the point of view of social subjection. From the point of view of machinic enslavement the sites of productivity, the vectors of enunciation, the "for itself" [*pour soi*] and "for the other" [*pour l'autre*], are not exclusively human. Machines, objects, procedures, diagrams, maps, and so on, are not waiting for the "biblical" spirit of living labor to restore life, mobility, and creativity to them. From the point of view of machinic enslavement, asignifying semiotics, objects, diagrams, programs, and so on, contribute to production, creativity, innovation, in the same way as "people" do. Like machines, humans are hybrids of "dead" and "living labor."

Machinic enslavement (or processes) precedes the subject and the object and surpasses the personological distinctions of social subjection. The latter, between living and dead, subject and object, are the result of the reterritorialization process centered on "man" and "labor." Sociology and industrial psychology operate a humanist reterritorialization, a "humanization" of work, which has nothing progressive about it; indeed, it is identical to the social subjection it legitimates. Instead of being considered an operation of power, capitalism's distribution of places, roles, functions, and jobs is identified with man's very emancipation. By attributing "status and social place [...] [work] contributes decisively to the construction of identity... it allows one to act on the world, on other people and oneself."[45]

Sociology and industrial psychology only recognize "work" ("work assigned," "work accomplished," "work experience," etc.) and completely neglect the fact that "work" is always "capitalist labor," that the concept itself exists nowhere else but in capitalist society. They project the category "labor" onto the past and the future by making it a "universal" spanning all of history.

The political dimension of the distribution of "labor"[46] is forgotten in favor of an analysis of self-realization. "Work is a bodily and existential experience that man makes of the limits and uncertainty of his actions [...]. The work we do (or are deprived of) plays a decisive role in each person's psychic and somatic thought."[47]

Sociology and industrial psychology confuse "work" with the "political program" the workers' movement created in response to "wage slavery." It was not labor as such that guaranteed emancipation. Self-realization, identity formation, and social recognition through work have always been at the heart of the capitalist—and socialist—project itself. The reverence for and celebration of work expressed by France's last president[48] are more than the products of ideology and opportunism. We must look to something other than "real full employment," genuine "work-value." For the social-democratic functions with which work has been invested—income guarantees, social recognition and mobility, the meaning and confidence in the future—are no longer borne out by work or employment. Starting with machinic enslavement, we must conceive a reterritorialization that leads to something other than "work=value." We must seize the opportunity of desubjectivation opened by machinic enslavement so as not to fall back on the mythical-conceptual narratives of producers, workers, and employees. This is one of our most urgent tasks if we are to invent new political subjectivations.

5. The Dual Function and Processing of Subjectivity

> Power uses signifying semiotics, but never loses itself completely in them, and it would be a mistake to imagine that it could fall victim to its own signifying methods or ideologies.
> —Félix Guattari, *Molecular Revolution*

What is the relationship between asignifying semiotics and semiologies of signification in the exercise of capitalist power? Their actions coalesce and complement one other. Economic and political power is inconceivable without the production of subjections and significations that determine for each person the position one is to occupy (you are a man, you are a woman, you are a worker, you are a boss, etc.), the way to behave, the function to fill (you have to produce for yourself, for your family, for the State, etc.), the way to think, and to express oneself. If you do not think and if you do not act the way the State wants and as the market demands, your thoughts and behavior will have to adapt, they will have to be made compatible with these significations.

> There is no moment when we are not encircled by power formations. In our societies people must not gesticulate overmuch, we must each stay in our proper place, sign on the dotted line,

recognize the signals we are given—and any failure may land us in prison or the hospital.[49]

As Foucault reminds us, power—which is simply an action upon an action—determines possibilities, probabilities, potentialities, and virtualities, which must continually be territorialized and integrated into the molar dimension of institutions and significations, to become embodied in the roles and behaviors of individuated subjects.

Money, for example, creates deterritorializing effects insufficient in themselves. The economic imperatives that result from them (for example, reducing the debt, cleaning up government accounts, imposing "sacrifices" on the dominated, etc.) must be interpreted and translated into discourse, thought, and action by the media, political parties, unions, experts, and State administrators and addressed to public opinion, to each social group and every individual. The State, the media, and the experts ceaselessly produce narratives, stories, and statements that continually reinfuse with meaning the asignifying operations of credit money, which, in its specific function (diagrammatic, asignifying), has no use for subjects or objects, persons or things. Money and profit recognize only an abstract and deterritorialized subjectivity and an equally abstract and deterritorialized object (Marx): any subjectivity whatsoever and any kind of object whatsoever without territory, existence, or subjectivity. Subjections attach this deterritorialized subjectivity to roles and functions in which individuals in turn become alienated.

Conversely, if we remain at the level of social subjection and signification, power is reduced to an icon, an image, a representation for contemplation (about which, in reality, we are rarely fooled).

Discourses, narratives, and significations capture subjectivity only at the level of representation, consciousness, images, and significations. To take hold, to act on subjectivity, to determine where and when to act, another type of process is needed, a molecular process of subjectivity carried out through machinic enslavements that circumvent representation, consciousness and signification. Enslavement mobilizes both more and less than the person and the individuated subject insofar as it intervenes at infra-personal and supra-personal levels.

The two modes combine and complement one another: signifying semiotics effectuate a molar processing of subjectivity that targets, solicits, and interpellates consciousness, representation, and the individuated subject, whereas asignifying semiotics effectuate a *molecular* processing of the same subjectivity, mobilizing partial subjectivities, states of non-reflexive consciousness, perceptual systems, and so on. We should again emphasize that the destitution of the subject and his semiologies through capitalist deterritorialization "still does not invalidate human semiotics." The recourse to "human" semiotics has a well-defined goal: to control and modulate the processes of deterritorialization and reterritorialization realized and assured by the asignifying semiotics of technico-scientific systems, economics, and the collective resources of the State, destroying previous existential territories, their values, and their way of life.

An example of the non-reactionary use of signifying semiotics is that of the workers' movement. In the nineteenth century, the latter was able to invent a revolutionary reterritorialization that, rather than simply defending those whom capital was destroying, went beyond capitalist deterritorialization: proletarian internationalism, mutualization, and transnational class solidarity went beyond man in the singular.

The ambiguities, uncertainties, and upheavals which periods of great change, like ours, have experienced can be in part explained by this twofold movement of deterritorialization and reterritorialization. In the Marxist language Guattari employs, the "worker" is deterritorialized in "production" by asignifying semiotics and can thus also be the agent of revolutionary rupture as well as of reactionary reterritorialization.

Capitalism produces crises, indiscriminate and concomitant advances toward a post-human world as well as spectacular retreats toward man. It moves to a world "beyond the human," and it must reterritorialize itself according to that which is most petty, most vulgar, and most cowardly in "man" (racism, chauvinism, exploitation, war). And this incessantly renewed return to "man" (with no possibility of humanism) is justified by the obsessive fear that through deterritorialization and asignifying semiotics, by taking advantage of them as well as acting against them, one might construct a politics beyond the human, in other words, beyond exploitation, racism, war, and colonization, beyond man's power over women and over all other existents (living and non-living).

6. Pasolini and Neo-Capitalism's Semiotics of Immanence

> On the one hand, we have an infantilization of the products of subjectivity with a standardization and homogenization of modes of expression and relations with the world, on the other hand, an exponential expansion of non-denotative functions of language.
>
> Children and adolescents do not understand their development, at least for the most part, by way of signifying discourse. They resort to what I call forms of asignifying discursivity: music, clothing, the body, behavior that signals recognition—as well as to all kinds of machinic systems.
>
> —Félix Guattari, *Révolutions Moléculaires*

> This language of production and consumption—and not the lan-
> guage of man—appears as implacably deterministic. It only wants
> to communicate functionally; it doesn't want to perorate or exalt
> or convince—advertising slogans see to all that.
>
> —Pier Paolo Pasolini, *Heretical Empiricism*

Pasolini is surely one of the first authors to have grasped the nature and functioning of the sign systems of "neo-capitalism." The way in which he frees himself from the limits of linguistics and semiotics as those fields developed over the nineteenth and twentieth centuries intersects, at many points, with the work of Guattari.

The "general semiology" he looks to elaborate recognizes the continuity between nature and culture modernity had broken by concentrating all subjectivity on the subject and by depriving the object of all capacity for expression. Drawing on his experience in film, he created, following Peirce's example, a new semiology starting from the question of the image. By refusing to view the latter as a production of the brain or the result of our system of perception, he is able to overcome the dualisms of the image and things, of consciousness and the object. The shot of Jerry Malaga's hair and Umberto Eco's "real" eyes are part of the same continuum of images that constitute a world that is, consequently, a cinema in itself, a cinema in nature, a metacinema. As in the first chapter of Bergson's *Matter and Memory*, the eye is in things themselves; things are luminous by themselves with no consciousness illuminating them.

By situating the eye in things, cinema undermines the anthropomorphic conception of expression and action. Things express themselves by themselves, constitute focal points of subjectivation; they have a power of expression, a "luminosity," a capacity for proto-enunciation and action specific to them and that in no way depends on man.

1. The Languages of Consumption-Production

What interests us in Pasolini's "general semiotics" is how the language of things functions as a "nonverbal discourse," as a power for the proto-enunciation of reality itself and, therefore, as a site of subjectivation. As with Guattari, expression is not reserved only to linguistic signs. On the contrary, in capitalism, expression and enunciation belong first of all to asignifying and symbolic semiotics.

For Pasolini language is "one of the many possible systems of signs" and not "a privileged system unto itself."[50] Action, behavior, and physical presence are semantic fields, sites of non-linguistic communication. The physical presence of Rome's or Bologna's rundown suburbs and their architecture "speak," just as in Guattari; they function as vectors of subjectivation. Things are sources of discursivity, "dumb, material, objective, inert, merely present," which act as vectors of enunciation.[51]

Things are "iconic signs," images, which communicate or express something. This sensitivity to the language of things themselves comes from Pasolini's work as a filmmaker rather than from his work as a writer. The gaze, aided by the camera, forces him to become conscious of and to catalogue all the things that a film shot contains. The writer transforms things into words, that is, into symbols, into the signs of a verbal system which are "symbolic and conventional while the 'signs' of the cinematographic system are nothing more or less than the things themselves in their materiality and reality."[52] It is as a film director that he was confronted with the immediacy of the "expressive presence" of things.

Nonverbal discourse is "endowed with a persuasive power which nothing verbal possesses."[53] We can forget what we have been taught through words but we can never forget what we have learned through things.

The first image from Pasolini's life is a white curtain, and this image spoke to him "objectively" and communicated the world of his bourgeois childhood to him, the universe in which he was living. We also find a curtain, although "red," in Guattari, which also speaks, communicates, and expresses something.

> The somber red color of my curtain enters into an existential constellation with nightfall, with twilight, in order to engender an uncanny effect that devalues the self-evidences and urgencies which were impressing themselves on me only a few moments ago by letting the world sink into an apparently irremediable void.[54]

Guattari specifies the color's modes of expression, in other words, the way in which a thing can function as a focal point or vector of subjectivation. Even if we cannot say that the color red "speaks," it nonetheless constitutes, by arranging human elements (perception, memory) and non-human elements (the curtain, dusk), the existential foundation of all expression and all speech: "What is in the curtain, what is in the twilight, what is in my memory, *is given as an enunciative nucleus*. Yet it couldn't be said that representation is involved. The latter is present solely as part of an existential function. [...] This existential function is organized in a way totally different from that of denotation and signification."[55]

The particular assemblage (color, curtain, evening, memory, perception, etc.) effects an aggregation, a condensation, of existential elements which, although non-discursive, are at the basis of enunciation.

As with Guattari, although the language of things is unable to establish invariable and stable significations, it can produce models of behavior which possess the force of example and the self-evidence of physical presence. Nonverbal semiotics, asignifying semiotics (the operative technico-scientific languages of industry) and symbolic semiologies profoundly transformed Italian subjectivity during the 1960s and 1970s. Neo-capitalism is the "second and final bourgeois revolution" whose "culture produces codes that engender behavior."[56] Codes do not first act through verbal language and its functions of representation, denotation, and signification. Neo-capitalist culture puts models of desire into circulation and imposes models of subjection (models of childhood, the father, the mother, etc.). "It launches (subjective) models the way the automobile industry launches a new line of cars."[57] Capitalism manufactures the individual, molding his body and his psyche, equipping him with modes of perception, semiotization, and an unconscious, endeavoring to introduce a "bourgeois property-owner in every worker."

Since the 1960s, capitalism has required from the "deterritorialized worker, someone who goes beyond his professional expertise, who follows technological innovations or even develops a certain creativity, a certain interest. Furthermore, a consumer is needed who can adapt to market developments."[58] Pasolini offers the existential version of the new type of worker laid out by Guattari. "Power needs a different type of subject" endowed with what Pasolini calls "existential flexibility"—the counterpart to the economic flexibility of the labor market—an "absolutely formal elasticity in 'existences' so that everyone becomes a good consumer."[59]

The cultural model offered to the Italians (and to the rest of the world), a model to which they must conform (in the way they dress, the shoes they wear, their hairstyles, their actions and gestures), bypasses representation and the cognitive dimensions of subjectivity to affect existence itself.

"It is above all in lived experience, in the existential, that we find conformity to the model, and thus in the body and behavior as well."[60] The semiotic efficiency of nonverbal discourse is formidable because it affects existential functions (Guattari) through domesticating effects: "What has to be educated, shaped, is the flesh itself, the flesh as mold of the spirit."

These models of conduct and subjectivation are imposed through a "physical language," a "language of behavior," which, because nonverbal, "is no longer rhetorical in the humanist sense, but pragmatic in the American sense."[61]

Neo-capitalism asserts the primacy of languages of clarity, precision, functionality, and instrumental and pragmatic efficiency by vacating them of the expressive dimension of humanist languages. During a historical period in which verbal language has become completely conventional and empty, subjected to the translatability, the centralization, and the imposed equivalency of languages of infrastructure, "this physical and gestural language is of decisive importance."[62]

Neo-capitalism always acts and expresses itself through "mixed semiotics," albeit by reversing the semiotic hierarchies in which languages of superstructure (school, law, university, etc.) were once dominant.

> The culture of a nation like Italy is expressed above all through the language of behaviors or physical language, plus a certain quantity—completely conventional and extremely vacuous—of verbal language.

Together with the spread of non-denotative language acting through mimetic contagion, through affect, arises the molding of language through "technique." "The technological phenomenon, like a new spirituality, permeates language from the roots to all its extremities, all its phases, and all its particularities."[63]

At the same time as a national language, a sole and unique signifying substance is imposed, in particular through the educational system and television; the collective structures of the State and mass communications carry out a centralization of symbolic semiotics through a new culture of the image, producing a new, paradoxical, hideous "expressivity." The hold on subjectivity is therefore less due to speech, language, representation, ideology, or consciousness than to the languages of production and consumption (to the asignifying semiotics of economics and the symbolic semiotics of consumption).

2. Intolerance and the Italian "Cultural Genocide"

Without a collective assemblage of "revolutionary" enunciation deployed at the level of neo-capitalist development, the effects of the languages of infrastructure (industrial, media, bureaucratic, etc.) are catastrophic since Italians become the victims of the consequent anthropological mutation. Following the Marx of the *Communist Manifesto*, Pasolini speaks even of "cultural genocide."

Deprived of their popular culture, the "new poor" live the disparity between the new neo-capitalist culture of mass consumption and their own economic conditions. It is impossible for them to acquire what mass consumption dangles before them "because of the poverty that persists, disguised by illusory improvements in the standard of living." The disappearance of the old popular cultural models and the socioeconomic disparity produce the frustration, violence, guilt, and aggressiveness that Pasolini identifies above all in the behavior and presence of young people's bodies.

Before neo-capitalism incorporated and subordinated society in its totality, the poor experienced a "segregation and marginality" that allowed them to conserve, reproduce, and reinvent their culture and forms of expression. The lumpenproletariat of the 1950s were "blacks" in all but name, over whom the bourgeoisie limited its control to police repression without bothering to "evangelize" them, in other words, without bothering to impose cultural models or models of subjectivation. From this point of view, fascism was still a part of the world of the first capitalism, or more specifically, it stood at the intersection, at the threshold, of the old and the new capitalism. The languages of production and consumption represent a more considerable internal revolution of fascist dictatorship.

> Fascism offered a monumental, reactionary model, although it went unheeded. The various distinctive cultures (of the peasants, the lumpenproletariat, the workers) continued undisturbed to identify with their own models, for repression was limited to getting them to acquiesce in word alone.[64]

With its "languages of infrastructure," neo-capitalism strikes at the roots of existence. It does more than demand submission or obedience, it molds and modulates individuals' subjectivity and lives. Government is a government of "souls," as Foucault later writes.

> Various forms of fascism had transformed them into puppets, servants, and perhaps in part into true believers, but it didn't really reach the depths of their souls, their way of being. Consumption

touched their innermost selves, it gave them other feelings, other ways of thinking, living, other cultural models. Unlike under Mussolini, there was no superficial, scenographic regimentation, but rather a real regimentation that altered and robbed them of their souls.[65]

Historically, fascism had exploited rhetorical values like heroism, patriotism, and family, whereas the "new fascism is [...] a pragmatism that acts as a cancer on all of society—the national tumor of the majority."[66]

By imposing familialist forms of life and sexuality, the new fascism of culture, public relations, and mass consumption is "almost racist," producing a "false tolerance." The "new tolerance" of consumption, public relations, and mass culture threatens to turn into a new and more disturbing "intolerance."

The "new tolerance," today's "political correctness," produces paradoxical effects, since, although within neo-capitalism "the elites are much more tolerant toward sexual minorities than in other periods, by way of compensation the vast majority has become more blatantly intolerant, more violent and revolting than ever before in Italian history."[67]

This intolerance, which spread like a micro-fascist cancer only a short time after Pasolini's death, has found its macro-political expression in the Northern League, the party of every intolerance and every reactionary reterritorialization.

Pasolini was undoubtedly the first to grasp the power of languages of production and consumption and especially those expressed through television (which he in fact demanded be temporarily shut down). Power destroyed the old freedoms, those of "the poor," workers, and the proletariat, and created others by appropriating "the demands—let us say the liberal and progressive demands—of liberty and, by making them its own, changed their nature and made them worthless."[68]

The normalization, standardization, the leveling of ways of life and behavior are no longer exclusively the result of discipline and confinement (of which the Roman "*borgate*" were a paradoxical example), but rather the work of the "most subtle, cunning, and complex" technologies of power to which semiotics surely belong. The latter express and institute consumer society's "mass hedonism," an apparently more tolerant and liberal power that is in reality, according to Pasolini, more intolerant and more destructive than fascism.

3. The Death of the Sacred and Machinic Animism

Pasolini is very much aware of the paradoxical situation capitalism creates. On the one hand, it destroys popular cultures and their sacred "animist" vision of nature, things, and the cosmos. On the other hand, through machinic assemblages, it creates the conditions for delineating new continuities between subject and object, between nature and culture. Like Guattari, Pasolini registers these contradictory tendencies: first, the objectivation and complete rationalization of nature and the cosmos that makes them exploitable; second, the possibility of a machinic animism that might make them sacred again (Pasolini) or "re-enchant" them (Guattari).

Pasolini has brilliant theoretical intuitions he gained as a filmmaker. Destined to disappear under the capitalist contagion, "popular" culture paradoxically possesses an understanding commensurate with capitalist machinism and, especially, filmic machinism. Before the "language of reality" became "natural," before it was overtaken by filmic apparatuses, it was beyond the reach of our consciousness. Now, as in animist traditions, cinema operates an acculturation, an animation,[69] and a "subjectivation" of nature such that it is impossible to distinguish it from culture.

Capitalism profoundly transforms subjectivity by destroying the "oral" culture of dominated classes. The symbolic semiotics which were once used in primitive societies (of which a large part had been reproduced in the peasant and lumpenproletariat communities of modern Italy) and which, at the time of the first industrial revolution, manifested worlds, values, ways of life heterogeneous to capitalism, are fated to disappear.[70] The culture and language of infrastructures (the language of "production-consumption"), superimposed on other cultural and linguistic strata, transform them until they are eliminated. "Subaltern class culture [almost] no longer exists: only the economics of subaltern classes exists."[71] The culture that was dying under Pasolini's eyes was peasant (and "lumpenproletariat") culture, transnational and trans-epochal culture, which came from the depths of history (or better, from the absence of history). To have an idea of what capitalist deterritorialization has meant, one need only be familiar with the abrupt drop in the West's rural population,[72] an exodus which has quickly spread to other parts of the world, marking the end of a phase begun in the Neolithic period.

The peasantry's disappearance has brought with it the disappearance of processes of subjectivation and animist and polytheistic beliefs that survived despite the capitalization and expropriation carried out by the Church. But what touches Pasolini the poet most is the effacement of the "sacred" and the loss of the attitude toward the world and toward others which the animist conception of the world holds.

The "characteristic feature of peasant civilizations is not their finding nature 'natural,'"[73] but rather "animated," subjectivated, sacred. Where capitalism seeks to desacralize things and people, to make them objects in order to measure, exchange, and capitalize them, Pasolini looks instead to "resacralize them as much as possible." Against the capitalist process that requires us to perceive only the "inanimate, mechanical" appearance of things, against the "objective and scientific" conception of reality, Pasolini opposes the "subjective" consistency of the same reality.[74]

Some of this "religion" ended up in his "semiotics," for, as with Guattari, there is no break, fissure, or abyss between sign and reality, between content and expression, culture and nature. Pasolini's animism is a kind of expressionism since the sign is immanent to the real. In his polemic with Umberto Eco, Pasolini asserted that his semiotics does not naturalize cultural codes but "transforms nature into cultural phenomena: it transforms all life into speech."[75]

Nature as culture is expressive nature; it speaks to itself because there is a "continuum without any solution of continuity" between a person who says "oak tree" and the oak tree itself. The latter is not the referent of the sign "oak tree," but a sign itself, an iconic sign, just as the living person is not the referent of the sign "person," but a "living-iconic" sign itself. A person and an oak tree are the "im-signs" of reality which cinema merely reproduces.

Subjectivated nature, animated culture, is a "Vedic-Spinozan" God, says Pasolini, which speaks with itself. Everything that exists, whether plant or rock, expresses, sings, the glory of this immanent "God."[76]

Even if man were to lose his "imperialist" claim to be endowed with what all other existents lack—the power of enunciation and expression—"the nonverbal is nothing other than another verbality" such that the signs of verbal languages do no more than translate the signs of nonverbal languages and in particular languages of action.

What we have lost with the disappearance of these non-anthropomorphic cultures and religions we can reinvent with the equally non-anthropomorphic machinisms of capitalism.

The cinema reveals that reality is not a collection of "*res*" but of "actions." Action (as much Lenin's as that of an obscure Fiat employee, Pasolini would say), the first and primary language of people and things, is the source of all other forms of expression. The image does not only represent, it acts pragmatically on the real and on subjectivity; for it makes us see, intervenes, acts on what "man" and "human" subjectivity cannot see and do.

Science, industry, and art have used the image "diagrammatically" for a long time. Computer-assisted imagery, for example, captures, as in a dynamic diagram, the functional articulations of a situation or system which it allows one to anticipate, forecast, and intervene. It participates directly in the production of its "object." This function of the image, an iconic mapping that both registers and creates possibilities, is also identified by directors like Godard, who denounces the way in which the film industry cancels it out. Society maintains the possibility of using the cinema and its images as science uses diagrams and microscopes to "see" the infinitely small or the telescope to "see" the infinitely large that escapes man and his language in order to construct "iconic cartographies" that multiply possibilities for action. Like a diagram in movement, the cinema: in order to see, decide, choose, and act.

Confronted with and attracted by filmic machinism and its "animism," Pasolini offers us a political reading of "diagrammatic" action and its possibilities. The action of the image is indubitably "machinic" (or diagrammatic), in the process of "moving away from classical humanist ideals" and of being lost in what Pasolini calls the "pragma" of languages of infrastructure. Along with other audiovisual techniques, cinema seems to be the language of this pragma; it seems to function in complete harmony with capitalist deterritorialization. But cinema can also represent a chance for salvation, a possibility for a change of course, precisely because it expresses this pragma—"and it expresses it from the inside; by producing itself, by taking it as its starting point, by reproducing it."[77] The cinema machine is completely inside the real. But what makes it an apparatus for subjection and enslavement can also be turned into new processes for subjectivation provided that one recognize the nature of machinic assemblages, that one abandon the anthropological and humanist perspective that imbues so much of critical thought.

The immanent power of im-signs prefigures the formidable political power of audiovisual machines like television. Signs do not exist in the world of superstructures but make up operative semiotics, power signs, which act on both the real and on subjectivity.

Action-images can also sing the glory of the "Lord," like the little birds in *The Hawks and the Sparrows*, in other words, they can sing the emergence of a new political subjectivity or sing the glory of capital, that is, vulgarity, arrogance, and the impotentized power of the machinic image like Berlusconi's, whose rise Pasolini had anticipated with surprising lucidity.

4

Conflict and Sign Systems

> I am convinced that if extraterrestrials landed in São Paulo tomorrow, there would be experts, journalists, and all sorts of specialists to explain to people that, really, it is not such an extraordinary thing, that the possibility had already been considered, that a special committee on the issue has long been in place, and, most important, that there is no reason to panic, because the authorities are here to take care of things.
>
> —Félix Guattari, *Molecular Revolution in Brazil*

What semiotics are brought into play in political conflict? What meanings, stories, and signs do journalists, experts, and scholars produce? Is it an ideological battle? We will attempt to problematize these questions starting from a specific case: the 2003 labor dispute among precariously-employed French cultural workers—the "intermittents du spectacle."[1]

The motto of the Coordination des Intermittents et Précaires,[2] "We are the experts!" raises two different kinds of question. The first concerns the nature and functions of the expert or specialist: "Who is an expert?" and "What do specialists know and what can they do?" Faced with the increase in expertise, studies, data, and statistics, whose rise is directly proportional to the intensity of the conflict, intermittent workers have asked themselves, on the one hand, what special experience and what legitimacy the experts have that allow them to develop and build knowledge with regard to their practices. On the other hand, they have questioned what the experts "can do," in other words, the ways in which the experts participate in decision-making and in the socioeconomic choices that bear on labor, employment, and unemployment conditions.

The second set of questions the motto raises reflect on the Coordination's own practices: "What do we know?" and "What can we do?" In other words: What is the value and import of our experiences and our words in the production and distribution of knowledge *about us*? Why are our words and knowledge limited and naïve and thus disqualified while "specialist" knowledge represents "objectivity" and "universality"? What power do we have as a group, a collective, an association, to play a part in the decisions that concern us? Why is our speech institutionally termed "non-political"?

In short, the motto "We are the experts!" puts into question the composition and legitimacy of the assemblage that "knows" and the composition and legitimacy of the assemblage that "decides." The issue can be put like this: "Why don't we have the right to participate in the collective arrangement that problematizes and explores the possibilities our work, employment, and unemployment represent? And who has the right and the legitimacy to make decisions about our lives?"

The mobilization of intermittent workers seems to follow the two paths typical of "minority" struggles which question both the procedures of the production of democracy and the procedures of the production of knowledge. The fight against cultural-labor market reforms constitutes a critique of the knowledge produced by institutions (the State, trade unions, business organizations, the media, the social sciences, etc.) which assert what must be taken for "true" and "false" with regard to economics, social rights, and culture. It also constitutes a critique of the procedures through which the institutions governing unemployment insurance define problems, come up with solutions, and make decisions.

The Coordination's struggle foregrounds and contests the existence of the three transversal practices crisscrossing apparatuses of knowledge production, those of the production of democracy and of the production of communication: division, delegation, monopoly. The *division* of the population into experts and laymen, into representatives and represented, into communications professionals and the public, implies, on the one hand, the *delegation* of knowledge, power, and speech to the experts, representatives, and communication professionals; on the other hand, it ensures the centralization of and monopoly over the production of knowledge in laboratories and think tanks, the centralization of political decision-making within institutions, and the centralization of the production of public speech within media newsrooms. The production of knowledge is legitimized through agreements among specialists made behind closed doors. Political representation entails the centralization of and monopoly over decision-making such that political arrangements are made and unmade among the few. In the same way, a small number of journalists ensure a monopoly for themselves over what is said in the media and what information goes out. By way of these three main practices, which constitute techniques for controlling behavior and technologies of subjection, the roles and functions, the rights and duties, the freedoms and constraints of our societies are divvied up.

The battle waged by intermittents over speech, categories, and discourses ran up against a new strategy and new semiotic techniques:

silence the non-expert, the "citizen," and the public by making them speak; arrange for their exclusion by making them participate; keep them at a distance by consulting them, by listening to their grievances through an army of journalists, experts, and researchers. We live in a "common world" designed by the semiotics of marketing, advertising, consumption, television, and the Internet. Access to these shared semiotics is not only not denied, it is imperative: one must join in, one must take an active part. The exclusion of the governed and the neutralization of their singular speech result from the inclusion of their form of expression within a given common semiotic space. In surveillance societies, a shortage of speech is not the problem but rather its overabundance, the consensus and conformism that its circulation presupposes and produces.

Public space is saturated with a circulation of signs, images, and words and with a proliferation of mechanisms of subjection which, while encouraging and soliciting speech and expression, prevent singular expression and neutralize heterogeneous processes of subjectivation. For singular speech to be possible, shared communication must first be interrupted, one must leave the infinite chatter of the media consensus, force ruptures in public space, just as, in order to "see," one must remove oneself from the incessant bombardment of visual clichés. In other words, for one to exist politically and to exist at all, rather than enter the common world, the latter must be singularized, that is, one must impose existential and political differentiation by creating new cleavages, new divisions. The specificity of a common world, its singularity, and its difference, must be asserted "at a time when the leveling effects of information and social participation are every day reinforced."[3] Singularity, division, and difference are not given in advance: they have to be invented and constructed.

Semiotic regimes play a strategic role in the building of this common world that they did not have, or that they had in a different way, in disciplinary societies. After *Archeology of Knowledge*, Foucault returned to the production of utterances only in his last lectures. In his lectures at the Collège de France,[4] he briefly examines the relationship between economic control and the control of public opinion. Liberal government of society is a government of the population whose dual aspect must be taken into account. First, it is a government of the "biological" reproductive conditions of the human species (regulation of births and deaths, demographic management, regulation of production, risks, etc.); second, it is a government of the public, over public opinion. As Foucault points out, economists and publicists emerged at the same time. Since the eighteenth century, the governing of society bears on both the economy and public opinion. In this way, governmental action has extended from its biological roots in the species to the surface created by "the public." From the species to the public: therein lies an entire field of new realities and, consequently, new ways of acting on behavior and opinions in order to modify the ways of doing and saying of the governed.

Today's semiotic governmentality relies on the differential management of the public (subsequently transformed into audiences), which replaces the hegemonic management of opinion in disciplinary societies. The optimization of "semiotic" differences aims at the homogenization of subjectivity (a leveling of heterogeneity which has no precedent in human history)[5] and takes the form of a new conformism of difference, a new consensus of plurality.

It is in this new context that intermittent workers began a struggle focused on the statements and meanings of categories of unemployment, employment, and work in a shared public space occupied by the semiotic regime of journalists, experts, and researchers. The categories of unemployment, employment, and work serve as so many catchphrases, so many clichés, which regulate and limit our ways of acting and thinking. The awesome assemblage of university laboratories, consulting firms, democratic institutions, and media chiefs stands as a veritable semiotic wall against which the intermittents collided.

In the conflict, signifying semiotics which mobilize consciousness and representation come into play at different levels. They put into discourse the problems important to a society and time period by constituting them as catchphrases and deploying them in worlds and universes of meaning. They then ensure the interpretation and transmission of these catchphrases and universes of meaning for more and more differentiated publics by at once giving speech to and stripping it from the governed. Finally, they make these catchphrases and worlds and universes of meanings the conditions for individuals' subjection, the conditions for their production as subjects.

Problematization

Given that we arrive at the solutions the questions we ask "deserve," Foucault and Deleuze make determining problems one of the major stakes of politics. Dominant utterances, representations, and meanings function as a "grid" that affects our way of perceiving, feeling, and understanding. Everything that happens, everything one does and thinks, everything that one could think and do within the social and economic field, is passed through this grid of statements and meanings that makes up the horizon of interpretation and expression of the world. To call employment and unemployment "the" problem of an age means defining a framework that sets the limits of the possible, stating what is important and perceivable, defining what is legitimate and what is not, and circumscribing forms of political action and speech. It is in this way that, for Foucault, the power to formulate questions is a power of politicization, that is, a power to introduce new objects and new subjects within the space of politics and to make them the stakes of a polemic and a struggle.[6] Problematization introduces into public space not only new objects and subjects, but also "rules of action, modes of relation to the self,"[7] in other words, modes of possible subjectivation. The intermittent movement, by breaking the conceptual framework of the institutional consensus between the unions, bosses, and the State, by emphasizing "new social rights" rather than "the right to work," directly attacked the "monopoly" on problematization, introducing new problems and new questions and thus completely new stakes for thought and action.

The right to problematize employment and unemployment is reserved for "social partners" alone (the "co-determination" between employers and workers). Here, as in other domains, decisions are made within institutions that have long abandoned the public sphere of political division and confrontation. The ways of evaluating and measuring deficits, costs, and investments as well as the questions relative to their import and purpose have been removed from all public problematization, from all controversy, and entrusted to specialists (economic interest groups, experts, researchers, State administrators, etc.). The institutions for mutual aid and solidarity born from workers' struggles, managed and co-managed by members' representatives (employers' and workers' unions), have long stopped promoting the "democracy of labor" or the "democracy of production." The democracy of labor and production has been transformed into the "oligarchical" power of certain union and management players. The co-determination of French universal health care based on the Fordist model of industrial relations fails to take into account the "interests" of all these new subjects (the unemployed, precarious workers, women, the sick, handicapped, students, etc.) and neglects the new social and political divisions which neoliberal differentiation has produced since the late 1970s.

The power struggle provoked by the intermittent workers' movement created a brief opening in and disruption of this monopoly on problematization.

Moreover, the worse the "jobs" and "unemployment" "crisis" has become, the more these words have paradoxically ceased to denote realities worthy of examination and instead have changed little by little into stock phrases for thought and action, helping produce the clichés of consensus. The latter now pass for the "truths" (those of liberalism) that one is supposed to *believe*: If employment is unilaterally considered the right question, then it is the right solution. Thus, to raise employment, taxes on business must be reduced, to increase labor-market flexibility, the level of social protections must fall, and so forth. None of these "truths" has ever been demonstrated for the simple reason that they are indemonstrable.

The watchwords on employment and unemployment constitute the unnamable and unspeakable focal points from which the narratives and discourses of power issue, from which the possibility of speech and knowledge of those governing is born. They represent the unarticulated and inarticulatable presuppositions of discursive practices (the non-discursive focal points of enunciation). Like discourses pertaining to the "reform" of unemployment insurance, economic discourse is first of all structured by a non-discursive reality that reflects power relations, the desire for wealth, inequality, exploitation, and so on.

The institutionalization and selection of problems and solutions operated by signifying semiotics establish an initial split between government and the governed. Those who govern have the power to define problems and formulate questions (which they term "the possibilities") and establish in this way what is noteworthy, important, relevant, feasible, worth acting on and speaking about, whereas the freedom of expression of the governed is exercised within the limits of already codified "doing" and "saying," both already settled by the problems and solutions of those who govern.

As Deleuze and Guattari remind us, problems and significations are always the problems and significations of the dominant reality; the communications machine of signifying semiotics exists only to produce and repeat this self-evidence. The problems and frameworks of statements and dominant significations represent real semiotic barriers to the intermittent workers' movement. All that fails to fit within the consensual definition of employment and unemployment is literally inaudible, incommunicable, and untransmittable to journalists, experts, and researchers. As one could easily see throughout the conflict, beyond most journalists' bad faith or intellectual poverty, the issue was not cognitive but ethico-political. Even the most open and well-informed people literally did not understand what was going on because the Coordination's words, in order to be understood, presupposed a modification, a displacement, of the problem.

The Interpretation and Transmission of Catchphrases

With the catchphrases "employment" and "unemployment" and the consensus that results, the semiotics of journalists, experts, and researchers set in motion an enormous interpretative and narrative machine as well as a powerful machine for subjection from which the universe of significations and sense of liberalism emerge. In the past, the exclusive privilege of the politician—namely, speech—which determines and states problems, which establishes limits on saying and doing, is today constituted at the intersection of the non-discursive practices of the market and an assemblage of statements reducible—without great exaggeration—to an assemblage of experts, scholars, and journalists. Everything that has happened, is happening, and will happen is interpreted by these three according to the "grid" of problems and statements of modern-day capitalism (jobs, growth, the market, competition, etc.).

But why in our security states does the assemblage of the journalist, the expert, and the scholar replace the politician? Why does their expertise tend to replace the space in which the political confrontation of differing perspectives once occurred? Because the contemporary democratic system functions according to the belief that there is no dispute, no dissent, possible concerning the implicit presuppositions of the social consensus. If there is agreement that the fundamental social issue is employment, the difference in opinions between the labor union (to guarantee the rights of non-executives) and business management (to guarantee the prerogatives of "human capital") can easily be reconciled by the expert. His mediation/interpretation is largely sufficient in itself.

The pacific machinery assigning roles and functions among politician, expert, scholar, and journalist only breaks down when, as happened during the intermittents' struggle, the consensus (on employment) is repudiated, when a political force (the associations) retracts its assent to the implicit presuppositions conveyed by the dominant catchphrases-statements and produces "another collective assemblage of enunciation" from which singular speech can be deployed. To do so, it is not enough to "liberate" speech from the apparatuses of power; it must be constructed. That is when the networks of power are confronted with a completely new situation.

Freely drawing our inspiration from the work of Michel de Certeau, we can describe the constitution, interpretation, and transmission of catchphrases produced by the assemblage of experts, researchers, and journalists in the following way. The researcher has the task of interpreting the statements that define what is important, what is noteworthy, for society and, if needs be, to explain them using his specialized knowledge. The expert acts as a mediator and translator of this specialized knowledge in the language of political, economic, and state-administrative decision-makers. In turn, the media selects, interprets, and transmits the researcher's and expert's statements by reformulating them in the language of public opinion, by circulating them within the shared semiotic space among different audiences. The discourse on employment, unemployment, and work thus has its speakers, interpreters, and translators as well as its "shifters," which ensure the coherence between different types of statements (the concepts of scholars, the judgments of experts, and the opinions of journalists) and between the apparatuses that produced them (the university, the media, the think tank, etc.).

We can slightly adjust de Certeau's theory in asserting that the balance of power between the journalist, scholar, and expert weighs largely in favor of the first, since the media calls less and less on outside analysis (of the intellectual or expert). Indeed, scholars and experts "are thus forced to become journalists if they want to conform to the norm" of modern-day communications.[8] With the assemblage of scholar, expert, and journalist we have a first "regime of signs" of interpretation and communication. The regime entails certain conditions: First, that signs refer to signs indefinitely, since the discourse produced is absolutely tautological and arbitrary; second, that there are categories of specialists (researcher, expert, journalist) whose "job it is to circulate these signs, to say what they mean, to interpret them, to thereby freeze the signifier"; and third, "there must still be subjects [different audiences] who receive the message, who listen to the interpretation and obey."[9] It should not be hard to see that by way of this assemblage we are describing a metamorphosis of "pastoral power," a new "priest" and a new "flock." The assemblage takes the public in hand employing the semiotic technologies of a "government of souls."

The Scholar of Conflict

The work of Pierre Michel Menger, head of research at the Centre national de la recherche scientifique, research director at the École des hautes études en sciences sociales, director of the Centre de sociologie des arts, and "specialist" in the sociology of labor and the arts, perfectly matches the description of how these assemblages function, since his work provides the media with statements ready-made to be passed along, "sound bites" perfectly adapted for governing public opinion so as to ensure the success of "reform." On the one hand, they make intermittent employment an "exception of the job market," and, on the other hand, permanent employment the instrument and measure of the need to regulate the "far too many" intermittent workers overwhelming cultural production. By making the category of permanent employment the goal and essence of social and economic activity, Menger sets the limits on possible and reasonable activities on the cultural job market (every-thing outside his framework is disqualified as naïve, irrational, utopian, etc.). The employment policy for the cultural sector this scholar proposes poignantly shows how disciplinary apparatuses are supposed to work in a surveillance society. His most recent book is based entirely on the disciplinary distinction between normal (standard employment and unemployment) and abnormal (occasional employment and unemployment), as its title clearly indicates: *Intermittent Workers: Sociology of an Exception*.[10]

For Menger, "just as these jobs are not ordinary, we are not dealing with ordinary joblessness [...]. The rules governing intermittent workers' unemployment cover atypically atypical risk. But exceptional flexibility has considerable consequences."[11] Extraordinary unemployment and employment, atypical risks and coverage of atypical risks, exceptional flexibility—this is the language of the disciplinary "exception." Menger wraps his arguments about the cultural sector and intermittent status in a scholar's formalism that aims to reduce and confine the issues raised by the intermittents' movement to the reassuring framework of the abnormal, the exceptional, and the atypical. The job policies to implement must eradicate the exceptional and reestablish the normal functioning of the job market, which provides for both the return of the entrepreneur's function (his autonomy) and the reimposition of the employee's (his subordination) in order to assign each their place ("their rights and duties," in the politician's and scholar's jargon) within the division of labor. To put it in Durkheimian terms, a "direct and organized hierarchy" must be reestablished in a job market made unruly by behavior out of line with the norm of capital-labor relations. We know that the normal functioning of the job market is not "natural" but rather must be produced and reproduced via the continuous intervention of job policies. This is what "reform" is meant to do.

Undaunted by paradox, Menger even manages to blame intermittent employment for neoliberal policies: "There is no use condemning widespread job insecurity if we fail to realize that it is the system of intermittent employment itself that creates insecurity [...]. The failure of the job market is part of the very principle of intermittent work."[12] The assertion neglects the fact that over the last thirty years insecurity has also spread to all sectors of the economy. In any case, his remarks are disproven by the reality of those working in the job market's cultural sector who are not covered by intermittent workers' unemployment insurance.[13]

In professions whose activities do not provide the rights of intermittent employment the same (but worse) phenomena of underemployment and insecurity have also emerged. Without a compensation regime like that of intermittent workers', individuals either have recourse to basic welfare benefits or must take on several jobs in order to survive. To turn Menger's viewpoint on its head, we might say that if inequality is more acute in these sectors of the cultural job market (and in every sector where discontinuous employment exists), it is precisely because of the absence of a compensation regime that accounts for the discontinuity of employment and the forms of work and training in a flexible economy. Poverty, underemployment, and enormous disparities in income are not a function of the intermittent regime but of the flexible organization of the culture industry and the way its job market functions.

What is happening here is what has already happened in other parts of the economy over the last thirty years: a policy of full employment (creating "real," stable, full-time jobs) that neglects the actual conditions of production and divides and fragments the job market by creating a growing disparity among incomes. It serves only to further differentiate, to further multiply, inequalities and thus to create the ideal terrain for neoliberal control of the job market so that it can further install itself and extend its reach. Employment policies are subordinated to the logic of liberalism because they do no more than segment and subsequently differentiate and increase the competition between "guaranteed" and "non-guaranteed" work, between secure and insecure employment, and in this way enable the policy of "optimizing differences," of differential management of inequalities, of control of behavior on the job market.

Unemployment and Invisible Work

"Unemployment" plays a strategic role in neoliberal significations and narratives. Neoliberal analysis ends up at the same disciplinary distinction between normal (unemployment benefits as instituted after the war) and abnormal (unemployment benefits as used, abused, and appropriated by intermittent workers). As with all the experts of cultural-sector employment policies, Menger would like to bring the unemployment benefits whose use has been perverted by intermittent work (because the benefits finance cultural and artistic activity as well as intermittent workers' lives) back to their so-called natural function of simple coverage against the risk of job loss. But Menger, like most experts, seems to ignore that within a system of "flexible accumulation," unemployment changes meaning and function. The clear and distinct separation between employment and unemployment (unemployment as the wrong side of employment) established within a very different system of accumulation (the standardization and continuity of production and, thus, stability and continuity of employment) has transformed into an ever-narrower imbrication of periods of work, periods of unemployment, and periods of training.

When we look at the cultural sector, the first thing that jumps out is the discrepancy between labor and employment. The duration of the latter covers the duration of real work only in part. Intermittents' labor (education, apprenticeship, the circulation of knowledge and know-how, the forms of cooperation, etc.) includes periods of employment and unemployment without it being reducible to either.[14] The time of employment only partially corresponds to the labor, education, and cooperative practices intermittents undertake. The developments are not recent but date back to the 1980s. Hence, unemployment cannot be reduced to a period without labor activity. Unemployment benefits not only cover the risk of job loss but also guarantee income continuity, serving to produce and reproduce the overlapping of all these practices and temporalities for which the worker is in this case not totally responsible as he would be in other sectors.

Menger's focus on ("cultural") employment and the type of solutions he advocates prevent him from grasping the economic changes we are now living through. Given the situation of intermittent workers, the CERC (Council for employment, incomes, and social cohesion) report on job security[15] is completely right. For it considers the phenomena we observe among intermittent work the rule rather than the exception or an abnormality: "The straightforward split between employment and unemployment, between salaried work and free-lance work, has been replaced by a kind of 'halo' of employment, a fluid status, at once unemployed and salaried, for example, or free-lance and salaried, while the types of labor contract have multiplied (regular short-term, intermittent, or interim work contracts)."[16] The supposed "exception" of intermittent work is becoming the rule of the salary-based system, just as the intermittent associations have been arguing since 1992. The "ordinary" or "traditional" categories Menger would like to reestablish for the system of intermittent work hardly function even within "normal" sectors of the economy. Contrary to his assertions, the difference between intermittent unemployment and unemployment in other sectors represents a difference in degree and not in kind.

The "grand narrative" of employment (or full employment) is thus interpreted, spoken of, and staged according to two non-contradictory discursive logics: the protection of long-term salaried workers and the protection of the entrepreneur and business. The reason these discourses are not contradictory is that they condemn the system of intermittent employment but for different reasons. On the one hand, neoliberals do so because, although they exploit the system's mobility and flexibility, they do not want to pay the price for it in terms of unemployment insurance ("It kills competition," "It makes people lazy"). On the other hand, with increasing precarity, there is the risk that the continuity of income and rights that intermittent work guarantees (even partially) despite discontinuous employment could be imitated in other sectors of precarious work. Unions and the left, for their part, want nothing to do with the intermittents either, since their objective is full employment, in other words, "real jobs" for "real artists" and "real professionals" (though they leave this last part out). Intermittent work is only a last resort that must be eliminated on the way to the "stable employment" with which the unions are more comfortable.

It is not hard to understand the role the "scholar" Menger has played in the battle over discourses and signs. The theoretical concepts and interpretations of the conflict he has advanced have been picked up by the media because his discourse on employment in the cultural sector, the deficit, the necessary regulation and standardization of the "far too much," and so on, has synchronized perfectly with the crucial moments of the intermittents' struggle and with the interpretive framework of journalists, experts, politicians, and union bosses. His concepts have provided the watchwords that circulate in the media, reinforcing and validating by way of this circulation their accuracy and staying power.

The press and, above all, radio and television feed these interpretations into the discourses and speech circulating within institutional and social networks. They select experts' statements and their content, translate them into a language for everyone, making the information both attractive and easily digestible. They are in this way active agents in its appropriation and transformation. The statements the media chose throughout the intermittents' struggle in order to channel, transmit, and anchor them in social networks, public opinion, and ordinary language are (no surprise here) those which translate those statements on employment, the law of supply and demand, and business in terms reflecting the "necessary" and "inevitable" regulation of the "too much."

The media also chooses among statements from the intermittent workers' movement, erecting what we have called veritable "semiotic barriers" on the Coordination's demands, limiting them to claims for the protection of unemployment insurance specific to "artists." The media barely picked up on the "spectacular" week-long occupation of the roof of the French national employers' union's headquarters. This was because the Coordination had climbed up there demanding an overhaul of the State agency on employment[17] and, specifically, a thorough review of the unemployment system and not only that part of it relating to intermittent work, a demand far exceeding the context of a cultural and artistic exception in which journalists were happy to confine the intermittents' struggle. Although one could find in the media some sympathy for and interest in those "artists" who fought with the determination of a bygone age, there was nonetheless a complete black-out on everything that went beyond the idea that the same media had of the functions and roles of art and artists in society. The multitude of "lay" voices expressing themselves throughout the conflict held almost no weight among the media chiefs who used them at best for man-in-the-street public opinion. For the media, a legitimate, expert voice was enough to silence the jabberers who failed to understand that if the job market is regulated, it is only for its own good.

The Narrative-Function of Signifying Semiotics

The media does more than communicate catchphrases. It actualizes them, deploys them, in worlds and universes of images, words, and signs through stories and narratives that constitute the real rather than describe it. De Certeau effectively synthesizes this new narrative-function of signifying semiotics: "The media transform the great silence of things into its opposite. Formerly constituting a secret, the real now talks constantly. News reports, information, statistics, and surveys are everywhere. No story has ever spoken so much or shown so much. [...] Narrations of what's-going-on constitute our orthodoxy. Debates about figures are our theological wars. The combatants move forward camouflaged as facts, data, and events. They present themselves as messengers of a 'reality.' [...] But in fact they fabricate [it], simulate it, use it as a mask, accredit themselves by it, and thus create the scene of their law."[18] The injunction conveyed by the asignifying semiotics of figures, statistics, and deficits is translated into a discourse that issues the command to "Be quiet!" This is what, between the lines, journalists in the press, the television host, and political representatives express with the help of statistics and surveys: "'These are the facts. Here are the data, the circumstances, etc. Therefore you must...' Narrated reality constantly tells us what must be believed and what must be done."[19]

Stories and narratives actualize employment and unemployment into worlds and universes of discourse and meaning. Unemployment is at once interpreted and narrated as an *illness* of the social body that must be cured through employment and as the *event* of security societies that must be continually talked about and continually staged through the figures and statistics that call on and appeal to the speech of experts, scholars, and the unemployed themselves. And all this serves no other purpose than to internalize through the public relations machine the inequalities the economy exacerbates. "Narratives" have a conjunctive function since they compensate for the growing "disjunctures" created by the division of labor, the differential treatment instituted by public employment policies, and strategies of segmentation of the job market. While communicating fear, discourses on unemployment also promote a project for mobilizing the public for the future. Signifying semiotics produce restorative meaning by providing through employment a common frame of reference for the multiplication of "differences" (inequality of status, income, access to insurance, etc.). The common reference is meant to bind the differences together to establish a common goal. In the battle for employment, discourses, stories, and narratives produce the possibility for a reality reconciled with itself. They provide the image of the rediscovered unity of society (against social conflict), the image of security (of employment) that erases fear.

Unemployment thus allows for the unrelenting repetition of narratives that constitute individuals as victims of the market and globalization (the political and left-wing trade union version) or as responsible for their situation because of their own behavior (the neoliberal right-wing version). But the "grand narrative" of employment does not have the same power of subjection and internalization as the story of the "nation" or "progress." It is a little "dream" of security that requires the mobilization of the entire society for infinitesimal changes in unemployment whose calculation itself is subject to every kind of manipulation imaginable.

The Subjection Machine

> Do you know what you have to do to keep someone from speaking in his or her own name? Have him say "I."
> —Gilles Deleuze, *Two Regimes of Madness*

> I know very well that people in *favelas* couldn't care less about psychoanalysis, Freud, or Lacan. But the abstract machines of subjectivation produced by psychoanalysis through the media, magazines, films, and so on, are certainly also present in what takes place in the *favelas*.
> —Félix Guattari, *Molecular Revolution in Brazil*

A final function exercised by signifying semiotics has to be examined. The latter are not limited to constructing, interpreting, and transmitting catchphrases. The functioning of the semiotic machine for interpreting and transmitting them is indistinguishable from the functioning of a subjection machine. One might even say that the purpose of interpretation and transmission is the production of subjection.

In security societies a plurality of sign regimes coexist. We have already analyzed one of them, the circulation/transmission of "statements-watchwords." The process of subjection represents another. Here, signs no longer refer to signs within a circle closed upon itself but rather to the subject. Signs, significations, and statements do not refer to their own reproduction but to the limits of their circulation constituted by the use the subject makes of them in order to act on and for himself. It is a major failing in all of postmodern communications theory (Baudrillard, Virilio, etc.) that it restricts itself to only the first system of signs while neglecting the specificity of the process of "subjectivity production" and the relation to the self. If the latter is the source of new forms of domination, it can also be an opportunity for a radical break with the relations of power and knowledge of security societies. In this second semiotic regime, signs and their functioning are one of the conditions of the process of of subjectivity production.

Deleuze and Guattari's analysis of psychoanalysis can also help us to understand how semiotic subjection machines function. Psychoanalysis represents a process of disciplinary subjection; because of its incitement to speak, it functions as an apparatus that is able, on the one hand, to "pin" the subject-function on the body of the individual and, on the other hand, to prevent singular statements from being formulated. Psychoanalysis emerged and developed at the moment when disciplinary societies began to turn into control societies. Thus, while the psychiatric hospital is a disciplinary apparatus practicing its techniques on the bodies and mental reality of the sick within a closed space, psychoanalysis is a security apparatus exercising power through speech on the bodies and mental reality of the "sick" within an open space.

Such as it is analyzed in *Anti-Oedipus*, psychoanalysis invented strategies for the construction of the subject which were deployed in two principal ways: by "discrediting" the singular speech of the individual through interpretation and, once discredited, by reconstructing it as a "civilized" subject's speech in accordance with the behavioral model of subjects within the "family." Everything the "patient" says is interpreted through a particular framework or a small number of utterances (papa, mama, phallus, castration, or signifier, the symbolic, or lack in the more deterritorialized Lacanian version) meant to uncover the repressed meaning of singular speech. Starting from the discrediting interpretation which relocates the origin and the sense of the utterance in the familial triangle or in the signifier, and by basing itself on the patient's enunciation, psychoanalysis resocializes the subject by constructing him as an individual who accepts, adapts to, and identifies with the dominant model of individuation of capitalist society (the family) and its psychic apparatuses (id, ego, superego).

What interests us in Deleuze and Guattari's work is the fact that the generalization of this apparatus of subject production is not guaranteed in completely developed security societies by psycho-analysis but rather by the "pastoral" communication and techniques of the welfare state. The functions of control over and standardization of enunciation and the functions of subjection assured by psycho-analysis (as described in *Anti-Oedipus*) are picked up, unified, and generalized by mass communications as a material apparatus and by linguistics and analytic philosophy as a theoretical apparatus (dealt with in part in *A Thousand Plateaus*). Psychoanalysis put the final touches on a series of "technologies for the construction of the subject" which in turn spread to the social sciences and today constitute in a simplified and impoverished form the ways in which the media functions.[20] Focusing on television, we can sketch out a broad outline of how these security apparatuses of subjection work, apparatuses which act on and through speech by "shutting up" the public and making it speak according to the rules of the common space of communication.

Like psychoanalysis, television functions based on a small number of already codified statements (its "grid") about the dominant reality (in our example, this means the economic statements of the market, competition, and employment/unemployment), which it seeks to make the statements of individual subjects.

There is nothing natural about the subject-function in communications and language. On the contrary, it must be constructed and imposed. According to Deleuze and Guattari, the individuated subject is neither a condition of language nor the cause of utterances. In reality, the latter are not produced by us, as subjects, but by something else entirely: "multiplicities, masses, and mobs, peoples and tribes, collective arrangements; they cross through us, they are within us, and they remain unknown to us."[21] This multiplicity that exceeds the individual makes us speak; and it is from this multiplicity that we produce utterances. There is no subject, there are only collective assemblages of enunciation that produce utterances. "[T]he utterance [is] always collective even when it seems to be emitted by a solitary singularity like that of the artist."[22]

The television machine extracts from these collective assemblages, from the multiplicity of verbal and nonverbal semiotics that traverse and constitute them, a subject of enunciation who must mold himself to a subject of utterance, in other words, a subject caught up in statements corresponding to television "reality," and who must adapt to a fixed framework of prefabricated enunciations. Television pushes us to speak as subjects of enunciation as if we were the cause and the origin of our statements, whereas we *are spoken by* the communications machine of which, as subjects of utterances, we are no longer anything more than one of the effects.[23]

If, for example, you are interviewed on television (whether on a literary program, a talk show, or a reality show), you are instituted as a subject of enunciation and subject to a machine which takes over your speech and remotely guides your singular expression through a semiotics attaching you to the dominant utterances. As in psychoanalysis, television is able to pass off utterances that conform to the dominant reality of capitalism as the utterances of individuals by dint of *interpretation* (and discrediting) and *subjection* machines.

Television uses all the linguistic and non-linguistic, verbal and nonverbal, constituents of the enunciation. First, you fall under the control of a non-discursive machine that interprets, selects, and standardizes your attitude, movements, and expressions before you even start speaking. Television functions based on a small number of ready-made utterances as well as on a selection and imposition of nonverbal semiotics (a certain intonation, a certain length and cadence of speech, certain behavior, a certain rhythm, certain gestures, certain clothes, a certain color pattern in the design, "costumes," a certain arrangement of the space in which you speak, a certain framing of the image, etc.). As a subject of enunciation, you are fit to a prefabricated audiovisual semiotics. Your voice, your gestures, and your intonation conform more or less amenably to codified apparatuses of expression.[24] As soon as you open your mouth, you pass through the interpretations of the discursive machine. The journalist is but one terminal which, with the help of other terminals of the interpreting machine (the expert, the specialist), determines the possible remaining gaps between your enunciation, your subjectivation, your signification, and the utterances, the subjectivation, the significations, expected of you. Nothing unexpected ever happens on television, and if it does, even something slightly out of place, it is immediately noticed—that is how thoroughly everything is codified. At the end of the interview, you are a subject of utterance, a subject caught in utterances in conformity with televisual logic, an effect of the semiotics of the interpretation machine, whose experience is that of a subject of enunciation, the absolute cause and origin of what is said.

With regard to psychoanalysis, Deleuze speaks of the "crushing of enunciation" by a preexisting code. This is not suffered negatively as repression but rather positively as encouragement to speak up, as a prompt to express oneself, such that the subject "has the impression of talking [...] but he will never be able to get to what he really has to say." Try as one might, the entire interpretive and subjectivation machine "exists to suppress the conditions of real expression."[25] The more you express yourself, the more you speak, the more you become part of the interactivity of the communication machine, the more you give up what it is you have to say because the communicational apparatuses cut you off from your own collective assemblages of enunciation and connect you to other collective assemblages (television) which individualize you as a split subject, as a double subject—both the cause and effect of utterances.

Psychoanalysis experiments with techniques for controlling and producing subjectivity. By concentrating on the enunciation rather than utterances, these techniques then migrate to other domains, especially the media, management, the individual monitoring of the unemployed and welfare recipients, and so on: "While, to achieve their ends, religions act by direct suggestion, by the imprint of standardized representations and statements, at least to begin with psychoanalysis gives free reign to a certain individual expression [...]. While religion, dare I say it, straitjackets subjectivity in the open air, psychoanalysis gets rid of some of the ballast of statements in order to concentrate its efforts on remodeling enunciation. [...]

[S]o-called 'free interpretation' is rapidly channeled by a pitiless semiotic remote control."[26]

De Certeau comes to the same conclusions: the proliferation of statements, messages, and signs prevents the conditions for a singular enunciation from emerging. The continuous drone, the incessant circulation of words and signs from the common semiotically standardized world, "create an absence of speech." Public space, saturated with signs, communications and discourse apparatuses, makes it impossible for people to form an enunciation that might be called their own.[27] In order to articulate a "real" enunciation that re-singularizes a "shared semiotics" which has the capacity to create new rifts, "polemical" points of view with which we might express ourselves, we must interrupt the circulation of the languages, signs, and media semiotics meant for "everyone, but true for no one."

All the apparatuses of enunciation in our security states (surveys, marketing, elections, union and political representation, etc.) are, on the one hand, more or less sophisticated variations of the independent and responsible speech production of the "individuated subject" ("human capital") and, on the other hand, refashionings of the creative/destructive process of its "free speech." As a voter, you are called on to express your opinion and to exercise your freedom of choice as a subject of enunciation; however, at the same time, you are spoken for as a subject of utterance, since your free expression is limited to choosing between possibilities that have already been codified by others, between alternatives ("right" and "left") that prevent you from exercising the power of problematization. Am I being asked the right question? Does it concern me? Is it really important to me? For a long time now voters have answered "no"; they abstain or they vote to eliminate the least worst choice others have already made. If a small gap remains between your enunciation and that which is expected of you, opinion polls are there to steer you in the right direction.[28]

With the proliferation of opinion polls, your voting decision ends up fitting into prefabricated molds, not instantaneously (during the election) but over time. In the same way, marketing and advertising provide daily training in the choice to make between alternatives set and offered by the market and business. Elections, marketing, and advertising mutually reflect and reinforce each other.[29] Like opinion polls, like marketing and union and political representation, elections presuppose prior consensus and agreement on problems and issues. Given this, it is understandable why the communications machine might function as a huge collective psychoanalysis. It translates what you say into another language, it shifts the origin and the sense of your words and explains to you your true utterances and actual desires (by giving them voice), which businesses can then plug into.

Television perfectly exemplifies how security apparatuses of power function in the way that Foucault describes, since it assures the governmentality of souls through the production of "freedom" (of speech and expression). Free speech is not a natural given one needs only to respect and protect. It is a correlate of the apparatus of power which must be produced and reproduced. The art of governing has "the function of producing, breathing life into, and increasing freedom" but through "additional control and intervention."[30] It is necessary, Foucault says, to "produce freedom, but this very act entails the establishment of limitations, controls, forms of coercion, and obligations relying on threats."[31] Security apparatuses at once produce and destroy freedom. The freedom they produce is one of enunciations and expressions codified and homogenized by the media. The freedom they destroy is that of inventing, creating, experimenting with singular forms of expression and speech.

On the rare occasions when activist groups have been invited to televised debates, we see how the subjection machine works. The "freedom of speech" and expression exercised within such strictly codified limits and conditions transforms into an injunction to conform speech to the prefabricated models of communication, to shape activists' statements to fit the template of statements and forms of thought of the journalists and experts with whom they are often faced.

For media to work, it needs individuals to accept, actively or passively, their implicit presuppositions, their forms of enunciation, and codes of expression. If this does not happen, as with an intermittent association member during a live interview on French television, the interviewer immediately senses the threat of alterity and, although usually calm and civilized with guests who accept the implicit presuppositions of televisual enunciation, he goes stiff, displaying a verbal aggressiveness and violence that betrays his fear of a non-preprogrammed broadcast. Because what frighten the members of the media are events they do not create themselves. They must immediately translate everything that happens into their own vocabulary. That is why, when confronted with a "real" event like the intermittent movement, the media's first objective is to isolate the person speaking from the connections that make up his collective assemblage (assemblies, collective action, the Coordination) and force a spokesperson, a representative, a leader, out of him, someone who both speaks for the others and expresses himself according to the media's codes, temporalities, and syntactical and lexical constraints (he will then, according to journalists, be "understood" to the public). The media is composed of apparatuses conceived and constructed to be always "at home" in the "common world" of democratic speech and expression, whatever happens and wherever they appear. During one of the intermittent workers' collective actions, for example—the occupation of a television news program—intermittents demanded the "right to blunder" when communicating, in other words, they refused the media codes governing speech and expression and refused to be caught in the apparatuses of subjection, to allow themselves to be cut off from their own assemblage. In this way, they revealed the conditions in which singular speech can be spoken.

The communications machine is thus a selection machine, implicitly following the same rules as those of co-determination, which sets limits on political and union representation and therefore on legitimate speech. If one wants to have a spot between "legiti-mate" representatives and the mere man-on-the-street the media normally welcomes in order to mask its flagrant lack of "reality," one has to make a lot of noise or make oneself known through "unruly" activity to be on the news. In any case, inevitably this will still not be enough since the media can only communicate within the limits of the "issues" it has defined in advance.

The political task before us is to discover, deploy, and give consistency to collective logics, to the people who are in us and who make us speak and thanks to whom we produce utterances.

This is what Deleuze and Guattari have in mind when they set "a whole field of experimentation, of personal and group experi-mentation" against both psychoanalysis and traditional political organizations.[32]

5

"Scum"[1] and the Critique of Performatives

> We govern one another in conversation through a whole series of tactics.
> —Michel Foucault, *Dits et écrits*, vol. 4

> The relationship established between replies in a dialogue—the relationship of question-response, assertion-objection, affirmation-agreement, offer-acceptance, order-execution—is impossible between unities of language.
> —Mikhail Bakhtin, *Speech Genres and Other Late Essays*

What is the relationship between social machines and discursive machines? We are going to examine this relationship within the specific context of Nicolas Sarkozy's 2005 French presidential campaign, which unofficially began while he was still Interior Minister. Our hypothesis is the following: discursive machines are something other than language [*la langue ou le langage*] since they imply a multiplicity of signifying and asignifying semiotics, technologies, functions, and so on, that do not operate according to performative logic but in a completely different register. They intervene in the social as part of a strategy of governing conduct that functions as the event-generating dynamic of an "action upon an action."

In order to account for the political function of language, both the theories of certain feminists in the United States and post-operaist theories in Europe draw on analytic philosophy and especially on performatives in such a way that understanding linguistic agency seems to me very difficult. Since the mid-1990s we have seen a return in force of analytic philosophy and Saussurean linguistics at a time when few would have expected it given the post-structuralist critiques of the 1960s and 70s and the political critiques of the semiotics of power.

1. The "Absolute" Performative

The turn to performatives by post-operaist Italian theory (Paolo Virno,[2] Christian Marazzi,[3] and to a lesser degree Negri/Hardt[4]) is quite surprising given that it seems to have resulted from a misunderstanding about the very definition of performatives. Thus its avatars seek to radicalize performative theory by introducing the category of "absolute performative" (Virno). Yet it retains only a portion of J. L. Austin's definition,[5] namely that the enunciation accomplishes rather than describes an action. By saying "Court is hereby in session," "I order you in the name of the people…" "I promise you…," one does not observe a situation or a state of affairs but rather does what one says.

According to Austin's theory, the force of the performative is that it entails a "social obligation" (in the case of a promise, it engages the person who says it at the risk of "losing face"; in the case of a question, the person to whom the question is addressed is supposed to respond at the risk of interrupting the conversation). In accomplishing the performative utterance, the speaker assigns himself a role and assigns his listener a complementary role. The force of the performative resides in the distribution of "rights" among speakers. The performative determines obligations such that language functions as a kind of vast institution "incorporating an array of conventional roles that correspond to the range of socially recognized speech acts."[6]

What is strongly emphasized is the "conventional" function of language as a reproduction of social obligations, in other words, its function of reproducing already instituted social relations.

This second and fundamental condition of the performative is inexplicably abandoned in the post-operaist theory of language such that the utterance "I speak," which is not a performative, is transformed into an "absolute performative," a verbal form that, according to Virno, characterizes "today's communication society from top to bottom."

In fact, "I speak" cannot be a performative since the result of the utterance is mere information from which no "obligation" follows. It institutes no "right," no convention, no role, no distribution of powers.[7] Even if it accomplishes what it states, it is nevertheless not a performative. "I speak" is an utterance that communicates something but it does not act on the "other." It does not create a new situation for an interlocutor which would oblige him to account for the fact that the utterance was addressed to him (by responding, obeying, not obeying, respecting a promise, not respecting it, etc.).

If we stick to Austin's theory, I see almost no case in which "I speak" might be considered a performative.

The definition of "absolute performative," reduced to the simple function of foregrounding the "event of language" without instituting an obligation (the fact that one speaks, that one intervenes, that one establishes an intersubjective relation), totally neutralizes the importance and implications of Austin's theory.

Performative theory upended both the categories of linguistics and Austin's theory itself. For one must remember that the theory was criticized and surpassed by its very inventor. After having distinguished the performative (what one does when one speaks) from the constative (a description of a state of affairs), Austin abandoned the opposition: all utterances are performative, since even constatives serve to accomplish a speech act.

After some hesitation, he argued against considering performatives a linguistic exception and introduced a new category, the illocutionary act, which encompasses the performative as a particular case. In this second version, all of our utterances (and not only performatives) serve to accomplish a certain social act that institutes an obligation.

Although linguists accepted the first version, they, like Benveniste, rejected the second. Because it puts the former radically in question, linguistics has by and large failed to exploit its possibilities. This is what we will attempt to do.

2. Emancipation Through the Performative

Judith Butler emphatically underscores what Virno neglects: the assignment of roles and ranks to which the performative attaches speakers.

In the United States, the "performative" is used by activists fighting against pornography and racist "hate speech." Austin's categories leave the musty halls of the university for the courtroom. According to defenders of women's rights and of ethnic minorities, pornography and hate speech are performative utterances insofar as they are not merely the expression of a point of view or an opinion (and as such protected by the First Amendment of the

US Constitution); they go beyond describing a situation. These utterances act on listeners by constituting those to whom the speech is addressed as dominated. The utterances do not simply reflect a social relation of domination, they describe, establish, or reestablish that power structure through the sole power of speech. By assigning women and minorities specific social roles, the performative utterance is thus similar to an action that neutralizes the agency of people to whom it is addressed and who, as such, might be brought before a judge.

Judith Butler's politico-linguistic program of rethinking the performative in order to appropriate the "political promise of emancipation" it holds seems to me problematic.

We will develop an initial critique of this return to the performative and its supposed emancipatory promise by drawing on Foucault's work. In his 1982/1983 lectures, published as *The Government of Self and Others*, he took the performative as the "counterexample" to the political rupture initiated by someone rising in an assembly in order to "tell the truth" [*dire vrai*]. The performative represents a "form of enunciation which is exactly the opposite of *parrhēsia*."[8]

Parrhēsia constitutes a rupture with the dominant significations, an "irruptive event" that creates a "fracture" by creating both new possibilities and a "field of dangers." The performative, on the other hand, is always more or less strictly institutionalized such that its "conditions" as well as its "effects" are "known in advance." In this way, it is impossible to produce any kind of rupture in the assignment of roles and distribution of rights (to speak). The irruption of true discourse "determines an open situation, or rather opens the situation and makes possible effects which are, precisely, not known." Inversely, the conditions and the effects of the performative enunciation are "codified." "*Parrhēsia* does not produce a codified effect; it opens up an unspecified risk."[9]

Just as the performative codifies enunciations, utterances, and their effects, it also institutionalizes speakers and listeners, their respective roles and ranks, and the public space of their acts. The "subjects" that emerge here take no risks and do not engage themselves "personally." They fit their speech and their subjectivities to the established forms of linguistic conventions.

To accomplish a performative utterance, the "status of the subject" is indispensable, yet if I baptize someone, the only thing required in order for it to be performed is the "priest function," whether or not I believe in God. What makes "Excuse me" a performative is what I say. Whether I am sincere or not is of no importance.

In other words, the performative "ritual" in no way engages or commits the subject, whereas truth-telling [*dire vrai*] establishes a "pact of the speaking subject with himself" and a pact with the listener. "He says that he really thinks this truth, and in this he binds himself" as much to the content of the utterance as to the act of enunciation itself, and he assumes all the risks and consequences of doing so.[10]

The parrhesiastic enunciation not only produces effects on others but firstly affects the enunciating subject, producing a transformation of his condition (an existential transformation, according to Guattari). "I think it is this retroaction—such that the event of the utterance affects the subject's mode of being [...] that characterizes a type of facts of discourse which are completely different from those dealt with by pragmatics."[11] With the performative, there is no invention or transformation of the subject possible.

Subjectivation is a power of affectation of the self by the self which, as such, is not linguistic. It defines a self-positioning, a self-existentialization (as Guattari would say), which, although employing words and propositions of language, radically removes us from the laws of linguistics and even those of pragmatics. Foucault is very clear: "With *parrhēsia* we see the appearance of a whole family of completely different facts of discourse which are almost the reverse [...] of what we call the pragmatics of discourse."[12]

The ontological consequences of the relation to self, which Butler completely neglects, are what allow Foucault to depart from the logic of power as well as from the structuralism of language (and even from his own work on "sex"). If one seeks a politics of emancipation, it is here and not in the appropriation and reversal of the performative that we will find it.

Former Interior Minister Sarkozy's definition of suburban Parisian youth as "scum" ("Have you had enough of this scum? Well, I'm going to get rid of them for you!") seems to reveal the wrongheadedness of positions invoking "performatives" in order to explain the power of words. It also makes one rightly suspicious of the capacity of the theory to account for the political "force" of language.

What were the effects of the "hate speech" then-Interior Minister Sarkozy uttered before the television cameras? While the word "scum" did not neutralize French suburbanites' agency, it did activate that agency on a scale unimaginable prior to the enunciation. Instead of constituting the young residents of the projects as dominated, the enunciation mobilized them as rebellious, insubordinate, based precisely on their refusal to accept the assignation "scum." The force of the revolt did not depend on "another kind of performative" or on its appropriation, as Butler maintains, but on an existential affirmation (Guattari) first manifested through a suspension of dominant meanings and social functions. It entailed a relation to the self (Foucault), in other words, an act that exceeds the linguistic or pragmatic framework.

Similarly, it is difficult to understand why Butler considers performative Rosa Park's refusal to give up her seat to a white man. There is nothing performative about it, or if there is, then we have to change the meaning of the term. It is an *act* of resistance, of self-positioning, of affirmation, showing itself in a *gesture* of refusal without speech. The act precedes both thought and speech; it constitutes the breaking point in dominant meanings and the negation of the distribution of roles and social functions.

Subjective mutation is not primarily discursive, since it touches the focal point of the non-discursive in subjectivity beyond which there is no going back. It is starting from this existential dimension that subjectivity emerges and takes on consistency through, only secondarily, a multiplicity of semiotics which also includes language, myths, and narratives. But it is only starting from the asignifying, unnamable, untellable dimension that there can be meaning, language, and narrative.

Still, the theory of the performative represents an important shift in linguistics. Contra Saussurean doctrine, we can no longer admit the separation between language [*langue*] and speech [*parole*], the former supposedly establishing meanings prior to any kind of use and the latter restricted to communicating them according to the speaker's intentions. We can no longer accept the definition of language as a means of communication, as an exchange of information.

Instead of moving beyond the movement Austin inaugurated, Virno and Butler, even if in different ways, close off the enunciation from language, as if language [*langue*] could exist autonomously, secrete meanings through syntactic, phonetic, or grammatical structures, generate agency over others, and explain the force of transformation of language [*langage*] and signs. They accredit the initial theory of the performative which even Austin abandoned.

3. Bakhtin and the First Theory of Enunciation

Life can only be understood as an event
—Mikhail Bakhtin, *Speech Genres and Other Late Essays*

Our second series of criticisms of the performative draws on Guattari's and Bakhtin's work. Instead of starting from language [*langue*] in an approach to the enunciation, one encumbered by huge difficulties and obvious reservations, as if the enunciation were, as Guattari says, language's "far-off suburb," these authors follow a path exactly opposite the one taken by linguistics. The pragmatics of the enunciation precedes phonology, syntactics, and semantics. The enunciation, and in particular its *non-discursive* component, represents for Guattari the "active core" of linguistic and semiotic creativity. Whereas for Bakhtin an approach to the enunciation that is not exclusively linguistic is indeed possible,[13] Guattari argues that, in order to think the production of subjectivity, a radical split has to be made between the "production of meaning and sense" and "existential production."

Turning to Bakhtin as a critic of the performative may seem paradoxical, since the essential features of his theory of enunciation were elaborated immediately after the Russian Revolution and therefore well before the invention of performatives. Paradoxical as well because in his theory the performative quite simply has no place; as in Austin's later work, "every speech act," and not only performatives, "is a social act" which engages speakers, creates obligations, and assigns roles.

Despite the homology of the terms they use, there are remarkable differences between Austin's theory and Bakhtin's. First of all, the latter establishes a difference in kind between language and grammar on the one hand and enunciation on the other, between the word and proposition of language and the utterance, between the (linguistic) meaning and the sense (of the enunciation).

He finds a new "sphere of being," the "dialogic," unknown to linguistics and the philosophy of language and not limited to mere replies between speakers in a dialogue. A dialogic relation can also be established between texts, scientific theories, and works of art separated in space and time.

In the dialogic sphere, relations are relations of sense expressed through language and signs yet remain irreducible to either. The dialogic relation is a specific relation that is part of neither a logical nor a linguistic system as in the structuralism of Saussure or Lacan; nor is it part of a psychological system, because it cannot be detached from the individual subjective consciousness of the speaker. The relation presupposes a language (and a logic, a semiotics, or psychology) but does not exist within the system of language (or in a logical or semantic system or psychology).

The force, expressivity, and agency of language [*langage*] do not derive from *langue*, from its grammatical structure; they do not emerge from differences or from a combinatory of signifiers but from the dialogic relations whose language constitutes a necessary but not sufficient element.

In order for words, propositions, and grammatical rules to form a complete enunciation, a "speech act," a "*supplementary* element" is needed (an ethico-political element and, more specifically and more radically, an *existential* element, an "*existential function*," as Guattari would say) that "remains inaccessible to every linguistic categorization or determination, whatever it may be."

Separated from the enunciation (from the "speech act"), words, grammatical form, and proposition are "technical signs," "material," simple "possibilities" in the service of an only potential meaning.

The individuation, singularization, and actualization of this potentiality of language which allows words and propositions to be transformed into a complete enunciation, into a "whole," are realized by pre-personal affective forces and post-personal ethico-political social forces external to language but internal to the enunciation.

It is impossible to isolate a category like performatives because every speech act is addressed to someone or something, responds to someone or something, entails an "obligation," and presupposes a "response" (or a "responsive attitude"). The "response" ("one can agree or disagree with it, execute it, evaluate it, and so on") is a constitutive element of the utterance. For the enunciation, "nothing is more terrible than a lack of response."[14]

Butler seeks to oppose the performative command with the possibility for unforeseeable and uncodified response and reaction.[15] This can only come up short since the problem of the "response," that is, the possibility of acting differently when addressed concerns all enunciations and not solely performatives (which is the same conclusion Austin comes to while neglecting some of its consequences). On the other hand, the command cannot be countered by a different type of performative act but only through a dialogic relation that exceeds all linguistic categories, whether performative or not.

Even if the response's syntax is inscribed in the "structures" of language, it is not produced by language but rather by the dialogic relation with the other. The "end" of the utterance, its realization (accomplishment), which makes it a request, an order, and so forth, is given by the dialogic relation and not by linguistic forms, whether or not performative.

> The first and foremost criterion for the finalization of the utterance is the possibility of responding to it or, more precisely and broadly, of assuming a responsive attitude toward it (for example, executing an order). This criterion is met by a short everyday question, for example, "What time is it?" (one may respond to it), an everyday request that one may or may not fulfill, a scientific statement with which one may agree or disagree (partially or completely), or a novel, which can be evaluated as a whole.[16]

There is indeed a grammatical "end" and "finalization" of the propositions of language that make them intelligible. But grammatical intelligibility is a necessary but not sufficient condition of the verbal exchange. An intelligible, effectuated linguistic proposition within the linguistic order "cannot evoke a responsive reaction."[17]

Only the speech act and not linguistic propositions has the property of accomplishing an enunciation, for it is through address and response that *it expresses values, points of view, emotions, affects, sympathies, and antipathies with regard to the situation, to the other, to utterances and, in particular, to utterances referring to the "true, the just, and the beautiful."*

The response is always a self-positioning, a self-affirmation, and it is only through this positioning that one can respond, speak, and express oneself.

Every speech act is an ethico-political act because it aims for "agreement" or "disagreement." Every speech act is a "question" asked of others, oneself, and the world. Bakhtin's theory of enunciation implicates the world as a problem, an event, as something that always remains to be accomplished. This is unlike Austin's theory of the performative and illocutionary act, which considers the world as a set of conventions, as an institution, as a distribution of powers, rights, and duties to be reproduced. By its nature, every speech act and not only the performative acts on others by restructuring the possibilities for action.[18] The speech act is an event which creates indetermination by opening possibilities that "subjectively" engage speakers in a singular relation occurring "here and now." Every enunciation is an historic event even if it is "infinitely small."[19]

Unlike structuralism, which attempts to confine the enunciation within the combinatory rules of language, and unlike Austinian speech act theory, the enunciation represents a "micro-politics" and/or "micro-physics" of relations between speakers. The enunciation is not produced according to the linguistic model via a speaker's active speech process and a listener's passive processes of perception and understanding. On the contrary, the latter takes full part in accomplishing the act. As in Foucault's late theory of power relations, the other is "active" and "free."[20] In the event of enunciation, the other establishes its dynamics and orients its actualization. Enunciation is a co-production of a *polemical* and/or *cooperative* co-actualization of linguistic virtualities, worlds of values, and the existential territories in which they occur.

Like the Foucauldian strategic relations of power, the dialogic relations of enunciation open a field of possible responses/reactions that can only be determined, can only be actualized, in and through the "doing" of enunciation.

In this way, it is easy to see that the nature of the enunciation is not performative but dialogic, "strategic," and event-generating. Bakhtin, like Foucault, has an "agonistic" and "polemical" view of the enunciation; the latter resembles a "battle"[21] between speakers or, better still, it functions as a "strategy" for governing the behaviors of others manifested through a whole series of techniques and linguistic and semiotic tactics.

The parallel Foucault establishes between the course of a conversation and the governmental techniques we noted at the start are perfectly expressed in Bakhtin's description of the dynamics of the enunciation, which have nothing to do with the institutionalization or distribution of roles implied by the performative.

> When constructing my utterance, I try actively to determine this response. Moreover, I try to act in accordance with the response I anticipate, so this anticipated response, in turn, exerts an active influence on my utterance (I parry objections that I foresee, I make all kinds of provisos, and so forth). When speaking I always take into account the apperceptive background of the addressee's perception of my speech: the extent to which he is familiar with the situation, whether he has special knowledge of the given cultural area of communication, his views and convictions, his prejudices (from my viewpoint), his sympathies and antipathies— because all this will determine his active responsive understanding of my utterance.[22]

4. The Micro-Politics of Voice and Gesture

We already find in the Bakhtin Circle's first articles published in the 1930s this micro-political (polemical and/or governmental) relation of enunciation. Where linguistics and Lacanian structuralism *see* differential relations between signs or between signifiers, Bakhtin, like visionaries, idiots, or madmen, "*hears* voices and their dialogic relationship" and the self-affirmation, the existential territories (Guattari), and the values maintaining them.

In an important article in which Bakhtin is considered at length, Guattari observes that, according to the Russian philosopher's theory, in each enunciation there are both "pre-individual voices," which express "volitive-emotional" evaluations ("sensible affects," in Guattari's terminology), and "social voices," ethico-political voices which express the beautiful, the just, and the true—universes of "values" in Guattari's vocabulary. These voices extend *beyond* articulated language. Voice/intonation, not yet caught in the "phonetic abstraction" of language, is always produced "on the border of the verbal and the nonverbal, the said and the unsaid" and "it endows everything linguistically stable with living historical momentum and uniqueness."[23] It is through the voice that the address to the other is made. And this address is first affective and ethico-political before it is linguistic. "Intonation makes it sound as if the world surrounding the speaker were still full of animate forces—it threatens and rails against or adores and cherishes inanimate objects and phenomena."[24]

In voices we find the animation of nature, of the cosmos (animism), Guattari describes. Contrary to what linguistics and the philosophy of language claim, pre-signifying corporeal semiotics (gestures, bodily attitudes, movements, facial expressions, etc.) here play a decisive role, since it is through the body that values first emerge. "Intonation and gesture have a close interrelationship" that originates in the body, that furnishes "the originary raw materials for this expression of values."[25] The notion of gesture must be understood in a "broad sense including miming as facial gesticulation."[26]

Gesture, like intonation, "always has latent within itself the germ of attack or defense, of threat or caress." This is the reason why every enunciation always makes the speaker play the "role of ally or witness," "enemies, friends."[27]

The voice works with, uses, and organizes linguistic and semiotic elements not only by choosing and combining, but also by operating a singularization of language which can be defined as strategic, since it distributes and "names" the speakers according to a proto-political model structuring the space of speech according to power relations between speakers.

The voice expresses itself, feels, and vibrates within a "sympathetic atmosphere," one of "complicity," "confrontation," or "discomfort" vis-à-vis the addressee.

In each voice, there is a twofold address. The voice is addressed not only to the addressee but also to "the object of enunciation," which acts as the third element in enunciation such that the addressee is called on to be both "judge and witness" and, therefore, "ally" or "enemy."

Even the poet, Bakhtin says, must "continually work with his listener's sympathy or antipathy, agreement or disagreement."[28]

Only when the voice penetrates and appropriates words and propositions do these latter lose their linguistic potential and transform into an expression that appeals to friends and wards off enemies, that threatens or flatters, repels or pleases, opening to the risk and indetermination of enunciation.

5. Discursive Strategies

It is now easy to understand why in the case of Sarkozy's utterance ("You are scum") we are in no way dealing with a performative but with a "strategic" utilization of enunciation within the given power relations the former minister was attempting to modify to his advantage. "Hate speech" ought not to be understood, as Americans do, as a force accomplishing what it says but rather as an "action upon possible actions," an action opened to the unpredictability, to the indeterminacy, of the response-reaction of the other (of others).

The enunciation "You are scum" takes place within a given sociopolitical situation in order to modify that situation. By appealing to "friends" and designating "enemies," the enunciation threatens the latter and reassures and reinforces the former. It seeks out allies, and in order to build new alliances it conjures up as enemies the immigrant, suburban youth, the "lazy," the "unemployed," "thugs," etc. It looks to reconfigure political space by calling on others as "judges and witnesses," obligating them to position themselves, to express a point of view, to make a value judgment, which is always at once affective and ethico-political. Finally, it seeks to construct a public space in which fear of, rather than friendship with the "other" prevails.

The space-time opened by the enunciation is not that of the performative; it is the space-time of indetermination, unpredictability, the dialogic event, the "battle discourse," which seeks to hold sway over others, over their behavior, by restructuring their field of action. The effects are not predetermined as with performatives, where the speaker, the utterance, and the listener are already instituted.

Here the speaker and the "audiences" he addresses on television (enunciation and machinic speech, we should emphasize) are open to the becoming of the event. Would the insulting enunciation allow Sarkozy to win the presidential election through a strategy meant to weaken the other candidates of his own or the opposing camps? Would he win votes among the xenophobic electorate of the extreme right? Would he succeed in forcing the "Left" to respond by accepting the political debate over security? He had no idea himself (even if in the reactionary and fear-ridden Europe in which we live the strategy had and has been proven to work).

In any case, the "response-reaction" of the "scum" highlights the dialogic nature of every speech act.

As we know, every enunciation implies understanding, a "response-reaction," "active responsiveness," "taking a position," a "point of view," an "evaluative response." And this one provoked them all beyond what even their author could have hoped.

Revolt occurs first of all as an asignifying existential crystallization, as the emergence of focal points of subjectivation that take on consistency through a multiplicity of materials of expression. The crystallization of the response, the singularization of "understanding," takes place not only linguistically—far from it. The materials of expression are not solely linguistic; the vectors of subjectivation, the focal points of enunciation, are multiple. They are not limited to language and to linguistic interlocution, as Rancière would have it.[29] Revolt is in itself the sign of the capacity to interrupt, suspend, the dominant significations and to create "gestures," acts, signs, and perhaps even words according to modalities which may not be those of the speaker. There is an ontological difference between "asking" and "responding," as Bakhtin reminds us; for the two belong to absolutely irreducibly unique space-time blocs, two existential territories, two very different ways of speaking.

Well before Sarkozy's remark, the youth from the projects had inverted, just as Butler would hope, the meaning of the term "scum" with which power addressed them. Their way of speaking was defined by the same people as "speaking *caillera*," suburban slang for *racaille* ("scum"). They did not have to wait for the supposed performative of Sarkozy's words to "twist" the insult.

The political space opened by the enunciation changed before our very eyes. Several "strategies" confronted each other: on the one hand, the affirmation of "city youths" as political subjects, on the other, the presidential candidacy. We saw the effects of the enunciation unfold in real time, following the rhythms of the riots, the positions of political forces, experts, unions, and intellectuals—the whole thing orchestrated by media machines.

The results of the enunciation could not be anticipated in the way they might be when a judge declares, "I find you guilty in the name of law"; the enunciation continues to modify the social and political body even now that the riots have been suppressed and the media is no longer training its cameras and mikes on the suburbs. No one knows what the "focal points of asignifying existential affirmation" alit during the November nights of 2005 might one day produce.

6. The Reproducible and the Non-Reproducible

But let us return to the performative and to the reappraisal Butler, by way of Derrida, wishes to accomplish. The simple repetition of the sign (not of its semantics but of its existence as mark) is supposed to be enough to break with the distribution of roles, functions, and rights instituted by the performative. In order for it to repeat itself, the sign-mark must detach from the context. The autonomy of the sign-mark with respect to the context in which it is made (which represents the core of Derrida's polemic with Searle) is supposed to determine a "point of rupture" with "dominant meanings." Her position, which equals in its formality and abstraction the differential logic of language (Saussure) and of the signifier (Lacan), gives us a misleading picture of how rupture and repetition function in and through language.[30]

In every enunciation, the "point of rupture" never follows from the autonomy or independence of the mark but rather from the singular speech act, from subjective affirmation, and from the *ethico-political positioning* that founds and supports it.[31]

We can distinguish in the enunciation between what is reproducible (all the elements of language, the mark as well as the syntax and the semantic content) and what is not (the subjective act of enunciation).

These two dimensions—reproducible and non-reproducible—can be easily discerned both in the address and in the response to which the enunciation gives rise. Guattari draws attention to a text from 1924 in which Bakhtin distinguishes five linguistic (reproducible) and extralinguistic (non-reproducible) constituents of the enunciation:

> (1) the phonic side of the word, the musical constituent proper; (2) the referential meaning of the word (with all its nuances and variations); (3) the constituent of verbal connections (all the relations and interrelations that are purely verbal); (4) the intonational (on the psychological plane—the emotional-volitional) constituent of the word, the axiological directedness of the word that expresses the diversity of the speaker's axiological relations—ethico-political and more specifically social values (pre-individual voices and post-personal social voices); (5) the feeling of verbal activeness, the feeling of the active generation of signifying *sound* (included here are all motor elements—articulation, gesture, facial expressions, etc.—and the whole inner directedness of my personality).[32]

The first three constituents of enunciation, constituting the linguistic and semiotic elements, represent its "reproducible," reiteratable parts, whereas the remaining two are non-reproducible elements, the absolutely singular elements created for the first time through and in the act of enunciation. The fourth constituent is the specifically dialogic one since it expresses both affective evaluation ("the emotional-volitional") and social evaluation (the axiological).

The last constituent, the feeling of the creative activity of speech, expresses the relation to the self, the ontological force affirmed through existential positioning. It constitutes the non-discursive element that generates not only the physical reality of the word but also "meaning and evaluation." Through the utterance, the speaker occupies an active position (he realizes an existential self-positioning, as Guattari would say) with respect to the world and to others: "that is, a feeling of moving and assuming a position as a whole human being—of a movement into which both the organism and the meaning-directed activity are drawn, because both the flesh and the spirit of the word are generated together in their concrete unity."[33]

If we now move from the "polyvocity" and heterogeneity of the semiotic linguistic and non-linguistic elements of the address to those of "understanding," we encounter the same multiplicity of reproducible and non-reproducible features. In understanding, which is an active "reaction-response," we find a series of elements realized through the extralinguistic forces of the dialogic relation:

(1) Psychophysiologically perceiving a physical sign (word, color, spatial form). (2) Recognizing it (as familiar or unfamiliar), understanding its (general) reproducible *signification* in language. (3) Understanding its significance in the given context (immediate and more remote). (4) Active-dialogic understanding (disagreement/agreement). Inclusion in the dialogic context. The evaluative

aspect of understanding and the degree of its depth and universality.[34]

The final, properly dialogic element is the most important because it singularizes, gives "existential" consistency to, the reaction-response. From this, one selects, orders, and finalizes the enunciation.

Linguistic understanding is not the same thing as dialogic understanding. The latter always entails taking a position, making a judgment, an action-response within dialogic relations. Responses express a "sympathy, an antipathy," an "agreement, sympathy, objection, execution, and so forth."[35] Every response "refutes, affirms, supplements, and relies on"[36] preceding utterances.

At the end of his introduction to John Searle's *Speech Acts*, Ducrot asks, "Do the elements of language, besides their polemical value, have independent conceptual (and semantic) content? Is there in language a nucleus of meaning irreducible to the activity of enunciation?"[37] Is there an expressiveness to language independent of enunciation? Bakhtin gave his answer in the 1920s, as Peirce did[38] before him: the enunciation logically and practically precedes *langue*.

7. Language That "Precedes and Exceeds the Subject"

If we start from the enunciation rather than from language, if we start from the speech *act* rather than from the autonomy, the "exteriority," and "supremacy" of the signifier (or, in the contemporary version, of performative "force"), if we start from what is reproducible and what is not reproducible in the enunciation, we can put the matter differently of what, in language, "precedes and exceeds the subject."[39] Butler can only conceive language as a transcendence that precedes and exceeds us because we become a subject only by entering into the normativity of language and following its rules.

With Bakhtin, there are indeed linguistic elements (phonetic, grammatical, syntactic, etc.) and chains of utterances that precede the subjectivation and individuation process. Yet, contrary to Butler, they cannot exceed that process because the realization of the enunciation is not accomplished through its conformity with the rules of grammar (Wittgenstein) or the institutional distribution of performative roles, or for that matter through a chain of signifiers (Lacan), but rather through event-generating dynamics. What "precedes" us is always and necessarily activated in the enunciation and is each time "transfigured in what is created" by the speech act, which establishes a dialogic relation in which the subjective forces of existential affirmation alone accomplish (complete) the utterance.

> An utterance is never just a reflection or an expression of something already existing outside it that is given and final. It always creates something that never existed before, something absolutely new and unrepeatable, and, moreover, it always has some relation to value (the true, the good, the beautiful, and so forth). But something created is always created out of something given (language, an observed phenomenon of reality, an experienced feeling, the speaking subject himself, something finalized in his world view, and so forth). What is given is completely transformed in what is created.[40]

Despite Butler's preoccupations, we can conceive a "non-essentialist" thought without positing the preexistence of language as a "radical and originary dependency." The subject, his means of expression, the objective of his discourse, the relationship with others and their utterances, and the utterances that circulate in public space occur and transform in and through the event of enunciation. There is no originary subjectivity because the subject and the relationships prevailing in the subjectivation process are always yet to be realized, actualized, and constructed. The subject is not an effect of language; language is not the cause of the subject. For the subject is not constituted through a preexistent linguistic structure but through a self-positioning, a self-affirmation, matched with words, others, and the world.

> An object is ready-made, the linguistic means for its depiction are ready-made, the artist himself is ready-made, and his world view is ready-made. And here with ready-made means, in light of a ready-made world view, the ready-made poet reflects a ready-made object. But in fact the object is created in the process of creativity, as are the poet himself, his world view, and his means of expression.[41]

With Bakhtin, we can push our critique still further. In reality, what precedes the subject is not language, grammar, and their rules, but what Bakhtin calls "speech genres." We can only learn language by way of "chains of concrete utterances" whose use, in differentiated verbal spheres, develops relatively stable types. We learn to speak, we "become a subject" not through grammar and syntax, but through immersion in these genres of which the first are those of colloquial discourse.

Speech genres operate at the intersection of language "structure" (what is reproducible) and then each time singular enunciation (what is non-reproducible). Through these language enters life and life enters language.

The "chain" of speech genres does not act as a structure or a molar constraint in the way that "chains of signifiers" do in Lacan. They function as an assemblage composed of a multiplicity of ways of speaking, responding, disagreeing, and cooperating. The "chain of utterances" is open, fractal, constantly changing, and it provides more or less freedom to the "intention" of the speaker. Although just as normative and prescriptive as language, speech genres are much more "changeable, flexible, and plastic."[42] Speakers discover in speech genres the possibility of forming their expression and their "intention" (address, response, position, etc.) in more or less creative, more or less stereotypical, ways.

The difference between speech genres has firstly to do with the degree of "freedom" or "constraint," of standardization or creation, of reproduction or novelty, they encourage or thwart in relationships between speakers. Bakhtin classifies what analytic philosophy regards as performative among *the most standardized, the most stereotypical speech genres*, for they entail the reproduction of political relations and of existing linguistic conventions.

> [I]n certain spheres of everyday life (questions that are purely factual and similarly factual responses to them, requests, orders, and so forth), in certain business circles, in the sphere of military and industrial commands and orders, we encounter verbal spheres in which speech genres are maximally standard by nature and where the creative aspect is almost completely lacking.[43]

If class relations introduce a major difference between the address and the response of speakers, they are still and always relations marked by conventions (speakers' hierarchical positions, social standing, rank, wealth, fame, etc.). For enunciation and creative expression, a space-time is needed other than that of conventions, hierarchy, and subordination, one where sympathy, trust, and mutual understanding prevail, where the other is perceived and felt to be a friend and of the same status.

> In addition to these standard genres, of course, freer and more creative genres of oral speech communication have existed and still exist: genres of salon conversations about everyday, social, aesthetic, and other subjects, genres of table conversation, intimate conversations among friends, intimate conversations within the family, and so on. [...] The majority of these genres are subject to free creative reformulation (like artistic genres, and some, perhaps, to a greater degree).[44]

Creativity is not a product of language but an ethico-political assemblage of which language is only one constituent part. "Freedom" requires that a discourse be infused with deep trust, with sympathy, sensitivity, and the benevolence of one's responsive understanding, in other words, with a politics other than that of standardization.

The colloquial and intimate genres are linguistic apparatuses that encourage creativity because the speaker and addressee "perceive their addressees in exactly the same way: more or less outside the framework of the social hierarchy and social conventions, 'without rank,' as it were. [...] In familiar speech, since speech constraints and conventions have fallen away, one can take a special unofficial, volitional approach to reality. [...] Intimate speech is imbued with a deep confidence in the addressee, in his sympathy."[45]

Creativity or the simple reproduction of the enunciation depends on the presence or absence of relations of hierarchy or subordination, sympathy, or "discomfort," the affects of friendship and enmity, trust or distrust. Standardization or creative differentiation depends on the micro- and macro-politics of the enunciation and not on the structures of language or performatives.

8. Transcendence and Guilt in Language

In the new "critical" versions of performative theory (Žižek, Butler), the speaker still seems burdened by the transcendence, error, and guilt of the religious man. He finds himself in a relation of "radical and orginary dependency." The latter no longer exists with regard to the divinity but to "a language whose historicity exceeds in all directions the history of the speaking subject"[46] such that our power to act depends "paradoxically" on the power of language (on its exteriority, on its autonomy, etc.).

Given that the subject engages in and through language and that the rules of language transcend us, subordination to language and, more generally, to the laws of "power and knowledge" in place is the condition of possibility for speaking. Butler unjustifiably and inexplicably attributes the point of view to Foucault, when in fact it is a verbatim reiteration of Lacan, for whom the "freedom" of the subject "becomes bound up with the development of his servitude."[47] As in Lacan, the "negative" (castration, repression, lack, loss, etc.) does not manifest the contingency of power relations but rather a universal necessity of the human condition, a condition of our very existence, which one must assume and surpass dialectically.[48]

According to Bakhtin, however, the speaker does not experience language as "servitude" because he is immersed in a living and heterogeneous world different from that described by Butler and Žižek. In the utterances in which he is immersed, he hears the voices of normativity and injunction but also the voices of creation and freedom. He hears the heterogeneity of points of view, judgments, and values; and in this way, he hears the struggles, registers the sympathy and antipathy, agreement and disagreement, and trust and distrust they express.

> For any individual consciousness living in it, language is not an abstract system of normative forms but rather a concrete heteroglot conception of the world. All words have the "taste" of a profession, a genre, a tendency, a party, a particular work, a particular person, a generation, an age group, the day and the hour.[49]

The speaker does not find himself thrown into *one* space-time "saturated" with *power* one can escape solely through the dialectic pirouettes of the work of the negative. Instead, he exists in a multiplicity of *power relations, in a great variety* of space-time blocs in which the voices and harmonics of standardized speech genres as well as those of the "intimate and familiar" genres resound, in which relationships among them and with utterances are conducive to creativity. The development of space-time blocs of one or the other kind does not depend on language (Saussure), grammar (Wittgenstein), or performatives (Butler and Žižek), but on the micro- and macropolitics of language (the centrifugal and centripetal forces—of which linguistics and structuralism are obviously a part—that shape language) and on micro- and macro-politics *tout court*.

9. Variants and Invariants

The chain of utterances configured as a fractal multiplicity of non-totalizable speech genres within a structure is an evolving reality. In the reality of verbal exchange, syntactic forms and speech genres do not have the stability of grammars and dictionaries. These are constantly varying, always in the process of being made and unmade.

> [S]ome forms are undergoing grammaticalization while others are undergoing degrammaticalization. It is precisely these ambiguous, borderline forms that are of the greatest interest to the linguist: this is precisely where the developmental tendencies of a language may be discerned.[50]

Hence the impossibility of confining these relationships to a linguistic structure (Saussure's and Lacan's structuralism, Wittgenstein's "grammar," or Austin's illocutionary acts). The organic link between language, speech genres, and speech acts "cannot become lexical, grammatically stable, and fixed in identical and reproducible forms, i.e., cannot itself become a sign or a constant element of a sign, cannot become grammaticalized."[51]

Linguistics appears obsessed by the desire to reduce the indeterminacy, risk, and instability created by the event-capacity of enunciation to a fixed grammatical or syntactic structure, to norms of enunciation, to the invariants of the official language. Bakhtin's theory, on the other hand, calls for a "science of singularity" whose object is the organic link between the reproducible and the non-reproducible, between linguistic and non-linguistic elements, between the given and the created, an organic link which is "attained in the concrete historical act of the utterance, exists only for the given utterance, and only under the given conditions of its realization."[52]

Before Deleuze, Guattari, and Foucault, Bakhtin turned from constants to the consideration of variants and variations.[53] Foucault remarks that one must "reveal functions of discourse which are not simply those of expression (a relation of forces already constituted and stabilized) or reproduction (a preexisting social system)."[54] The decision to privilege variants or invariants is not only indicative of a linguistic or stylistic affinity but above all a political move, since language and grammar are primarily State policies conveyed by centripetal, centralizing forces that format language politically.

10. Still More on "Scum"

The strategic or governmental nature of Sarkozy's enunciation can now be refined using Bakhtin's categories. A concrete and singular utterance is a "link in the chain of speech communication," to which it is connected not only through contemporaneous utterances but also through past utterances and those to come.

There is not only the *synchronic* dimension of language, of signifiers, but also and especially the *diachronic*, temporal dimension of enunciation and speech genres. An utterance must above all be considered a response to previous utterances insofar as it refutes, affirms, supplements, and relies on them, assumes that they are known and, in one way or another, "counts on them." At the same time, it is constructed in anticipation of a response to come, one which the enunciation necessarily presupposes (a response that can take place now or in the far-off future).

Sarkozy's statement on immigration is not the first but rather belongs to a chain of utterances with a long history. The target of his words (the immigrant, the foreigner, the delinquent) is not new either. "The object, as it were, has already been articulated, disputed, elucidated, and evaluated in various ways. Various viewpoints, world views, and trends cross, converge, and diverge in it."[55]

The chain in which Sarkozy's statement is a part belongs to a linguistic "heritage" shared by the left and the right. It responds to, relies on, and complements the French Communist Party's utterances (the slogan "Let's make French!" proclaimed as French-made bulldozers raze immigrant homes in Paris's "red" suburbs); those of the National Front ("The French first!"); as well as those of the Socialist Party ("We cannot be a home for the world's poor" or the "suburbs" "feral children"). But we can also find more remote echoes and resonances in the voices of the bourgeoisie defining the nineteenth-century proletariat in the same way it does the suburban youth of today: "scum."

The future president's insult was not only connected to racist statements of the past but also to those to come. "Scum" is not a performative injunction addressed to the young immigrants of the suburban projects, but a speech act aiming to shape a situation and the subjectivity of the "French" who must subsequently position themselves with respect to the utterance.

> But from the very beginning, the utterance is constructed while taking into account possible responsive reactions, for whose sake, in essence, it is actually created. As we know, the role of the others for whom the utterance is constructed is extremely great. We have already said that the role of these others, for whom my thought becomes actual thought for the first time (and thus also for my own self as well) is not that of passive listeners, but of active participants in speech communication. From the very beginning, the speaker expects a response from them, an active responsive understanding. The entire utterance is constructed, as it were, in anticipation of encountering this response.[56]

The historicity of language does not include a past and a future that "exceed in all directions the history of the speaking subject" (Butler). Like grammatical rules, genres of discourse, and so on, these temporalities constitute only the conditions of the event of enunciation. In the here and now of the event, the past, present, and future coexist (the present of the past, the present of the present, and the present of the future, according to Augustine's formulation). Temporalities are put back into play and "transfigured" in the event of enunciation. History and its temporalities, language and its temporalities, are but the conditions the event reconfigures in order to create something new.

The former president's enunciation revealed at once a continuity and break with the utterances that preceded it. "Scum" is the repetition ("refrain" [*ritournelle*]) of the power that holds these disparate (linguistic and extralinguistic) elements together through an existential (reactionary) affirmation that sees in the nation, in the fear of and the contempt for the foreigner, in work, authority, and order, his universe of values and "existential territories."

It is therefore impossible to discover significations, the power of transformation and subjectivation, simply from the semantic, phonetic, or grammatical structures of language.

To accomplish an enunciation always means asserting power over extralinguistic constituents that are at once somatic, ethological, mythographic, institutional, economic, political, and aesthetic.

6

The Discursive and the Existential in the Production of Subjectivity

But why do they have to continuously return to this irrational, religious, etc., stuff? Why? In a given state of subjectivity, there is no other way [...]. If in order to exist we absolutely have to have recourse to this kind of thing, it isn't surprising that people rush headlong into it, even if they know that rationally it doesn't hold water.

There's no getting rid of molar strata. Schizoanalysis cannot replace organizations.

—Félix Guattari, "Machine abstraite et champ non-discursif," Seminar of March 12, 1985

1. The Existential as Machinism

The collective forms of today's political mobilization, whether urban riots or "union" struggles, whether peaceful or violent, are all motivated by the same issue: on the one hand, the refusal of representation and, on the other, the experimentation with and invention of forms of organization and expression in rupture with the modern political tradition founded on the delegation of power to representatives of the people and classes.

Representative democracy has progressively transformed into a mechanism of the State; political parties and trade unions have become, through a process spanning the entire twentieth century, an integral part of State institutions. The crisis affecting the West since 2007 has subsequently transformed political democracy and social democracy. The former is completely subordinate to the logic of neoliberalism to the extent that Marx's remark, which has too often been ridiculed, that "the State is but a committee for managing the common affairs of the bourgeoisie," has again become relevant. One needs only change "bourgeoisie" to "creditors" and you have the function of political representation in a nutshell. Even a weak political democracy like ours is still too democratic for neoliberal politicians. Social democracy, on the other hand, does no more than represent and defend the social strata of full-time employees, and in particular retirees, without, however, really managing to succeed.

The protests that have exploded more or less everywhere on the planet reveal that within representative democracy "there are no possible alternatives." In this regard, Guattari opens more than one avenue for reflection, uniting a critique of representative politics and a critique of the representational functions of language. Signifying semiotics (language, writing) claim to "represent" all other supposedly pre-signifying modes of expression (corporeal, gestural, iconic) as well as asignifying ones (money, scientific equations, etc.). The latter supposedly lack something only language can provide in the same way that citizens and the social lack something that only political representation can provide.

In reality, linguistic "representation," just like political representation, constitutes a seizure of power, overcoding, hierarchizing, and subordinating other semiotics and other modes of expression. The two forms of "representation" in the systems of signs and political institutions go hand in hand and any kind of political break with them demands that both one and the other are overcome.

What are the conditions, besides those of analytic philosophy, structuralism, and Lacanianism, in which speech and signs operate in the "constitution of the self" in a way that bypasses both political and linguistic representation?

Examining the relationship between the *discursive* and the *existential*, Guattari redefines processes of subjectivation both on the macro- and micro-political levels. Paradoxically, by making the "existential," which is neither linguistic nor semiotic, an essential condition of enunciation, he carries out a major shift which neutralizes the power of representation.

While Bakhtin disillusions us with regard to the performative thanks to a conception of the enunciation that eludes every kind of structural or combinatory formalization of language, Guattari radicalizes the break with linguistics and pragmatics by examining what Bakhtin failed to examine in sufficient depth, namely, the relationship between the linguistic and the extralinguistic. The latter cannot be reduced to intersubjectivity (Bakhtin) or to social or economic infrastructures. Very late in his work, Guattari called this extralinguistic dimension existential.

According to him, we are living a paradox and a challenge to thought which linguistics is incapable of identifying or responding to:

> We are thrown into discursive systems and, at the same time, we are dealing with focal points of existential affirmation that are not discursive [...]. When a love machine or fear machine is activated, it is not due to the effect of discursive, cognitive, or deductive statements. It happens immediately. And this machine gradually develops different means of expression.[1]

Linguistic competence is not at the basis of the enunciation but rather an apprehension and existential appropriation of self and world, and it is from this existential/affective appropriation that language, discourse, knowledge, narrative, artworks, and so forth, become possible.

Speech thus has a dual function: to signify, communicate, and declare "politically," but also and especially "to produce assemblages of enunciation able to capture, territorialize, and deploy the singularities of a focal point of existential subjectivation and give consistency and durability to them."

On the one hand, the crystallization of subjectivation processes "is not the exclusive privilege of language; all the other semiotic components, all the other procedures of natural and machinic encoding play a part as well."[2] On the other hand, subjective mutation is not primarily discursive; to become discursive, it must reach the "focal point of non-discursivity at the heart of subjectivity [...]. In order to make stories, describe the world and one's life, one must start from this indefinable point, the breaking point of sense, the point of absolute non-narrative, the point of absolute non-discursivity."[3] Along with the signifying and denotative functions Guattari introduces the "existential function," which, although *non-discursive*, acts as the creative force of the enunciation.

Following the linguistic turn and Lacan's structural-linguistic psychoanalysis, Butler reduces subjectivity to the result of signifying operations. Guattari determines instead to map the various components of subjectivation in their fundamental heterogeneity by carrying out "the radical divorce between the production of sense, the production of signification, pragmatic production, and finally the production of subjectivity."[4]

The same semiotic links can work to "produce discourse" and to "produce existence,"[5] "the same statements that signify something in dream are taken in their subjective assemblage, giving them, rather than a meaning, existential significance."[6] They constitute the speaker as a subjective entity.

Unlike discursive pragmatics, existential pragmatics has to do with the production of the self, with the "ontological singularities of the self-appropriation of the self, the singularities of self-consciousness."[7]

Existence is a matter of self-positioning, self-affectation. Guattari's path runs parallel to Foucault's, who, practically at the same time, comes to the same conclusions. There is a difference in kind between the parrhesiastic enunciation that expresses the affirmation of the "self" and the discursivity of pragmatic linguistics, be it that of the pragmatics of the performative. In both cases, we use words, propositions, we make use of language, but the underlying logic is radically heterogeneous.

The constitution of the self is able to break with dominant meanings; it does not primarily bring signifiers, discourse, and meaning into play, but rather a power of self-affectation, a relationship of forces with itself. In Guattari this self-affirmation takes on a particular hue, since the "for self" [*pour soi*] and the "for others" [*pour les autres*], the focal points of enunciation, the vectors of subjectivation, are not exclusively human. Existence follows a "machinic logic," "in any case, something that doesn't in any way function according to the logic of discursive ensembles, but which I've just recently been calling the logic of existentialization."[8]

The words and propositions of language function according to the logic of sense by referring from one sense reference to another or according to a diagrammatic logic that bypasses representation, consciousness, and the "I" of the subject. Going beyond Bakhtin, for whom the word is almost everything in human life, Guattari introduces non-human semiotics and assemblages capable of initiating and organizing existentialization, action: "Speech remains an essential medium, but it's not the only one; everything which short-circuits chains of signification, postures, facial traits, spatial dispositions, rhythms, asignifying semiotic productions (relating, for example, to monetary exchange), machinic sign productions, can be implicated in this type of analytical assemblage. Speech itself—and I could never overemphasize this—only intervenes here inasmuch as it acts as a support for existential refrains."[9]

In the same way that material flows and social, economic, etc., flows, semiotic flows exist within actualized spatiotemporal coordinates, whereas the "relation to the self," "existential territories," and "universes of value" constitute the incorporeal, affective, intensive dimension of the assemblage which is not governed by ordinary space and time coordinates.

The existential eludes physical determination and causality and constitutes a non-energetic, non-informational "machinism." The transformations that take place in existence are incorporeal and, unlike the transformations studied by science, do not involve energetic and informational processes.

2. Disjunction and Conjunction of the Discursive and Existential

The relation to the self represents an incorporeal existential focal point, an autopoietic machine whose consistency, durability, and development depends, secondarily, on the multiplicity of actualized elements that it *traverses* and *reconfigures* (the discursive, the cognitive, but also institutions, the social, the economic sphere, etc.).

The "subjective matter" of "existentialization" uses discursivity in order to "appear to itself, to manifest itself to itself as a body without organs, as a pseudo-unity, but one which is in no way a totalization like that of the logic of ensembles."[10]

By establishing a difference in kind between the discursive (and the conceptual) and the existential, Guattari conceives not only the disjunction but also the conjunction of these two disparate logics: "semiotic logic" and "ontological pragmatics."[11]

Let us quickly enumerate the "dissymmetries" between these two logics. First, the discursive and the existential function based on heterogeneous "referents." The semiotic or discursive dimension "is part of a system of extrinsic references, in other words, it always implies that every element is discursive relative to another element which constitutes its referent," in such a way that its "truth, its essence," is external to its existence. According to existential logic, on the other hand, "the singular element is itself its own reference and generates its own reference, it secretes its world of reference."[12] Existential pragmatics is "self-referential, self-productive of reference."[13] Existence "produces itself within its own movement."[14]

Second, discursive logic is linear; there is one element, then another. It develops according to the temporality indicated by the "arrow of time." Existential affirmation is circular; it continually comes back to itself, it intensifies and gives consistency to existence or it disappears because incapable of crossing certain thresholds. Starting from this circular return, from the agglomeration, from the consolidation of this focal point of existentialization and this subjective emergence, existential affirmation *transversalizes* the actualized dimensions (economic, political, social, linguistic) by *configuring* them differently.

The third dissymmetry: repetition in discursive logic always produces discourse, combinations of discourse, whereas in existential logic repetition ("*ritournelle*") produces changes in subjective states which mold subjectivity. To say that existence is self-productive of reference means that "it is repetition relative to itself that is the reference."[15] The refrain ("empty speech"), unlike Derrida's and Butler's formal repetition of the sign-mark, has an existential function: it gives consistency to the relation to the self. In refrain-repetition, it is not the semantic content that is important but the repetition itself which produces a change in subjective state. Christic or Leninist refrains[16] are not defined in terms of sense but by the change in subjectivity they effect, the consistency, the crossing of the threshold, the agglomeration, and the transversality of subjectivity they make possible and engender. Christic or Leninist refrains initiate "a kind of universe, a framework, a stage, which corresponds to a production of subjectivity at the level of the collective."[17] Existential refrains may have a semantic content and constitute systems of expression, but they also function as a mode constitutive of another kind of universe that brings with it a "surplus value of possibles."

A fourth difference. Discursive ensembles articulate distinctive oppositions (speaker/listener, content/expression, subject/object, etc.) and personological oppositions ("I"/"you"), unfolding within extensive spatiotemporal coordinates of representation. Existential ensembles, on the other hand, follow a logic of intensities and affects established prior to the distinction of identities, persons, and functions. Affects, while non-localizable with regard to both their origin and their destination (fear or joy affect the speaker and the listener and make up transitional subjectivities[18]), can be precisely located based on the threshold of consistency they determine.

Existential pragmatics cannot easily be circumscribed by the logic of discursive ensembles, since content and expression are reversible (there is no background against which expression can be isolated, "anything can be content and anything expression"); the agents are not subjects and objects, but "subjectivities and objectivities," mutant entities—half-object, half-subject—which have neither inside nor outside, but generate interiority and exteriority. "They are becomings—understood as nuclei of differentiation."[19] The distinctive features of existential ensembles are not the subject and object, the "I" and the "you," but the threshold-crossings, the gradients of intensities.

Discursive logic implies exchange, whereas in ontological pragmatics existence is not exchangeable. "Existence is attached to its *topos*, totally; no form that would be a form of existence can ever be prized away. You are either there or you're not [...] and there is no existential negativity. Existence alone is itself every existent. And then, if existence is not, if nothing can be said about it, it cannot be called non-existent."[20]

Ontological or existential pragmatics is processual, irreversible, singular, and event-generating, whereas discursive logic is reversible, structural, ahistorical, and universal. The two logics are thus dissymmetrical functions of subjectivity. It remains to be seen how the conjunction between these two very different series comes about.

3. The Aesthetic Paradigm

The non-discursive does not denote the powerlessness of the ineffable, of the unsayable or irrational; it is the power of the virtual, the incorporeal, intensities, and affects that constitute so many focal points of proto-enunciations. The non-discursive is not formless matter waiting for differentiation, disciplinarization, or signifying or symbolic organization from language and "the Law" (both Lacanian). There is nothing mysterious about the non-discursive as there is in Wittgenstein. On the contrary, it is traversed by very rich semiotic and expressive dynamics, affects that function as existential territories, "emerging selves," focal points of human and non-human mutant subjectivations and proto-enunciation, that make up different self-producing machines.

How, then, must we articulate the relationship between the discursive and the machinic existential, the actual and the virtual, the possible and the real? A "scientific," "cognitive," or "bi-univocal" relationship cannot be established between these two levels because a radical asymmetry exists between the "discursive" and the "existential." The relationship can only be approached by what Guattari calls an "aesthetic paradigm."

The subjectivation process is not the effect of economic, sexual, linguistic, or social infrastructures (which would mean it has a referent external to itself). Instead, self-positioning, self-affectation, and self-referentiality—as openings to processuality, as the creation of possibles, as the impetus to becoming and mutation are originary. But these autopoietic focal points take on consistency only by transversalizing, repositioning, and reconfiguring all the domains considered to be "structural" (the economic, political, social, linguistic, sexual, scientific, etc.).

Subjective self-references "are obviously not sustainable as such, since they have no external referent, come under no extrinsic reference [...]. They cannot be maintained by themselves, they can only be maintained through a reinitiation of discursivity."[21] The enunciation of the relation to the self and the existential territories that support them always depends on a *détournement* of narrative whose primary function is not to produce rational, cognitive, or scientific explanations, but to generate complex refrains ("mythico-conceptual, phantasmatic, religious, novelistic") which give consistency to the emergence of new existential territories.

This does not mean a return to the irrational nor to the age of myth; it is a matter of breaking with the scientific paradigm in which the nineteenth and twentieth centuries including Althusser believed. Guattari turns to the aesthetic experience, not as productive of the work of art, but as a pragmatics of the relationship between the discursive and the existential, the actual and the virtual, the possible and the real.

> The paradox which aesthetic experience constantly returns us to is that these affects, as a mode of existential apprehension, are given all at once, regardless, or besides the fact that indicative traits and descriptive refrains are necessary for catalyzing their existence in fields of representation.[22]

The approach to existential territories is always realized by way of a certain discursive or semiotic localization, with the caveat that the latter is in no way scientific, objectivist, or rationalist. There is no other way to access existence but through self-existentialization. Knowledge of existence requires what Guattari, following Vico, calls a "topical art," an art of cartographies.

The self-relation to the self, self-affectation, and self-positioning draw on the signs, myths, narratives, and conceptualizations that, rather than acting as a translation (which is in any case impossible) of the existential into the discursive, serve as a cartography for localization and access to processes of subjectivation and to existential territories.

> Existence can be localized, mapped, and perhaps it fundamentally involves, for its promotion, localization, and production, something that is thoroughly antagonistic to the discursive process of objectivist procedures.[23]

Before bearing or transmitting messages, before having a discursive function, signifying semiotics act as existential "refrains." This does not mean a depreciation of language, of the concept or conceptual abstraction—far from it. The more *abstract* the cartography, the more diverse the possibilities for articulating the discursive and the non-discursive become; the more *arbitrary* the cartography, the more propitious the ground for their articulation.

According to Guattari, there are two types of cartographies. There are "concrete cartographies directly productive of what I will call existentialization, which generate a subjective territory at the same time as the cartography is deployed [i.e., the existential cartography of a person, group, or even a nation]; and then along with these there are speculative cartographies which do not produce territories, which are second-level cartographies, whose purpose is to think, organize, and articulate the relation between these two radically heterogeneous levels."[24] Hence the fundamental importance of theological, political, and philosophical debates.

The theological arguments at the dawn of Christianity or the debates among Bolsheviks around 1905 did not serve to establish *true* statements but rather cartographies capable of opening up possibilities for articulating the existential and the discursive, for inventing refrains capable of seizing subjectivity, of making it pass thresholds, of initiating a process.

The Marxist or Freudian theoretical discourses which claim scientific bases did not receive their "social validation" inasmuch as they crystallized, gave consistency and transversality to the emerging, mutant "focal points of subjectivation" of capitalism.

Like Marx, Freud did not found a new science (Althusser) but rather instruments for "mythico-conceptual"[25] localization which allowed, in the case of Marx, to create a "stage" (human history as the history of the class struggle) for mythico-conceptual performers (the proletariat as the subject destined to abolish waged labor and social classes) capable of realizing and semiotizing the singularity of subjectivity during the first industrial revolution. But always starting from an indefinable point, an unrepresentable asignifying point, which alone was supposed to enable the creation of subjectivation mechanisms, not in order to "tell a story," but so that history could be made. Within this framework, stories, concepts, and "myths" do not have a communicational, intersubjective, or cognitive function, they have an "aesthetic/existential" one.

The relationship is paradoxical ("it is not related, but it is not without relation"), since it is only through a certain use of discursive categories that one has access to existential effects and mutations.

> Here we find the source of Tertullian's paradox: it's because it is impossible for the son to be dead, buried, and resuscitated, that these facts must be held to be certain. It's because in many respects Freudian theory is mythical that it can trigger refrains of mutant subjectivation.[26]

Speculative cartographies function not only as passive localizers, but also as active initiators of subjectivation processes: "It is only because I think of God that I have the courage to march off to war and get myself killed [...]. And these can be completely abstract operators (God is relatively concrete!). [...] [They] open a pragmatic path to action, to existentialization, to an existential universe. That is, these are not elementary empiricist entities."[27]

It is at this point that Guattari returns to the Christic, Leninist, and Debussyst refrains as "thingamajigs" [*trucs*] ("semiotic acts" in the same way we say "speech acts"), which initiate subjectivation processes, bring us into other universes of reference, and encourage action. The discursive as such is not sufficient to grasp subjectivity, to engage it, or to spur it into action. In order for it to do so, *discourses, signs, and concepts must function as access points to new worlds, as the "diagrammatic initiators" of action.*

The sphere of action plays a central role in schizoanalysis. The act can help us understand the relationship between the discursive and the existential because its expression, which precedes representation, and, being "itself its own expression," functions as a "kind of cogito." A kind of cogito insofar as the act secretes its own reference, insofar as it is impossible to isolate a form from the act, insofar as it constitutes an emergent focal point from which processuality is triggered, one beyond which there is no going back.

For schizoanalysis, the act does not occur *ex nihilo*. It is not a dialectical passage between "everything and nothing, following binary logic," but a passage between heterogeneous dimensions. There is no act in itself, but instead "degrees of consistency in the existence of the act, existential thresholds relative to the act."

The conditions of the act are the actualized ensembles and virtual ensembles of the assemblage from which the act derives. Actualized ensembles constitute "the dimension of that which connects the act to behavioral stratifications, structures, systems, and segmentarities of every kind." With actualized ensembles, "the act always appears as the prolongation of something already present [*d'un déjà là*], of a certain representation of something already present, and within a teleological perspective of a certain project, itself represented as well." And yet, in the course of analysis, even if "everything is interpreted, everything is clear... nothing changes, nothing follows from this representation."[28]

Another dimension is needed in order for the act to occur, a dimension of the act that escapes representation, a "diagrammatic dimension," a machinic dimension. To act never means becoming conscious, to be conscious of, or to possess the representation[29] of something.[30] With existence and the act, "we no longer contemplate" as we do in representational or significational logic, "we are in a pragmatic relation; we articulate or aggregate it. It is the fact of acting, the fact that signaletic systems involve material processes, social, economic, and subjective mutations."[31]

The choice and the act refer neither to the subject's freedom nor to the dialectics of necessity and chance, since both are machinisms. For Guattari, the "existential" is machinic and the machinic is in no way synonymous with mechanical determinism. On the contrary, the machinism of the act means "producing modes of organization, quantification, which open up a multivalent future to the process— a range of choices—the possibility of heterogeneous connections, beyond already encoded, already possible, anticipated connections."[32]

It is machinism and not man that secretes options, matters of choice, and possibles. It is therefore always necessary to bear in mind that the act is neither anthropomorphic nor representative, which does not, however, mean that one is freed of all responsibility. Responsibility has other objects.

When the orchid 'chooses' the wasp in order to, in a way, co-opt it into its reproduction process, the wasp becomes a part of the orchid's world. But this does not at all happen in a mode of representation. It goes without saying that there is no memory or representational record in the mind of the orchid. There is no orchid brain! And yet, at the level of the orchid, a diagrammatic expression makes it such that something of the wasp belongs to the orchid. But what is that something? It cannot be located within spatio-temporal coordinates; it doesn't involve a quantity of movement. It is an incorporeal. The wasp-orchid marriage develops, then an incorporeal which is a certain machinic choice [...]. There was 'n' possibility before this machinic choice, but from the moment the choice was made, progressive development follows from there.[33]

The choice and the act both depend on machinism and on a certain kind of consistency of assemblages. Guattari often cites Lenin's example in order to account for the relationship between existential (revolutionary) affirmation and the consistency of collective, social, and political assemblages. The act is *causa sui et non ex nihilo* because in a singular situation there are thresholds, "actance crystals" (a certain political situation, a certain stage in the organization of the party, a certain phase of subjectivation of the working class, etc.), which, while they are not the cause of the act, determine the consistency of "optional matter" [*matière à option*]. In schizoanalysis there is no determinism because the act occurs only when there is a surplus value of possibilities, when there is a "possibility of playing a completely new tune, when there are relative fields of potential creativity established."[34] Potentialities and possibles that must be created.

4. The Current Crisis

The essence of the "current crisis" lies in the incapacity of capitalist forces to articulate[35] the discursive and existential dimensions, in the impossibility of assembling ensembles of actualized economic, social, and technological flows and the virtual and incorporeal dimension of subjectivity production, existential territories, and universes of value. If the production of subjectivity is not part of a social field, a "product," a politics, a language, and so forth, we are faced, as is the case today, with a pathology of subjectivity (racist, xenophobic, individualist, confined to one's own interests, etc.). The watchwords concerning employment, full-employment, wages, labor, the defense of the welfare state, and so on, which ought to be connected to subjectivity, do not lead to subjectivation processes, for they do not open onto new worlds, do not constitute optional matter for modern-day subjectivity.

The political problem lies in the articulation, the concatenation, of "processes converging to make technical, social, and economic machines and subjectivation processes work. If there is not this quadruple convergence, it doesn't work."[36] Subjectivation must occur within a system of flows that allow one to be "within material effects," those of economic, social, linguistic, production, "which at the same time have to give you the production of subjectivity." Neoliberal capitalism (and what remains of the workers' movement) has been unable to articulate the relationship between economic, social, and technological flows and the changes and becomings of subjectivity emergent in modern-day capitalism. Nor has it succeeded in articulating discursive meaning (economic, social, institutional) and existential meaning, because under current conditions, as much for the subjective figure of the entrepreneur as for the wage-earner, "there's no mythical consistency, and nothing makes you want to leave on the Crusades or start another October Revolution!"[37]

The articulation between heterogeneous levels does not happen spontaneously, it must be constructed, invented, worked on. The articulation is *singular* but not *necessary*; nor is it a work of *chance*.

We are always living a paradoxical situation. The mutations of subjectivity are sudden, occurring at "infinite speeds," says Guattari. What happens is given "straightaway, then, secondly, discursively; one says to oneself: Isn't it boring here? Isn't it nerve-racking? Isn't the ambiance great? This first given constitutes a disposition or a situation which is that I'm here, in the room, and the enunciation takes on consistency."[38]

What arises in these condensations, in these agglomerations, in these kinds of "enunciative clumps," is not on the order of knowledge. Existential crystallization makes it such that there is "a certain disposition between the way in which one arranges signs, sees plastic forms, feels time: it's organized like that prior to any other construction." These points of crystallization, condensation, and agglomeration are sufficient in themselves. They subsequently require "aesthetic" and "ethico-political" completion. "Aesthetic because there is an obviousness to the enunciation when there is a relationship of love or hate. That is how Spinoza puts it: we're never wrong, as I always say, even a dog immediately knows what's going on; he doesn't speak but clearly sees that we are about to hit or pet him." At the same time, "there is an ethico-political dimension because this matter is not only aesthetic, but is also wrapped up in transversal relationships with other completely heterogeneous levels,"[39] whether political, social, economic, artistic, and so on.

Work on these emergences is carried out according to a methodology of the "aesthetic paradigm," of the topical art of cartographies. Just as the artist must not wait for whatever kind of inspiration is going to come, political action must construct and invent tools and procedures of experimentation, research, and intervention aimed first of all at the production of subjectivity rather than at the economic, the social, or the linguistic.

The relationship between the discursive and the non-discursive, between the conceptual and the existential, instead of leading to silence ("What can't be said, mustn't be said"), must be worked on, conceptualized, semiotized, staged, told, and so forth, beginning with the unrepresentable. Rather than siding with Badiou's retrospective fidelity (fidelity to the event once the event has taken place), one must intervene in the emergence of focal points of proto-enunciation and proto-subjectivation.

Emerging crystallizations, condensations, and agglomerations reach their aesthetic and ethical completion at both the micro-political level ("Work on a point of subjectivation that is not discursive, a point of subjectivation that is melancholic, chaotic, or psychotic") and at the macro-political level (a point of revolutionary, reactionary, fascist, group, etc., subjectivation).

As existential functions, asignifying crystallizations are "wrapped up in meanings and denotations like in the dough of a Turkish delight." To work on means liberating them from the layers imprisoning them and putting them "in a position to proliferate [...], that is, to establish connections, associative networks of production, passages to other registers."[40]

"Languages" and signifying semiotics make up neither the conditions of production (cognitive capitalism) nor the conditions of politics (verification of equality à la Rancière). Like those of a potential politics, the conditions of production arise instead from the production of subjectivity and its articulation with the institutional, the economic, the social, the linguistic, and so on.

The great merit of Guattari's work lies in its problematizing the relationship between the discursive and the non-discursive, exploring the modalities of articulation of the existential with economic, social, and political flows. It highlights the weaknesses of contemporary, supposedly critical or revolutionary, theories. On the one hand, we have, with Badiou or Rancière, subjectivation that has no need to be articulated with social, economic, or cultural flows since it stands all by itself. Politics is considered independent, autonomous, with respect to what Rancière and Badiou call economics, simply because the view they have of economics and of capitalism in general is a caricature of the one proffered by economists themselves. Capitalism's force does not lie in the objectivism of "the laws of the market" but in the capacity to articulate economics (and communication, consumption, the welfare state, etc.) with the production of subjectivity in various ways. As we have argued extensively, what Badiou and Rancière call economics implies and exploits subjectivity through social subjections and machinic enslavements.

To say, with Badiou and Rancière, that political subjectivation cannot derive from Capital is obviously completely different from examining their paradoxical interdependence. In the first case, you have the illusion of a "pure" politics, since subjectivation, left adrift, never attains the necessary consistency to exist. In the second, you open up sites for experimentation and construction since subjectivation must, if it is to exist, take on consistency, *retraverse* and *reconfigure* the social, the political, the economic, and so on.[41]

Cognitive capitalist theories also fail to articulate the production of subjectivity and the heterogeneity of the discursive, the economic, the social, and so on, because everything is steered back to the actualized flows of "knowledge," to the linguistic, cognitive, and representational dimension, to the preverbal, pre-cognitive, and non-reflexive dimension. Knowledge is supposed to fulfill the functions—as multiple as they are implausible—of the creation of possibilities, aesthetic creation, and the production of subjectivity that have to do instead with the existential machinic.

The inventor of the new definition of capitalism shows unbridled faith in knowledge: "The cognitive experience is always a—small or large—process of world-making," of creating possibles, says Enzo Rullani. The "cognitive experience" also develops "world views, aesthetic codes" which, as they spread, "change people's values." "Knowledge" is not only at the basis of economic and aesthetic values, but also those of subjectivity production. Through cognitive experience, "we open to the possibility that it can change our perception of the world and ourselves, our actual identity."[42] He, like his disciples, blithely confuses the production of subjectivity with the production of knowledge.

Knowledge, information, and languages, as such, have no ability to create possibilities, to multiply optional matter. Knowledge like information and semiotic flows always function in a single direction: "They always discursivize." On the one hand, this means that they always remain on the same plane, never reaching the existential territories where the mutation of subjectivity takes place.

On the other hand, so-called cognitive capitalism has made concrete the concept of "anti-production," because it has saturated the public sphere with ignorance, commonplaces, and subjective impoverishment without precedent.

Anti-production is no longer limited, as in disciplinary societies, to the exclusive prerogatives of the State (army, police, etc.). In modern-day capitalism, anti-production is everywhere pervasive and no more so than in "cognitive production." It "introduces a lack where there is always too much," that is, it carries out a veritable destruction of the knowledge, cultures, and understanding that are not beholden to capitalist logic. The cognitive divestments that the "knowledge society" has enacted across the board in education, research, culture, art, and elsewhere, represent operations of power that require privatization, competition, hierarchization, profitability, and company spirit. They are part of an "anti-production" program, that is, a program for the homogenization and standardization of knowledge, understanding, and cultures.

Anti-production "doubles the capital and the flow of knowledge with a capital and an equivalent flux of *stupidity* [...]. Not only lack amid overabundance, but stupidity in the midst of knowledge and science."[43] Cognitive capitalism endows subjectivity not with knowledge but with stupidity, even when it is qualified (BA, MBA, PhD, etc.), even when it takes pride in the artistic, the cultural, and so on.[44]

"Cognitive" divestments ensure both economic impoverishment (precarity, underemployment, miserable wages for the new "cognitive" proletariat) and conformism with the business culture in knowledge, art, politics, and communication.

It is less a matter of cognitive or cultural capitalism, the knowledge society, and so on, than of the power and knowledge relations that seek to mold the subjectivity of the population on the whole such that it is capable of adapting and submitting to the techniques, modes of labor organization, consumption, communication, and urban and life environments governed by profitability and "stupidity."

The creation and production of the new are not made possible through knowledge, information, or communication, but through an existential mutation, a transformation, which involves the non-discursive focal points of subjectivity, of these existential territories, of these modes of subjectivation. That cognitive capitalist theory is unable to explain its own objects of study (innovation, the creation of something new, new knowledge) is synthetically demonstrated by the tautology advanced by one of its theorists, who defines this economy as "knowledge production through knowledge."

"Out of the mere processing of linguistic, cognitive, economic, etc., flows new subjectivity cannot emerge," nor new knowledge, nor any kind of innovation.

Even scientific and knowledge production is shifted from a scientistic or "cognitivist" paradigm to an aesthetic paradigm, in other words, science and knowledge are beholden to an act of subjectivation in Bakhtin's sense in a text Guattari cites: "'from within the world of cognition, no conflict is possible, for in that world one cannot meet with anything axiologically different in kind. Not science, but a scientist can enter into conflict, and do so, moreover, not *ex cathedra*, but as an aesthetic *subiectum* for whom cognition is *the performed act of cognition*."[45]

Only a rupture with the mode of subjectivation can secrete an existential crystallization productive of new references, and new self-positionings, which, in their turn, open the possibility for constructing new languages, new knowledge, new aesthetic practices, and new forms of life. To break with the dominant significations and the established forms of life, we must pass through points of nonsense, through the asignifying and non-discursive which in politics manifest themselves in the strike, revolt, or riot. The latter suspend time for a brief moment and create other possibilities from which, if they take on consistency, other subjectivations and existential crystallizations might proliferate.

In this alternative logic I'm superimposing on the discursive, the same elements of semiotic discursivity are taken in the opposite sense and, at that point, it's insofar as they produce—not discursivities compared among themselves—but insofar as they produce existence, sensible territories and universes. According to this logic, the constellations that emerge conserve the same elements, but in one case you have semiotic productions and in the other subjective productions.[46]

This cartography of the production of subjectivity, which breaks radically with analytic philosophy, with Lacanianism, linguistics, and a certain type of Marxism, profoundly changes the perspective from which to conceive a politics commensurate with the current crisis.

7

Enunciation and Politics

A Parallel Reading of Democracy: Foucault and Rancière

> Revolutionary discourse plays the role of parrhesiastic discourse
> when it takes the form of a critique of existing society.
> —Michel Foucault, *The Courage of the Truth*

The refusal to delegate to political parties and unions representation of that which divides society (property, wealth, power, and so on) as well as to the State representation of that which is common (citizenship, community) originates in a new conception of political action that came out of the "revolution" of May '68. The struggle for "an other life" and "an other world," the fight for political transformation and the transformation of the self, must go beyond both political representation and linguistic representation in favor of new forms of organization particularly attentive not only to the utterances produced but also and in particular to their modes of production.

Foucault's last lectures resonate with Guattari's aesthetic paradigm, with his understanding of politics as invention and experimentation, as well as with one of his fundamental conditions for this, the overcoming of the semiotics of subjective rupture. As a force for self-positioning and self-affirmation, the "existential function," while non-linguistic, constitutes an essential element in every—and especially political—enunciation. At the core of this new and original point of view bearing on non-representative "democracy," one finds the relationship between the existential and enunciation, between self-affirmation and political speech.

1. Two Equalities

In an interview given to a center-left revue, Jacques Rancière argues that Foucault was never interested in political subjectivation "not at the theoretical level in any case. He was concerned with power."[1] This is a somewhat hasty and offhand judgment since political subjectivation represents the fulfillment of Foucault's work. Indeed, we are faced with two radically different conceptions of political subjectivation. Contrary to Rancière, for whom ethics neutralizes politics, Foucauldian political subjectivation is indissociable from ethos-poiesis (the formation of ethos, the relation to the self). The necessity to conjoin the transformation of institutions, laws, and the transformation of the self, others, and existence represents, for Foucault, the problem of politics itself in its post-'68 configuration. The two different concepts of subjectivation reveal two rather heterogeneous political projects, as can easily be seen when comparing the authors' readings of Greek democracy.

The two approaches show remarkable differences not only in their conception of politics but also of language and enunciation. For Rancière, Greek democracy has demonstrated once and for all that the exclusive principle of politics is equality and that linguistic equality (the minimal equality necessary for comprehension among speakers) contains the principle of verification for political equality. Speech, whether it issues a command or poses a problem, presupposes agreement in language. Political action must augment and effectuate this power of equality, however little there may be, contained in language.

In Foucault's reading of this same democracy, equality constitutes a necessary but not sufficient condition of politics. Enunciation (truth-telling [*le dire vrai*]—*parrhēsia*) creates paradoxical relationships since truth-telling introduces differences of enunciation into the equality of language. This necessarily implies an "ethical differentiation." Political action is carried out within the context of "paradoxical relationships" between the equality of language and differences of enunciation, and between equality and the production of new forms of subjectivation and singularity.

2. "Truth-Telling" (*Parrhēsia*)

Foucault examines democracy by way of truth-telling (*parrhēsia*), in other words, the "seizure of speech" of someone who rises in the assembly and takes the risk of stating the truth concerning the affairs of the city. In analyzing democracy, Foucault returns to a classic theme of one of his masters, Nietzsche, that of the value of truth, of the will to truth or, still more, the question: "who" wants the truth?

The relationship between truth and subject is here no longer posed in the terms Foucault uses in his work on power. He asks: Through which practices and which types of discourse does power attempt to speak the truth of the mad, the delinquent, the incarcerated subject? How has power constituted the "speaking subject, the working subject, the living subject" as an object of knowledge? Starting in the late 1970s, his perspective shifted, articulated in the following terms: What truth discourse is the subject "susceptible and capable of saying about himself?"

The line of questioning that runs through his reading of Greek democracy is oriented by a typically Nietzschean question which in fact has to do with present circumstances: What does "truth-telling" mean after the death of God? Unlike Dostoyevsky, the problem is not how to behave in life if "everything is permitted," but rather: "if nothing is true," how should one live? If the concern for truth consists in its permanent problematization, what "life," what powers, what knowledge, and what discursive practices can respond to such a concern?

Capitalism's answer to the question is the constitution of a "market of life" in which people purchase the existence that suits them. It is no longer philosophical schools, as in ancient Greece, nor Christianity, nor the revolutionary project of the nineteenth and twentieth centuries, that furnish modes of existence, models of subjectivation, but rather corporations, the media, the culture industry, the institutions of the welfare state, unemployment insurance, and so on.

In modern-day capitalism, governing inequalities is inextricably linked to the production and governing of modes of subjectivation, to forms of life. Today's "police" operate through both the division and distribution of roles and the allocation of functions and through the injunction to conform to certain modes of life. All income, every benefit, and every wage are part of an "ethos" that prescribes and engages certain conduct, that is, a way of doing and saying. Neoliberalism represents at once the reestablishment of a hierarchy founded on money, merit, and inheritance, and a genuine "life fair" in which businesses and the State, by replacing the schoolmaster or the confessor, prescribe how to behave (how to eat, live, dress, love, speak, etc.).

Modern-day capitalism, its private enterprises and institutions, prescribe a care for and work on the self that are simultaneously physical and mental, a "well-being" and an aesthetic of existence, which mark out the new frontiers of the capitalist subjection and economic valorization indicative of an unprecedented impoverishment of subjectivity.

Foucault's last lectures provide an invaluable tool for problematizing these questions. His analysis first of all demands that one not isolate the political act as such, as Rancière does, for, according to Foucault, in doing so one runs the risk of missing the specificity of capitalist power. The latter articulates the political and the ethical, the unequal division of society, the production of models of existence and of discursive practices. Foucault asks us to bring together the analysis of forms of subjectivation and the analysis of discursive practices and "techniques and procedures for directing human behavior."[2] In short, subject, power, and knowledge must be thought both in their irreducibility and in their necessary relation. In moving from the mode of political subjectivation from which it derives to the sphere of personal ethics and the constitution of the ethical subject, *parrhēsia* offers the possibility of thinking the complex relations between these "three distinct elements none of which can be reduced to or absorbed by the others, but whose relations are constitutive of each other."[3]

3. *Parrhēsia, Politeia, Isēgoria, Dunasteia*

In his last two lectures, Foucault demonstrates that *parrhēsia* (the truth-telling of someone who rises in the assembly), *politeia* (the constitution that guarantees the equality of all citizens), and *isēgoria* (the statutory right of anyone to speak, regardless of social status, privilege of birth, wealth, or knowledge) establish paradoxical relationships between them. In order for *parrhēsia* to exist, in order for truth-telling to be effected, both *politeia* (the constitution guaranteeing equality) and *isēgoria* (all may speak publicly and have their say in the affairs of the city) are necessary. But neither *politeia* nor *isēgoria* say who will actually speak, who will in reality express a claim to truth. Anyone has the right to speak, but it is not the equal distribution of the right to speak that makes one speak in fact.

The effective exercise of *parrhēsia* depends neither on citizenship nor on legal or social status. *Politeia* and *isēgoria* and the equality these two declare represent only the necessary but not sufficient conditions for speaking publicly. What effectively makes one speak is *dunasteia*: the power, the force, the exercise, and the real effectuation of the power to speak that mobilizes the speaker's singular relations with himself and with those whom he addresses. The *dunasteia* expressed in enunciation is a force of ethical differentiation because it means taking a position in relation to the self, to others, and to the world.

By taking sides and dividing equals, by bringing polemic and dispute into the community, *parrhēsia* is a risky and indeterminate act. It introduces conflict, agonism, and contest into public space, which may end in hostility, hate, and war.

Truth-telling, the claim to truth voiced in an assembly (and we might also think of those assemblies in contemporary social and political movements, since Greek democracy, unlike modern democracy, was not representative), presupposes a force, a power, an action upon the self (to have the courage to risk telling the truth), and an action upon others in order to persuade them, guide them, and steer their conduct. It is in this sense that Foucault speaks of an ethical differentiation, a process of singularization initiated and opened by the parrhesiastic enunciation. *Parrhēsia* implies that political subjects constitute themselves as ethical subjects, capable of taking risks, posing a challenge, dividing equals according to their positions, in other words, capable of governing themselves and of governing others within a situation of conflict. In the act of political enunciation, in assuming public speech, a power of self-positioning manifests itself, a power of self-affectation, subjectivity affecting itself, as Deleuze very rightly puts it with regard to Foucauldian subjectivation.

Parrhēsia restructures and redefines the possible field of action for the self and for others. It modifies the situation, it opens a new dynamics, for it indeed introduces something new. "Even if it implies a status, I think *parrhēsia* is connected much less to status than to a dynamic and a combat, a conflict. So, a dynamic and agonistic structure of *parrhēsia*" that surpasses the egalitarian framework of right, law, and constitution.[4]

The new relationships which truth-telling manifests are not contained nor anticipated by the constitution, the law, or equality. And yet it is through them and only through them that political action is possible, that it occurs in reality.

Truth-telling thus depends on two heterogeneous regimes, one of right (of *politeia* and *isēgoria*) and one of *dunasteia* (power or force), and it is for this reason that the relationship between true enunciation (discourse) and democracy is "difficult and problematic." By introducing de facto difference within equality, by expressing the power of self-affectation and self-affirmation, *parrhēsia* institutes a twofold paradox. First, "there can only be true discourse through democracy, but true discourse introduces something completely different from and irreducible to the egalitarian structure of democracy," that is, ethical differentiation. Second, "the death of true discourse, the possibility of its death or of its reduction to silence,"[5] is inscribed in equality, for competition, conflict, agonism, and hostility threaten democracy and equality. Such has effectively taken place in Western democracies where there is no longer any space left for *parrhēsia*. Democratic consensus neutralizes *parrhēsia*, cancels the risk of truth-telling and of the subjectivation and action that follow from it.

4. Enunciation and Pragmatics

The difference between Rancière's and Foucault's positions emerges still more clearly when one further examines the relationship of language and enunciation with politics and political subjectivation.

For Rancière, when those who have no part in the community ("*les sans-parts*," the demos or proletariat) speak, this does not imply an awakening consciousness, the expression of a specificity of the person who speaks (his interests or his membership in a social group), but rather the equality of the logos. The inequality of domination presupposes the equality of speakers, since in order for the master's orders to be carried out by subordinates, master and subordinate must understand each other in a common language. The act of speaking, even in the case of highly asymmetrical relations of power (Menenius Agrippa's speech on the Aventine which aims to legitimate the hierarchical differences of the society), presupposes understanding within language, presupposes "the notion that the standard of equality is the law [...] of the communitarian body."[6]

For political action to be possible, it is first necessary to posit an equality that functions as the measure and ground of the argumentation and demonstration of the dispute between the rule (of equality) and the specific case (the inequality of the police).[7]

Once equality has been declared somewhere, its force must be realized. Once inscribed somewhere, it must be expanded and reinforced.

Egalitarian politics founds its legitimacy and arguments in the logic and structure of language. Politics consists in creating a "stage around any specific conflict on which the equality and inequality as speaking beings of the partners in the conflict can be played out."[8]

For Rancière, there is indeed a logic of language, but this logic is upset by the duality of the logos—"speech and the counting of speech." Speech is at once the site of a community (speech that states problems) and a division (speech that gives orders). Against this duality, political enunciation must argue and demonstrate "that there is one single common language" and establish that the ancient demos, just like modern proletarians, is composed of beings who, through the very fact of speaking and arguing, are capable of reason and speech and, by dint of this, equal to those who command them.

> The quarrel has nothing to do with more or less transparent or opaque linguistic contents; it has to do with consideration of speaking beings as such.[9]

Whereas Rancière plays with universals and discursive rationality ("The first requirement of universality is that speaking beings universally belong to the linguistic community"),[10] while at the same time distancing himself from them, Foucault describes subjectivation as an immanent process of rupture and constitution of the subject.

For Foucault, *parrhēsia*, to borrow a phrase from Guattari, "exits language," but it also exits pragmatics such as analytic philosophy defines it. There is no rationality or discursive logic because enunciation is not indexed to the rules of language and pragmatics, but rather to the risk of staking a position, to "existential" and political self-affirmation. There is no logic of language; there is an aesthetics of enunciation in that enunciation does not verify what is already present (equality) but opens to something new arising for the first time through the very act of speaking.

Parrhēsia is a form of enunciation very different from that advanced by the discursive pragmatics of performatives. Performatives are expressions, linguistic "rituals," which presuppose a more or less institutionalized status of the speaker and in which the effect that the enunciation must produce is already institutionally given ("Court is in session" declared by someone authorized to do so is but an "institutional" rehearsal whose effects are known in advance). Inversely, *parrhēsia* does not presuppose any status; it is the enunciation of "anyone at all." Unlike performative utterances, it "opens up an unspecified risk," "a possibility, a field of dangers, or at any rate, an undefined eventuality."[11]

The irruption of *parrhēsia* creates a fracture, marks an intrusion into a given situation, and "makes a certain number of effects possible" that cannot be known ahead of time. The effects of enunciation are not only always singular but affect and engage the enunciating subject first of all.

The reconfiguration of the sensible firstly concerns the person who speaks. Within the parrhesiastic utterance, the speaking subject undertakes a double pact with himself: he binds himself to the utterance and to the content of the utterance, to what he has said and to the fact that he has said it. The enunciation has a retroactive effect on the subject's mode of being: "in producing the event of the utterance, the subject modifies, or affirms, or anyway determines and clarifies his mode of being insofar as he speaks."[12]

Parrhēsia manifests the courage and the positioning of the person who tells the truth, who says what he thinks, yet it also manifests the "interlocutor's courage in agreeing to accept as true the hurtful truth he hears."[13] The person who speaks the truth, who says what he thinks, "signs, as it were, the truth he states, he binds himself to this truth, and he is consequently bound to it and by it."[14] But he also takes a risk "which concerns his very relation with those he addresses." Whereas the professor possesses a "knowledge of *technē*" and risks nothing by speaking, the parrhesiast not only risks provoking conflict, "but also hostility, hate, and war." He runs the risk of dividing equals.

Between the person who speaks and what he says, between the speaker and the person who accepts to receive his speech, an affective and subjective link is established, a "belief" which, as William James reminds us, is a "willingness to act."[15] The relation to the self, the relation to others, and the belief that binds them can be limited neither by equality nor by right.

5. The Crisis of *Parrhēsia*

Rancière views the crisis of Greek democracy as a simple pretext for aristocrats' desire to reestablish their privileges of birth, rank, and wealth, whereas Foucault, without neglecting this aspect, views the crisis of Greek democracy as centered around the relation between politics and ethics, equality and differentiation.

The enemies of democracy put their finger on a problem which the supporters of equality as the sole principle of politics (Rancière, Badiou) fail to see and which constitutes one of the pitfalls into which nineteenth- and twentieth-century communism fell for lack of practicable responses.

As the enemies of democracy argue, if everyone can have their say about the affairs of the community, there would be as many constitutions and government as individuals. If everyone can speak, then the insane, drunkards, and halfwits are authorized to express their opinions on public affairs in the same way as those best suited to do so—the experts, as many would have it today. In democracy, competition, agonism, and conflict between equals who claim to speak the truth degenerate into the seduction of orators who flatter the people in the assemblies. If there is uncontrolled distribution of the right to speak, "anyone can say anything or everything." Given that, how can the good and bad orator be distinguished? How can ethical differentiation be undertaken? The truth, the enemies of democracy claim, cannot be told within a political field defined by "a lack of difference between speaking subjects."

> [D]emocracy cannot make room for the ethical differentiation of speaking, deliberating, and decision-making subjects.[16]

These arguments immediately recall the neoliberal critiques leveled at the "socialist" egalitarianism motivating demands for equal wage increases and equal social rights for all: equality hinders freedom, equality prevents "ethical differentiation," it drowns subjectivity in the indifference of subjects of rights.

Like Guattari, Foucault warns us that one cannot oppose neoliberal "freedom," a freedom which, in reality, expresses the political will to reestablish hierarchies, inequalities, and privileges through "egalitarian politics." That would mean making short shrift of the critiques that political movements have leveled at socialist egalitarianism, well before liberal critics did so.

Foucault does more than denounce the enemies of democracy. Drawing on the Cynics, he upends the aristocratic critiques on their home turf: that of ethical differentiation, that of the constitution of the subject and his becoming.

Out of the crisis of *parrhēsia* emerges a "truth-telling" that is no longer exposed to the risks of politics. Truth-telling moves from its political origin toward the sphere of personal ethics and the constitution of the moral subject. But it does so according to an alternative: that of a "metaphysics of the soul" and an "aesthetics of life"; that of knowledge of the soul, of its purification, which allows access to an other world, and that of practices and techniques in order to test, to experiment, the self, life, and the world in the here and now. The constitution of the self, not as "soul," but as "bios," as a way of life. The alternative is already contained in Plato's text, but it was the Cynics who made it explicit and turned it against the enemies of democracy through its politicization. The opposition between the Cynics and Platonism can be summarized thus: the former articulate "an other life/an other world," thereby producing an other subjectivity and other institutions in this world, whereas for the latter there is "the other world" and "the other life," whose articulation would prove so profitable to Christianity.

The Cynics revoke the traditional theme of "true life" in which truth-telling had taken refuge. "True life" in the Greek tradition "is one which shuns disturbance, change, corruption, and the fall, and which remains without change in the identity of its being."[17]

The Cynics counter "true life" by claiming and practicing "an other life" "whose otherness must lead to the change of the world. An *other* life for an *other* world."[18] They reverse the theme of the "sovereign life (tranquil and beneficial: tranquil for oneself […] and beneficial for others) by dramatizing it in the form of what could be called the militant life, the life of battle and struggle against and for self, against and for others," "battle in this world against the world."[19]

The Cynics go beyond the "crisis" of *parrhēsia*, the powerlessness of democracy and equality, to produce ethical differentiation, by binding politics and ethics (and truth) indissolubly together. They politically dramatize and reconfigure the question of the relation to the self by extricating it from the good life, the sovereign life of ancient thought.

6. Two Models of Political Action

These two readings of Greek democracy are informed by two very different models of "revolutionary" action.

For Rancière, politics constitutes the reparation of a wrong done to equality, a reparation realized through demonstration, argument, and interlocution. In political action, those with no part in the community must demonstrate that they are speaking and are not merely emitting noise. They must also demonstrate that they do not speak an unknown or minor language but express themselves in and master the language of their masters. Finally, they must demonstrate through their arguments and interlocution that they are at once beings of reason and speech.

This model of revolutionary action, founded on demonstration, argument, and interlocution, aims at inclusion, "recognition," which, however litigious, very much resembles dialectical recognition. Politics brings about a division through which "they" and "we" oppose and take account of one another, in which two worlds split while at the same time recognizing that they are part of the same community. "The uncounted could make themselves count by showing up the process of division and breaking in on others' equality and appropriating it for themselves."[20]

If we want to find something resembling Rancière's model, we ought not to look at political democracy but rather at the social democracy that came out of the New Deal and the postwar years. The social democracy which one still finds in the co-determination doctrine of French social security represents, in its reformist incarnation, the "dialectical model" of the class struggle in which the recognition and dispute between "us" and "them" constitute the engine of capitalist development and indeed of democracy itself.

What Jacques Rancière defends in the social democracy of the welfare state is a public sphere of interlocution in which workers (reformist trade unions) are included as political subjects and work is no longer a private but rather a public affair.

> One feigns to hold as abusive gifts from a paternal and tentacular State the institutions of solidarity and security born in worker and democratic struggles and managed or co-managed by the representatives of contributors. Yet in struggling against this mythical State, it is precisely non-State institutions of solidarity that are attacked, institutions that were also sites where different capacities were formed and exercised, capacities for taking care of the common and the common future that were different to those of the government elites.[21]

The whole trouble with Rancière's position (and more generally with the left's) lies in the difficulty he has in critiquing and seeing beyond this model, a model which surely expanded democracy in the twentieth century but which today represents a genuine obstacle to the emergence of new objects and new subjects of politics. The model is constitutionally incapable of including political subjects other than the State, unions, and business associations.

Foucault's analysis of Greek democracy provides a completely different model. Why, in order to problematize political subjectivation, does he look to a philosophical school such as the Cynics', a "marginal" school, a "minority" school, a "popular" philosophical school without much doctrinal structure?

What Foucault suggests is the following: We have moved beyond the dialectical and totalizing politics of the "demos." "Whoever has no part—the poor of ancient times, the third estate, the modern proletariat—cannot in fact have any other part other than all or nothing."[22]

It is difficult to imagine the Cynics, just as it is post-'68 political movements (from women's movements to movements of the unemployed), affirming "we are the people," we are both the "part and the whole."

In Foucault's model, the issue is not ensuring that those who have no part are counted, nor their demonstrating that they speak the same language as their masters. The issue is a "transvaluation" of all values, which also and especially concerns those with no part and their mode of subjectivation. In transvaluation, equality combines with difference, political equality with ethical differentiation. We meet up with Nietzsche again in the Cynics, those who entered the history of philosophy as "counterfeiters," as those who debased the "value" of money.

The Cynics' motto, "deface the coinage," refers both to the debasement of money (*nomisma*) and to the debasement of the law (*nomos*). The Cynics do not ask for recognition, they do not seek to be counted or included. They criticize and scrutinize the institutions and ways of life of their peers through self-experimentation and self-examination and the experimentation and examination of others and the world.

The problem of the constitution of the self as an ethico-political subject requires a specific truth game. "[N]o longer that of the apprenticeship, the acquisition of true propositions with which one arms oneself, equips oneself for life and its events, but that of the attention focused on oneself, on what one is able to do [...] [T]hese games of truth do not come under *mathēmata*, they are not things that are taught and learned, but exercises one performs on oneself: self-examination; tests of endurance."[23]

Here the political truth games practiced in the constitution of an other life and an other world are not those of recognition, demonstration, and argument-based logic, but those of a politics of experimentation that brings together rights and the formation of ethos. The opposition between Plato and the Cynics inevitably reminds us of the differences between Rancière and Foucault.

7. Logos and Existence, Theater and Performance

For Rancière, politics only exists through the constitution of a "theatrical" stage on which actors perform the conceit of political interlocution according to a double logic of discursivity and argumentation that is at once reasonable (since it postulates equality) and unreasonable (since nowhere does this equality exist).

In order for politics to exist, a stage of "speech and reason" must be constructed on which one enacts and dramatizes, in the theatrical sense of the word, the gap between the rule and the deed, between police logic and the logic of equality. This conception of politics is normative. All action in which public space is not conceived as interlocution through speech and reason is not political. The actions of Parisian suburban youth in 2005, which failed to respect this model of mobilization, are not considered political by Rancière.

> The issue is not integrating people who, for the most part, are French, but ensuring that they are treated as equals. [...] The question is whether they are counted as political subjects, endowed with a shared language. [...] It would appear that this revolt was not political, as I understand the term, it did not constitute a stage of interlocution recognizing the enemy as belonging to the same community as oneself.[24]

It is true that contemporary movements actualize the political logic Rancière describes by constructing a stage of speech and reason in order to demand equality through demonstration, argumentation, and inter-locution. But in fighting to be recognized as new political subjects, they do not make this form of action the only one that can be defined as political. Still more important, these struggles play out within a context that is no longer that of the dialectics and totalization of the demos, a demos which is at once part and totality, "nothing and everything."

On the contrary, in order to impose themselves as new political subjects, they must break through the deadlock of the politics of the "people" and the "working class" such as it exists in the political and social democracy of our societies.

Political movements play off and with these different forms of political action, but according to a logic that is not limited to the staging of "equality and its absence." Equality is the necessary but not sufficient condition of the differential process in which "rights for all" are the social bases of a subjectivation that builds "an other life" and "an other world."

The young "savages" of the French suburbs, as one socialist minister called them, resemble in certain respects the Cynic bar-barians who, instead of the orderly dialectical games of recognition and argument, preferred to leave the theatrical stage and invent a different artifice, one that had little to do with the theater.

Rather than of the stage, the Cynics make us think of contem-porary art performances, where public exposure (in the double sense of manifestation and risk of danger) is not necessarily carried out in language, in speech, nor through signifying semiotics, nor even through a dramaturgy with characters, interlocution, and dialogue.

How does the subjectivation process that opens to "an other life" and "an other world" work? Not simply through speech and reason. The Cynics are not only "speaking beings" but also bodies that say something, even if the enunciation is not initially expressed through signifying chains. Satisfying one's needs (eating, shitting) and desires (masturbating, love-making) in public, provoking, scandalizing, forcing others to think and to feel, and so on—these are all "performative" techniques that call on a multiplicity of semiotics.

The walking stick, wandering, begging, poverty, sandals, bare feet, and so forth, through which the Cynics expressed their way of life, are nonverbal forms of enunciation. Gestures, actions, example, behavior, and physical presence constitute expressive practices and semiotics addressed to others through means other than speech. In Cynic "performances" language has more than a denotative and representative function; it has an "existential function." It affirms an ethos and a politics; in Guattari's terms, it helps construct existential territories.

There are two paths to virtue in the Greek tradition: the long and easy path that passes through the "logos," in other words, through discourse and school learning; and the short but difficult one of the Cynics, which is, "in a way, silent." The short or abbreviated path, without discourse, is that of practice and experimentation.

Cynic life is public not only by virtue of language, speech, but is exposed in its "material and everyday reality." It is a "materially, physically public" life that immediately reconfigures the divisions constitutive of Greek society, the public space of the polis, on the one hand, and the private management of the household, on the other.

It is not a matter of opposing "logos" and "existence," but rather of situating oneself in the gap between them in order to question ways of life and institutions.

For the Cynics, there can be no true life except as an other life which is "at the same time, a form of existence, manifestation of self, and physical model of the truth, but also an enterprise of demonstration, conviction, and persuasion through discourse.[25]

Like most contemporary critical theorists (Virno, Butler, Agamben, Michon, Žižek), Rancière betrays a logocentric bias. Despite his criticisms of Aristotle, we are still dependent on and stuck in the theoretical framework of Greek philosophical thought: man as the only animal with language and a political animal because he possesses language. By attacking the "distribution" that the logos establishes between man and animal, the Cynics attack the foundations of Greek and Western philosophy and culture.

> [I]n ancient thought animality played the role of absolute point of differentiation for the human being. It is by distinguishing itself from animality that the human being asserted and manifested its humanity. Animality was always, more or less, a point of repulsion for the constitution of man as a rational and human being.[26]

The Cynics dramatize not only the difference between equality and inequality but also the practices of the "true life" and its institutions by exhibiting a shameless life, a scandalous life, a life that manifests itself as a "challenge and exercise in the practice of animality."

8. The Distribution of the Sensible: Or, Division and Production

Despite Rancière's opposition between the ethical and the political, political subjectivation for him still implies an ethos and truth games. It requires a mode of constitution of the subject through speech and reason which performs the truth games of "demonstration," "argumentation," and interlocution. Even in Rancière (or against Rancière), politics cannot be defined as a specific activity, because it is joined to ethics (the constitution of a subject of reason and speech) and truth (discursive practices that demonstrate and argue). It is hard to see how it could be otherwise.

But if it is impossible to make politics an autonomous mode of action, it is also impossible to separate politics from what Foucault calls the "microphysics" of power relations.

The dualisms of the "distribution of the sensible," which organize the distribution of parts (the class division between bourgeois who possess speech and proletariat who emits only noise) as well as the mode of subjectivation ("us/them"), imply micropolitical relations. Molar divisions presuppose and derive from molecular relationships.

To a certain extent, we are committed to Foucault's methodology because in modern-day capitalism it is impossible to separate, as Rancière would like, "ethics" from "economics" and "politics."

The division of society into "classes" (or parts) is produced by the assemblage of discursive practices (knowledge), techniques for governing behavior (power), and modes of subjection (the subject). But this "dualist" distribution is not only the result of the transversal action of these three apparatuses (knowledge, power, subject). The latter are themselves traversed by micro-power relations that make the distribution possible and operational. Man/woman relations, father/children relations in the family, teacher/student in the school, doctor/patient in the health system, and so on, which developed by what Guattari calls "collective facilities" of subjection, are transversal and constitutive of the division into "parts." It is impossible to understand today's capitalism without problematizing the relationship between the molar (the major dualistic oppositions—capital/labor, rich/poor, those who command and those who obey, those who have the credentials to govern and those who do not, etc.) and the microphysical (power relations based in, pass through, and are formed *within* those with no part).

But it is above all impossible without appreciating how power invests the relation to the self, care of the self, "ethics."

The examination of the Cynics' way of understanding *bios*, existence, and "militant" subjectivation can provide the weapons for resisting the powers of contemporary capitalism, which makes the production of subjectivity the primary and most important of its effects (Guattari).

Foucault tells us that *parrhēsia*, in moving from the "political" realm to individual ethics, became a technique for governing behavior, in other words, a technique of power. "By encouraging you to take care of yourselves I am useful to the whole city. And if I protect my life, it is precisely in the city's interest."[27]

The techniques of government of the self and others, integrated and reconfigured by the pastoral power of the Christian church, have become ever more important in the welfare state.

In capitalism, the "great chain of concerns and solicitudes," "the care for life," which Foucault talks about in regard to ancient Greece, has been taken in hand by the State. To take care of the self, to work on the self and on one's own life, means concerning oneself with the ways of doing and saying necessary to occupy the place allocated to us within the social division of labor. Taking care of the self is an injunction to become a subject responsible for the function to which power has assigned him.

The concepts of *bios*, existence, and life do not send us back to vitalism, but rather force us to ask ourselves how to politicize these micro-power relationships through subjectivation, through a relation to the self, that breaks with subjections.

In Rancière's definition of politics, he seems to neglect what he analyses historically among nineteenth century workers: the work on the self and the formation of an ethos.

The formation of the ethos, *bios*, the "militant" existence the Cynics practice, is not a variety of "moral discourse." It does not represent the teaching or expression of a new moral code. The formation of ethos is at once a "focal point of experience"[28] and a "matrix of experience" in which are linked "forms of a possible knowledge, normative frameworks of behavior for individuals" (power), "and potential modes of existence for possible subjects" (the relation to the self).

Conversely, politics for Rancière is not primarily an experience. The "sensible" has nothing to do with an existential focal point because politics is above all a question of form, a formalism of equality. "What makes an action political is not its object or the place where it is carried out, but solely its form, the form in which confirmation of equality is inscribed in the setting up of a dispute, of a community existing solely through being divided."[29]

The problematization of these "focal points of experience" and the experiments in political rupture and subjectivation that result run throughout Western history, finally leading to the revolutionaries of the nineteenth and early-twentieth centuries and to the artists of the same period.

9. Equality and Difference

Foucauldian subjectivation is not only an argument about equality and inequality, a demonstration of the wrong done to equality, but a genuinely immanent creation situated in the gap between equality and inequality, reorienting the question of politics by opening up an indeterminate space and time for ethical differentiation and the formation of a collective self.

If politics is indistinguishable from the formation of the "ethical" subject, then the question of organization becomes central, although in a different way than in the communist model. The reconfiguration of the sensible is a process that must be the object of "militant" work, which Guattari, expanding on Foucault's thought, defines as "analytical" political work.

For Guattari, the GIP—Groupe d'information sur les prisons founded by Foucault[30]—can be considered a collective assemblage in which the object of "militantism" becomes twofold: militantism in terms of intervention, but also militantism in terms of those who intervene. The new militantism is continuously at work, not only on utterances produced, but especially on the techniques, procedures, forms of expression of the organization, the subject of enunciation that produces utterances.

Conversely, Rancière has "no interest in the question of the forms of organization of political collectives." He does not take into consideration the "alterations produced by acts of political subjectivation." In other words, he views the act of subjectivation only in its rare irruption, a subjectivation whose duration is nearly instantaneous.

He refuses to examine "the forms of consistency of the groups that produce them,"[31] whereas May '68 puts into question precisely their rules of constitution and functioning, their form of expression and democracy, for it is precisely the political act of intervening that is inseparable from the act of constitution of the subject whose subjectivation reconfigures not only molar divisions but molecular relations as well.

If the paradoxical relations between equality and difference cannot be inscribed in a constitution, in laws, if they can be neither learned nor taught but only experimented, then the question of the modalities of acting together becomes fundamental.

What must be experimented and invented in a war machine that articulates the being-together and the being-against is what Foucault argues is the specificity of philosophical discourse, and what, since the collapse of the dialectical model of the demos, has become the condition of contemporary politics. We must never pose "the question of *ēthos* without at the same time inquiring about the truth and the form of access to the truth which will be able to form this *ēthos*, and [about] the political structures within which this *ēthos* will be able to assert its singularity and difference. [...] [N]ever pos[e] the question of *alētheia* without at the same time taking up again, with regard to this truth, the question of *politeia* and the question of *ēthos*. The same goes for *politeia*, and for *ēthos*."[32]

For Rancière, only democracy, as an apparatus of both division and community, can reconfigure the distribution of the sensible, whereas Foucault is much more reserved and less enthusiastic about this model of political action. He recognizes its limits. Political subjectivation, while dependent on equality, surpasses it. The political question is, therefore: How can we invent and practice equality under these new conditions of subjectivation?

With Guattari, we can pose the question directly by looking at our current situation. How do we invent and practice both equality and "ethical differentiation" (singularization) while breaking with the machinic enslavements and social subjections of modern-day capitalism that have a dual hold on our subjectivity?

—September 2010

Notes

Introduction: Logos or Abstract Machines?

1. The present introduction was written following the publication of my book *The Making of the Indebted Man*, trans. Joshua David Jordan (Los Angeles: Semiotext(e), 2012), in the French original *La fabrique de l'homme endetté* (Paris: Editions d'Amsterdam, 2011). The chapters that follow were written prior to its publication.

2. Félix Guattari in Jean Oury, Félix Guattari, and François Tosquelles, *Pratiques de l'institutionnel et politique* (Vigneux, France: Matrice éditions, 1985), 65.

3. Félix Guattari, *La Révolution moléculaire* (Paris: Union générale d'éditions, 1977), 95.

4. Félix Guattari, "La Crise de production de subjectivité," Seminar of April 3, 1984. http://www.revue-chimeres.fr/drupal_chimeres/files/840403.pdf.

5. Karl Marx, *Grundrisse*, in *Selected Writings*, ed. David McLellan (Oxford: Oxford University Press, 2000), 410.

6. Félix Guattari, *Pratiques de l'institutionnel et politique*, op. cit., 53.

7. Rancière's and Badiou's political theories are utterly incapable of analyzing "types of subjectivity" since for these authors there is only one subjectivation process and it is always the same, whether they are dealing with the Greek polis, the slave revolt in ancient Rome, the French, Russian, or Chinese Revolutions, or May '68.

8. Félix Guattari, "La Crise de production de subjectivité," op. cit.

9. The political theories of Rancière and Badiou are simply unable to articulate subjective and political rupture with class composition and its enslavements and subjections.

10. Gilles Deleuze and Félix Guattari, *Anti-Oedipus*, trans. Robert Hurley, Mark Seem, and Helen R. Lane (Minneapolis: University of Minnesota Press, 1983), 378.

11. See the second chapter of my book *Expérimentations politiques* (Paris: Editions Amsterdam, 2009) where the question of rupture is examined in relation to the rise of political movements.

12. Ibid., 377.

1. Production and the Production of Subjectivity

1. Gilles Deleuze, *Negotiations, 1972–1990,* trans. Martin Joughin (New York: Columbia University Press, 1995), 180.

2. The "user" is only one of the forms of implication, activation, and exploitation of subjectivity in the service-relationship maintained by business or the Welfare State. Hence the limitations of all theories that make "use" the cornerstone of politics (see, for example, the otherwise remarkable work of Michel de Certeau).

3. Michel Foucault, *Discipline and Punish,* trans. Alan Sheridan (New York: Vintage, 1995), 202. Foucault seems to forget this conception of power as a machine or diagram when he turns to his analysis of the "relation to the self," "conducts," and the "government of men," when he moves from disciplinary societies to societies of control.

4. Ibid., 205, 207.

5. "Coded personological relations, of the type nobleman-valet or master-apprentice, are replaced by the regulation of generous 'human' relations essentially founded on systems of abstract quantification of labor, wages, 'skills,' profits, etc. In the last analysis, the socius is no longer a matter of the 'person' but of decoded flows." Félix Guattari, *Lignes de fuite* (La Tour d'Aigues, France: De l'Aube, 2011), 54.

6. Maurice de Montmollin, *Les Systèmes hommes–machines* (Paris: Presses universitaires de France, 1967), 138.

7. Ibid., 54.

8. "Whereas subjection involves the overall person, easily manipulatable subjective representations, machinic enslavement joins systems of representation and meaning in which individuated subjects become recognizable to and alienated from one another." Félix Guattari, *La Révolution moléculaire* (Paris: Union générale d'éditions, 1980), 93.

9. Gilles Deleuze and Félix Guattari, *A Thousand Plateaus,* trans. Brian Massumi (Minneapolis: University of Minnesota Press, 1987), 456–457.

10. Lewis Mumford, *The Myth of the Machine: Technics and Human Development* (New York: Harcourt, Brace, and World, 1967), 196.

11. Ibid., 195, 192.

12. Ibid., 196, 197.

13. Ibid., 199.

14. Ibid., 201.

15. Gilles Deleuze and Félix Guattari, *A Thousand Plateaus,* op. cit., 458. Translation modified.

16. Obviously, the claim "we have never been modern" (Bruno Latour) is no more than a catchphrase, since the modern individuated "subject" and "man" are absolutely

indispensable to the functioning of power. The diametrically opposite position is that of John Holloway, for whom liberating man from capitalist exploitation means "to recover the subject negated by objectivity." His political program is Kantian more than revolutionary since he argues for "the assertion of ourselves as our own true sun," restoring "ourselves to the center of the universe," for "we humans create the world in which we live." Subject and object are part of the same paradigm of modernity and exploitation. John Holloway, *Crack Capitalism* (New York: Pluto Press, 2010), 235, 242, 145.

17. For Badiou and Rancière, the production of subjectivity poses no difficulty at all since, whether we are talking about Greek society, 1948, the New Deal, or today, subjectivity is always the same. Thus the complete lack of analysis of the processes of subjectivation capitalism entails, the formalism of the definitions of power relations, and the return of a politics emptied of politics.

18. "Our opposition between despotic signifying semiologies and asignifying semiologies remains very schematic. In reality, there are only mixed semiotics, which partake of both to varying degrees. Signifying semiology is always haunted by a sign machine and, conversely, a sign machine is always on the verge of being reclaimed by signifying semiology. Still, it is clearly useful to recognize the relations of polarity the two define." Félix Guattari, *La Révolution moléculaire* (Fontenay-sous-Bois, France: Recherches, 1977), 346.

19. Theories that make "language primacy" the key to how semiotics operate in our societies risk missing how capitalism actually works. Capital functions from a multiplicity of semiotics and not only signifying and linguistic semiotics, as the theories of "cognitive" or "cultural" capitalism claim.

20. Félix Guattari, *Les Années d'hiver: 1980–1985* (Paris: Les Prairies Ordinaires, 2009), 294.

21. When one is no longer able to measure labor in time, as is the case in most areas today, "automatic" and "objective" evaluators are replaced by the subjective and continuous (in schools for students and teachers, in hospitals and public health systems for services and "workers," etc.). Note, for example, the conflict that erupted in France at universities and hospitals when new methods of evaluation were introduced, methods part and parcel of neoliberal techniques of government.

22. Friedrich Nietzsche, *Twilight of the Idols*, in *The Anti-Christ, Ecce Homo, Twilight of the Idols*, trans. Judith Norman (Cambridge: Cambridge University Press, 2005), 169.

23. Gilles Deleuze and Félix Guattari, *A Thousand Plateaus*, op. cit., 492.

24. With regard to sociology's anthropomorphism, see Emile Durkheim, for whom the "vital forces of society" recall Marx's "live labor," whereas "things," among which, apart from "material objects," "must be included the products of previous social activity—the law and the customs that have been established, and literary and artistic monuments" play the role of "fixed capital." Objects and products "are the matter

to which the vital forces are applied, but they do not themselves release any vital forces. Thus the specifically human environment remains as the active factor." *The Rules of Sociological Method*, trans. W. D. Halls (New York: The Free Press, 1982), 136. In the work of his rival, Gabriel Tarde, can be found the conditions for a nonanthropocentric sociology.

25. In the industrial production of a large corporation like Fiat, the human labor force accounts for only 7.5% of general costs. Guattari points out that the impact of a completely automatized business would affect society on the whole rather than workers alone.

26. "The real control of machinic time, from the enslavement of human organs to the productive assemblages, cannot be effectively measured based on a general equivalent. We can measure a time of presence, a time of alienation, a period of incarceration in a factory or prison; we cannot measure the consequences on an individual. We can quantify the apparent labor of a physicist in a laboratory, not the productive value he creates." Félix Guattari, *La Révolution moléculaire* (Paris: Union générale d'éditions, 1977), 74.

27. "I would argue that the differential relationship between capital flows and labor flows generates a surplus value that it would be accurate to call human, since the latter is produced through human labor; the differential relationship between financing flows and revenue flows is productive of a surplus value that should specifically be called financial surplus value; and, finally, the third relationship between market flows and innovation (or knowledge) flows generates a properly machinic surplus value." Gilles Deleuze, Seminar of February 2, 1972, http://www.le-terrier.net/ deleuze/anti-oedipe1000plateaux/0722-02-72.htm. In any case, innovation/ knowledge as such never produces value. "The market flow, which includes innovation and through which innovation turns a profit, is of a completely different kind and of a completely different, non-commensurate power [...]: it is not the same form of money that pays for innovation and, furthermore, determines the profitability of innovation." Ibid. The creation of machinic surplus value does not directly depend on science and technique but rather on capital; it is added to human surplus value and with it offsets decreases in profit. "Knowledge, information, and specialized education are just as much parts of capital ('knowledge capital') as is the most elementary labor of the worker." Gilles Deleuze and Félix Guattari, *Anti-Oedipus*, trans. Robert Hurley, Mark Seem, and Helen R. Lane (Minneapolis: University of Minnesota Press, 1983), 234. The capitalist machine operates on two fronts, exercising a strong "selective pressure" on machinic innovations and introducing "not only lack amid overabundance, but stupidity in the midst of knowledge and science." Ibid., 236.

28. Whereas the theory of value in the first book of Marx's *Capital* is an additive theory (the arithmetical sum of individual labor), and whereas surplus value is still conceived as "human surplus value," in the *Grundrisse* and *Results of the Immediate Process of Production*, Marx describes machinic enslavement without, however, developing a theory of "machinic" value. Guattari points out that the Marxian

conception of human surplus value corresponds to the accounting practices of capital but certainly not to its actual functioning. Budget accounting is often brought up again today in order to justify the counter-reforms aimed at pension funds, because their financing is calculated based on individual employment and wages. Only subjection is taken into account while enslavement does not enter into it. A "cosmic swindle," Deleuze would say. It should also be added that Marx was the first to make the collective of humans and non-humans (the factory) the fundament not only of production but also of politics.

29. Gilles Deleuze and Félix Guattari, *A Thousand Plateaus*, op. cit., 458.

30. Ibid.

31. Gilles Deleuze and Félix Guattari, *A Thousand Plateaus*, op. cit., 492, 469.

32. "Consumers' participation in production is extremely heterogeneous […]. We have shown that each of these activities can be qualified as work in the economic, sociological, and ergonomical senses of the term. They produce value for the business. […] As with the salaried employee, the consumer's activity is highly prescribed and regulated. It is often performed under the constraints of time, productivity, and outcomes, using specific tools." Marie-Anne Dujarier, *Le Travail du consommateur* (Paris: Editions la Découverte, 2008), 230–231.

33. Félix Guattari, *La Révolution moléculaire* (Paris: Union générale d'éditions, 1977), 80. "It would be completely arbitrary today to consider corporate employees without considering the multiple systems of deferred wages, public assistance, and social costs affecting, however you look at it, the reproduction of the labor force, systems which bypass the monetary circuit of the business and are taken on by multiple institutions and mechanisms of power." Ibid., 81.

34. "The notions of a capitalist enterprise and a paid job have become inseparable from the entirety of the 'social fabric,' which is itself produced and reproduced under the control of capital." Ibid., 90.

35. That desire equals possibility implies a new and revolutionary definition of desire. Desire only emerges when, following the rupture of previous equilibriums, relations appear that had otherwise been impossible. Desire is always identifiable through the impossibility it opens and the new possibilities it creates. It is the fact that a *process* arises which secretes other systems of reference from a world that was once closed. To clearly register the rupture with the classical conception of desire, Guattari emphasizes its artificial "nature." Artificial, deterritorialized, and machinic desire means that it is not a "natural" or "spontaneous" force. Desire is not the equivalent of what Freud calls "drive" or of what Spinoza calls conatus (striving): "Desire is never an undifferentiated instinctual energy, but itself results from a highly developed, engineered setup rich in interactions." Gilles Deleuze and Félix Guattari, *A Thousand Plateaus*, op. cit., 215. "There are no internal drives in desire, only assemblages." Ibid. 229. Desire is not a matter of fantasy, dream, or representation, but rather of production. To desire always means to construct an assemblage; to

desire always means to act in and for a collective or multiplicity. Desire is not a matter of individuals and does not result from the simple interaction of individual drives or conatus (intersubjectivity). It does not come from within the subject, it always emanates from the outside, from an encounter, a coupling, an assemblage. The classical conception of desire is abstract, because it identifies a desiring subject and an object supposed to be desired, whereas one never desires someone or something but always a person or a thing within a whole constituted of a multiplicity of objects, relations, machines, people, signs, etc. It is the assemblage and not the individuated subject that makes someone or something desirable. One never desires only a person or a thing but also the worlds and possibilities one senses in them. To desire means to construct an assemblage that unfolds the possibilities and worlds that a thing or person contains. "We always make love with worlds." Gilles Deleuze and Félix Guattari, *Anti-Oedipus*, op. cit., 294. Desire is first of all collective though "collective" is not with the same as intersubjectivity. A collective assemblage is indeed "a basis of relations and [...] a means of assigning agents a place and a function; but these agents are not persons, any more than these relations are intersubjective." Ibid., 47. Persons and things "intervene only as points of connection, of disjunction, of conjunction of flows and elements of this multiplicity." Ibid., 349.

2. Signifying Semiologies and Asignifying Semiotics in Production and in the Production of Subjectivity

1. "We (teachers, shrinks, social workers, journalists, etc.) are workers in an ultra-modern industry, an industry that provides the subjective raw material necessary for all other industries and social activity." Félix Guattari in Jean Oury, Félix Guattari, and François Tosquelles, *Pratiques de l'institutionnel et politique* (Vigneux, France: Matrice éditions, 1985), 51.

2. Félix Guattari, *Les Années d'hiver: 1980–1985* (Paris: Les Prairies ordinaires, 2009), 128.

3. Félix Guattari, "Schizoanalyse du chaos," *Chimères* 50 (summer 2003): 23.

4. Giorgio Agamben, *The Sacrament of Language*, trans. Adam Kotsko (Stanford: Stanford University Press, 2011), 68.

5. Pascal Michon, *Rythmes, pouvoir, mondialisation* (Paris: Presses Universitaires de France, 2005), 289.

6. "It is a question of rediscovering in the laws that govern that other scene (*ein andere Schauplatz*), which Freud, on the subject of dreams, designates as being that of the unconscious, the effects that are discovered at the level of the chain of materially unstable elements that constitutes language: effects determined by the double play of combination and substitution in the signifier." Jacques Lacan, *Ecrits*, trans. Alan Sheridan (London: Routledge, 1989), 218.

7. Jacques Rancière and Davide Panagia, "Dissenting Words: A Conversation with Jacques Rancière," *Diacritics* 30:2 (2000): 117.

8. Félix Guattari, *The Machinic Unconscious*, trans. Taylor Adkins (Los Angeles: Semiotext(e), 2011), 73.

9. Pier Paolo Pasolini, *Heretical Empiricism*, trans. Ben Lawton and Louise K. Barnett (Bloomington, Indiana: Indiana University Press, 1988), 63.

10. Ibid., 198.

11. Ibid., 15.

12. Ibid., 43, 48.

13. Hannah Arendt, *The Human Condition* (Chicago: The University of Chicago Press, 1998), 231.

14. Ibid., 4.

15. Ibid., 7.

16. Félix Guattari, *Schizoanalytic Cartographies*, trans. Andrew Goffey (New York: Bloomsbury, 2013), 2.

17. Félix Guattari, *The Machinic Unconscious*, op. cit., 43, 199. Translation modified.

18. The linguistic turn in philosophy and the social sciences, which concentrate on human language (and, with Wittgenstein, the study of ordinary language, which really changes nothing), completely neglects the specifically capitalist force of asignifying semiotics, those expressed through the "languages of infrastructures" (economics, science, technique, aesthetics, etc.). The relationship between language and forms of life, between ethics and enunciation, goes completely unnoticed.

19. Félix Guattari, *Molecular Revolution*, trans. Rosemary Sheed (New York: Penguin, 1984), 164–165.

20. Emile Benveniste, "The Semiology of Language," *Semiotica* 1 (1981): 10.

21. Félix Guattari, *La Révolution moléculaire* (Fontenay-sous-Bois, France: Recherches, 1977), 305.

22. Ibid., 178.

23. Félix Guattari, *La Révolution moléculaire* (Paris: Union générale d'éditions, 1977), 304.

24. Pier Paolo Pasolini, *Heretical Empiricism*, op. cit., 38.

25. Félix Guattari, *The Machinic Unconscious*, op. cit., 65.

26. Ibid., 63. Guattari quotes Alain Rey, "Langage et temporalités," *Langages*, vol. 8, no. 32 (December 1973): 58.

27. Gilles Deleuze, Félix Guattari, *A Thousand Plateaus*, trans. Brian Massumi (Minneapolis: University of Minnesota Press, 1987), 76.

28. The subjectivity produced by consciousness "cannot be assigned purely and simply to the order of representation." Félix Guattari, *Molecular Revolution*, op. cit., 126. It manifests "man's specific capacity for deterritorialization that enables him to produce signs for no purpose: not negative signs, but signs to play about with for fun, for art." Ibid., 127. The autonomy and arbitrariness of the play of significations have "contradictory consequences: [they open] possibilities for creativity, but [...] also [produce] a subject cut off from all direct access to reality, a subject imprisoned in a signifying ghetto." Ibid., 92.

29. Félix Guattari, *The Anti-Oedipus Papers*, trans. Kélina Gotman (Los Angeles: Semiotext(e), 2006), 258.

30. Félix Guattari, *Molecular Revolution*, op. cit., 169–170. Translation modified.

31. Félix Guattari, *The Machinic Unconscious*, op. cit., 27.

32. Ibid., 67.

33. Félix Guattari, *Molecular Revolution*, op. cit., 93. Guattari quotes Benveniste's *Problèmes de linguistique générale II* (Paris: Gallimard, 1974), 68.

34. "Personological: an adjective qualifying moral relations within the subjective order. The emphasis on the role of persons, identities, and identifications characterizes the theoretical concepts of psychoanalysis. The latter's Oedipus brings persons, typified persons, into play: it reduces intensities, projects the molecular level of investments onto a 'personological theater.'" Félix Guattari, *Les Années d'hiver: 1980–1985*, op. cit., 295.

35. Félix Guattari, *Chaosmosis*, trans. Paul Bains and Julian Pefanis (Bloomington, Indiana: Indiana University Press, 1995), 98–99.

36. Félix Guattari and Suely Rolnik, *Micropolitiques* (Paris: Les Empêcheurs de penser en rond, 2007), 401.

37. Félix Guattari, *The Machinic Unconscious*, op. cit., 66.

38. Pier Paolo Pasolini, *Heretical Empiricism*, op. cit., 58n. Translation modified.

39. His engagement with Deleuze's thought begins with the concept of the "machine," which Guattari elaborated in the 1960s. Most philosophers who, like Badiou, fail to recognize Guattari's original contribution to his and Deleuze's work together miss the hugely important political shift in the concept of the machine.

40. Félix Guattari, "Balance Sheet-Program for Desiring Machines," trans. Robert Hurley, *Anti-Oedipus*, Semiotext(e), vol. 2, no. 3 (1977): 117–118.

41. Félix Guattari and Olivier Zahm, "Entretien avec Olivier Zahm," *Chimères* 23 (Summer 1994): 50.

42. Félix Guattari, *Chaosmosis*, op. cit., 39, 40. "It is said that machines do not reproduce themselves, or that they only reproduce themselves through the intermediary of

man, but 'does anyone say that the red clover has no reproductive system because the bumble bee (and the bumble bee only) must aid and abet it before it can reproduce? No one. The bumble bee is part of the reproductive system of the clover'" just as man is part of the reproductive system of the machine. Gilles Deleuze and Félix Guattari, *Anti-Oedipus*, trans. Robert Hurley, Mark Seem, and Helen R. Lane (Minneapolis: University of Minnesota Press, 1983), 284–285.

43. "We are misled *by considering any complicated machine as a single thing*; in truth it is a city or society, each member of which was bred truly after its kind. We see a machine as a whole, we call it by a name and individualize it; we look at our own limbs, and know that the combination forms an individual which springs from a single center of reproductive action." Ibid., 285.

44. Ibid., 286.

45. "Labor is not first and foremost concerned with objects, it aims at the dynamics that animate objects. Labor is a relation of forces: the action of forces meant to orient other forces. It is not directly concerned with possession but with becoming. […] In work, there is not on one side the subject and on the other the object. To work, one's senses must adapt to the play of forces animating the object. […] In work, a prereflexive relationship with objects is manifest, which 'precedes consciousness' and 'undermines a clear separation between subject and object.'" Philippe Davezies, "Entre psychique et social, quelle place pour l'activité?" *La santé mentale en actes* (Toulouse: ERES, 2005), 123.

46. Félix Guattari, *Chaosmosis*, op. cit., 36.

47. Félix Guattari, *Molecular Revolution*, op. cit., 84.

48. Ibid., 127.

49. Money obviously has other functions that become clear through the interaction with other semiotic systems: at the "symbolic" level, money functions as an imaginary subjection of the individual. His purchasing power "manipulates him not only according to codes of social status" but also according to perceptual and sexual codes. The monetary economy "interacts constantly with the signifying encodings of language, especially through legal and regulatory systems." Félix Guattari, *La Révolution moléculaire* (Fontenay-sous-Bois, France: Recherches, 1977), 295.

50. What one calls purchasing power is in fact a non-power. Only the actions of the dominated can transform these impotentized signs into signs of power by making them function in a process of subjectivation independent of the economic law of purchasing power. In the self-valorization process of the dominated, they represent nothing other than the independent self-positioning of their own production and reproduction.

51. Félix Guattari, *Schizoanalytic Cartographies*, trans. Andrew Goffey (New York: Bloomsbury, 2013), 168.

52. Félix Guattari, *Molecular Revolution*, op. cit., 76. Translation modified.

53. "On one paper surface we combine very different sources that are blended through the intermediary of a homogeneous graphical language," i.e., the diagram. Bruno Latour, *Pandora's Hope: Essays on the Reality of Science Studies* (Cambridge, Mass.: Harvard University Press, 1999), 66. Latour very hastily concludes that "we have never been modern." Such is true only in terms of machinic enslavement. As for social subjection, we have indeed been modern and even hyper-modern. Capitalist deterritorialization continually reterritorializes itself on "man" and on the "individualism" of the subject, the individual, *homo economicus*, etc., which, systematically failing, falls back on the "collectivism" of nationalism, racism, fascism, Nazism, machinism, class exploitation, etc. By neglecting the connection between enslavement and subjection, Latour takes major political risks, for he is incapable of accounting for the dramatic endpoint toward which capitalism systematically tends. To say that "we have never been modern" is the symmetrically opposite error of those who see only subjection (Rancière, Badiou).

54. The panopticon "is the diagram of a mechanism of power reduced to its ideal form [...]: it is in fact a figure of political technology that may and must be detached from any specific use." Michel Foucault, *Discipline and Punish*, trans. Alan Sheridan (New York: Vintage Books, 1995), 202, 205.

55. Ibid., 202.

56. "When you write a function 'x = function of...' it looks static, but these are signs that function in order to grasp a series of processes that are of the order of real time and movement, that try to account for it." Félix Guattari, *Chimères* 23 (Summer 1994): 43.

57. Félix Guattari, *Schizoanalytic Cartographies*, op. cit., 22. Translation modified.

58. Radio broadcasting does not furnish "the orientation, limits, and structure of the space" of enunciation but only the relations among sound intensities. The radio "uses sound fragments less as sensory qualities relating to an object than as an unlimited series of modes and passive and active forces of affect." "'Sound carries elementary forces (intensities, pitch, intervals, rhythm, and tempo) that have a more direct impact on people than the meanings of words—that is the foundation of radiophonic art.'" Serge Cardinal, "La radio, modulateur de l'audible," *Chimères* 53 (2004): 51–52. Cardinal cites Rudolf Arnheim, *Radio: An Art of Sound* (Salem, Massachusetts: Ayer Company Publishers, 1986), 28–29. Speech along with television and computers are always being "machined."

59. Greek political orators would deliver a "speech meant to last a very brief period of time, in a space never to exceed that in which the human voice could be heard," before a limited number of people "momentarily removed from all other prevailing influences," a speech written by the orator in the same spirit. "The newspaper is meant for a much larger, although dispersed, audience, made up of individuals who, while they read their article, remain subject to all kinds of distraction, hearing the buzz of conversations around them, among friends or in a café, ideas contrary to those of the author." Readers, like radio listeners, never see the writer/speaker, nor his gestures, bodily movements, or facial expressions, and, unlike the radio, they do

not hear his voice or intonation. With his speech alone the orator affects his audience. On the other hand, several articles are needed to reach the same result, since an "article is but one link in a chain of articles, coming in general from multiple writers who make up the newsroom." The newspaper cannot express a set of coherent ideas, with a harmonious display of arguments, as with the orator's rhetoric. "The newspaper topic is made up of innumerable topics that are given every morning with the events of the day or of the day before. It is as if, in the middle of one of Demosthenes' harangues against Philip, messengers approached at every instant to give him the very latest news, and as if the story and the interpretation of all this information were to form the content of his speech." Gabriel Tarde, *Les Transformations du pouvoir* (Paris: Les Empêcheurs de penser en rond, 2003), 256–258.

3. Mixed Semiotics

1. The "accident" that hit Wall Street in May 2010 (the sudden 10% drop in share prices which in just a few seconds made billions of dollars go up in smoke—in 14 seconds stocks changed hands 27,000 times) originated in computer and data communications machines. The transformation of operators from *protagonists* into *spectators* was due to the technological and structural revolution of the American stock market. The invention of ever more powerful computers has changed the way in which investors interact with the market. Today, more than 90% of orders made on the New York Stock Exchange are automated. The largest part of transactions on Wall Street are made automatically without human intervention, for the speed with which people can calculate and act is much too slow relative to the mass of information and speed with which it circulates. "Since stock market transactions have been completely taken over by computers, speculators' ultimate weapon is speed. Ultrarapid buying and selling softwares, based on ever more complex algorithms on ever more powerful computers are now critical tools. A cut-throat arms race is taking place among traders […]. The lead time (the delay between the issue of an order and its execution) is around a millisecond, and the profits subsequently made amount to billions of dollars every year. Supercomputers scan dozens of exchanges in order to detect market trends, then place orders at the speed of light, leaving the much slower traditional investor in the dust. They can also detect the ceiling price a buyer sets (the price above which he won't buy a stock). As soon as it is reached, the computers buy up all the available stocks before the real-life buyer has the time to act, selling them at a higher price, and generally at the highest price possible—that is, at one cent below the ceiling […]. In response to the demand for maximum speed, small systems for automated transactions have emerged. They operate with the help of a few dozen employees set up in inexpensive offices far from Wall Street. Certain of these systems have become formidable competition for the traditional stock market. In July 2009, the New York Stock Exchange accounted for only 28% of market transactions in the United States and the NASDAQ just 21%. Two companies that most people don't know about, the BATS Exchange in Kansas City, Missouri, and Direct Edge in Jersey City, New Jersey, are competing to become the third largest American exchange, accounting for 10% to 12% of the market depending how one measures." Yves Eudes, "Les 'Geeks' à la conquête de Wall Street" *Le Monde*, September 2, 2009.

2. Félix Guattari, "Ritornellos and Existential Affects," trans. Juliana Schiesari and Georges Van Den Abbeele, *The Guattari Reader*, ed. Gary Genosko (Cambridge: Blackwell Publishers, 1996), 158.

3. Recall, for example, the trial of Jérôme Kerviel, the Société Générale trader, who was judged the "sole" guilty party in the loss of five billion dollars.

4. Conversely, in "Can the Subaltern Speak?" Gayatri Chakravorty Spivak advocates for a return to the "theories of ideology." The essay is surprising in many respects, for it manages an incredible number of misunderstandings and misinterpretations of Deleuze/Guattari's and Foucault's work. A claim like the following, chosen at random among so many, makes one embarrassed for the person who wrote it: "In the Fou-cault-Deleuze conversation, the issue seems to be that there is no representation, no signifier (Is it to be presumed that the signifier has already been dispatched? There is, then, no sign-structure operating experience and thus might one lay semiotics to rest?)." *Colonial Discourse and Post-Colonial Theory*, eds. Patrick Williams and Laura Chrisman (New York: Columbia University Press, 1994), 74. According to the French publisher, the essay represents "a veritable publishing event." It remains a mystery that one can give rise to a debate around such a hodgepodge of "stupidity."

5. Daniel N. Stern, *The Interpersonal World of the Infant* (London: Karnac Books, 1998).

6. Ibid., p. 71.

7. Ibid., 54.

8. Ibid., 67–68.

9. "The "sense of an emergent self" is also what the philosophers of difference (Berg-son, William James, Tarde) have examined since the late nineteenth century. "Pure experience" is the name James gives to "the immediate flux of life which furnishes the material of our later reflection with its conceptual categories" and its division into subject and object, self and other, spatiotemporal figures, etc. James further remarks that it is "new born babes, or men in semi-coma from sleep, drugs, ill-nesses" that experience or offer the experience of this emergent self and its organizing processes. "A Pluralistic Universe," *Williams James: Writings 1902–1910* (New York: Library of America, 1987), 782.

10. Daniel N. Stern, op. cit., 27.

11. Ibid., 72.

12. Ibid. 128, 124.

13. Ibid. 133.

14. Félix Guattari, *Chaosmosis*, trans. Paul Bains and Julian Pefanis (Bloomington, Indiana: Indiana University Press, 1995), 67.

15. Daniel N. Stern, op. cit., 176–177.

16. Judith Butler, *Gender Trouble* (New York: Routledge, 1999), 103. Butler underscores and indeed exacerbates a major difficulty in Foucault's thought: to maintain that power apparatuses are productive, that they are constituents of subjectivity, gender, etc., means that they come first, that they are originary. If they provide us with a new conception of power as "production," in opposition to the juridical understanding of the term, they no less imprison the theory in the web of power, as Foucault himself recognized. Deleuze and Guattari offer a way out of the impasse: "Of course, an assemblage of desire will include power arrangements [...], but these must be located among the different components of the assemblage." In short, "power apparatuses do not assemble or constitute anything, but rather assemblages of desire disseminate power formations according to one of their dimensions." Gilles Deleuze, *Two Regimes of Madness*, trans. Ames Hodges and Mike Taormina (Los Angeles: Semiotext(e), 2006), 125. Translation modified.

17. Félix Guattari, *Molecular Revolution in Brazil*, trans. Karel Clapshow and Brian Holmes (Los Angeles: Semiotext(e), 2007), 316.

18. Félix Guattari, *Chaosophy*, trans. David L. Sweet, Jarred Becker, and Taylor Adkins (Los Angeles: Semiotext(e), 2009), 243.

19. Ibid., 242.

20. Félix Guattari, "Agencements. Transistances. Persistances," Seminar of December 8, 1981. http://www.revue-chimeres.fr/drupal_chimeres/files/811208.pdf.

21. Félix Guattari, *Chaosmosis*, op. cit., 263–264. Translation modified.

22. Pier Paolo Pasolini, *Hermetic Empiricism*, trans. Ben Lawton and Louise K. Barnett (Bloomington, Indiana: Indiana University Press, 1988), 169.

23. Ibid., 172.

24. Félix Guattari, *Chaosmosis*, op. cit., 266.

25. Félix Guattari, *Chaosmosis*, op. cit., 267.

26. Ibid., 265, 267.

27. Pier Paolo Pasolini, op. cit., 172.

28. Félix Guattari, *Les Années d'hiver: 1980–1985* (Paris: Les Prairies ordinaires, 2009), 129.

29. Marie-Anne Dujarier, *L'idéal du travail* (Paris: Presses Universitaires de France, 2006).

30. Ibid., 28.

31. Ibid., 50, 108.

32. Ibid., 112.

33. Ibid., 115.

34. The Althusserian interpellation constitutive of the subject who is addressed by power ("Hey, you there!") would be totally ineffectual without the work of asignifying semiotics.

35. Ibid., 27.

36. Ibid.

37. Ibid., 160.

38. Ibid., 161.

39. "There no longer exists a single official voice but multitudes of functional measurements deployed for the sake of the hierarchy, each independent of the other." Ibid., 212.

40. Ibid., 164.

41. The Greek term 'hypomnemata' might be translated simply as "reminder." We owe the term's rediscovery and use to Foucault: "*Hupomnēmata*, in the technical sense, could be account books, public registers, or individual notebooks serving as memory aids." Michel Foucault, "Self Writing," *Ethics: Subjectivity and Truth,* trans. Robert Hurley (New York: The New Press, 1997), 209. Hypomnemata are, insofar as acts of self-writing, a modality of the constitution of the self.

42. Marie-Anne Dujarier, op. cit., 166.

43. Ibid., 29.

44. "Soon the processes themselves will be the major factor in evaluating work. It may even be that, more than work, the evaluation of processes will become the priority." Ibid., 164.

45. Ibid., 6.

46. As Marx remarks, in a quote Benjamin includes in his vicious critique of social-democracy's exaltation of work, "'the man who possesses no other property than his labor power' must of necessity become 'the slave of other men who have made themselves the owners.'" Walter Benjamin, "Theses on the Philosophy of History," *Illuminations*, trans. Harry Zohn (New York: Harcourt Brace, 1968), 259.

47. Christophe Dejours, "La critique du travail entre vulnérabilité et domination," in *Travail et santé*, (Toulouse: Erès, 2010).

48. As the former president Nicolas Sarkozy put it in a speech in 2007, "I am proposing the following choice to the majority party: social policy, work, education policy, work, economic policy, work, fiscal policy, work, business policy, work, immigration policy, work, monetary policy, work, budgetary policy, work." "I am asking you to make work your policy."

49. Ibid., 172.

50. Pier Paolo Pasolini, *Hermetic Empiricism*, op. cit., 265.

51. Pier Paolo Pasolini, *Lutheran Letters*, trans. Stuart Hood (New York: Carcanet Press, 1987), 26. In the past "what those outskirts of the city said to me in their coded language was: here the poor live and the life that goes on here is poor. But the poor are workers. And workers are different from you middle-class people." In the same places today, "those outskirts will say to you in their coded language: 'There is no more popular spirit here.' The peasants and the workers are 'elsewhere,' even if materially they are still here." Ibid., 35–36.

52. Ibid., 31.

53. Ibid., 37.

54. Félix Guattari, "Ritornellos and Existential Affects," op. cit., 160.

55. Félix Guattari, "Ritournelles et affects existentiels (Discussion)," Seminar of September 15, 1987: http://www.revue-chimeres.fr/drupal_chimeres/files/870915b.pdf.

56. Pier Paolo Pasolini, *Lutheran Letters*, op. cit., 39.

57. Félix Guattari, *La Révolution moléculaire* (Paris: Union générale d'éditions, 1977), 95.

58. Félix Guattari, *La Révolution moléculaire* (Fontenay-sous-Bois, France: Recherches, 1977), 217.

59. Pier Paolo Pasolini, *Écrits corsaires*, trans. Philippe Guilhon (Paris: Flammarion, 1976), 256.

60. Ibid., 86.

61. Ibid., 82.

62. Ibid., 79.

63. Pier Paolo Pasolini, *Heretical Empiricism*, op. cit., xix.

64. Pier Paolo Pasolini, *Écrits corsaires*, op. cit., 49.

65. Ibid., 269.

66. Pier Paolo Pasolini, *Entretiens avec Jean Duflot* (Paris: Editions Gutenberg, 2007), 182.

67. Pier Paolo Pasolini, *Écrits corsaires*, op. cit., 147.

68. Ibid.,145.

69. Sergei Eisenstein wrote remarkable texts on the animism in Walt Disney's cartoons. See *Eisenstein on Disney*, ed. Jay Leyda (London: Methuen, 1988).

70. One should recall that in E. P. Thompson's *The Making of the English Working Class* these same "oral" cultures play a central role, something Marxists all too easily forget.

71. Pier Paolo Pasolini, *Écrits corsaires*, op. cit., 110.

72. In the early twentieth century, it was 60 to 65% peasantry, in 2000, only 1.8%.

73. Pier Paolo Pasolini, *Entretiens avec Jean Duflot*, op. cit., 105.

74. Ibid., 36.

75. Pier Paolo Pasolini, *Heretical Empiricism*, op. cit., 283.

76. Ibid., 279.

77. Ibid., 133.

4. Conflict and Sign Systems

1. An "intermittent du spectacle" is a worker in the arts—artists or technicians in cinema, television, theater, etc.—employed on an irregular basis. The term designates a French legal status: above a threshold of hours worked in these domains in a given year, the "intermittent" receives public benefits when he or she is not employed slightly superior to those of basic unemployment insurance. The French word "intermittent" is retained throughout to indicate this specific type of French worker. Translator's note.

2. The Coordination des Intermittents et Précaires (Association of Intermittent and Precarious Workers) was formed in 2003 in order to protect intermittent workers' right to unemployment insurance which the government's national union for employment (UNEDIC) had put under threat. The Coordination carries out actions in defense of these workers' rights and against workers' (further) precarization. See http://www.cip-idf.org/. Translator's note.

3. Michel de Certeau, *Culture in the Plural*, trans. Tom Conley (Minneapolis: University of Minnesota Press, 1997), 111.

4. Michel Foucault, *Security, Territory, Population: Lectures at the Collège de France 1977–1978*, trans. Graham Burchell (New York: Picador, 2009).

5. Starting in the 1980s, consumption, mass communications, and mass culture have been part of an integrating and co-opting process of "singularity" such that the problem is now the following: How can one integrate singularities, differences, minorities, in the standardizing and leveling system of capitalist valuation and accumulation? "Corporate leaders are trying to create conditions for at least some singularization to be possible in the vectors of production. This means that in these stratified structures an attempt is being made to create sufficient margins to allow for these processes, as long as the system capable of co-opting them remains absolute." Félix Guattari, *Molecular Revolution in Brazil*, trans. Karel Clapshow and Brian Holmes (Los Angeles: Semiotext(e), 2007), 70. We are confronted with a multiplicity of choices, options, and possibilities that account for "specific" issues in order to circumscribe, block, and reincorporate certain problematics. This is why Guattari prefers to speak of "processes of singularization" rather than "singularity": "The whole problem comes

down to the cooptation and integration of singularity whose aim is to block and neutralize processes of singularization." Félix Guattari, *Chaosmose* (Paris: Galilée, 1992), 183.

6. "Problematization […] is the totality of discursive and non-discursive practices that introduces something into the play of true and false and constitutes it as an object of thought." Michel Foucault, "The Concern for Truth," trans. Alan Sheridan, *Politics, Philosophy, Culture* (New York: Routledge, 1988), 257.

7. Michel Foucault, "What Is Enlightenment?" trans. Paul Rabinow, *The Foucault Reader* (New York: Pantheon Books, 1984), 49.

8. Gilles Deleuze, *Two Regimes of Madness*, trans. Ames Hodges and Mike Taormina (Los Angeles: Semiotext(e), 2006), 143.

9. Ibid., 15.

10. Pierre Michel Menger, *Les Intermittents du spectacle: sociologie d'une exception* (Paris: Éditions de l'EHESS, 2005).

11. Pierre Michel Menger, *Profession artiste: extension du domaine de la création* (Paris: Textuel, 2005), 45.

12. Ibid., 59.

13. In 2005, a study by the Ministry of Culture showed that half of the artists affiliated with the Maison des Artistes (an "association responsible for managing the social security regime of artists in the visual and graphic arts") declared making less than 8,290 euros annually. If we look at one of the criteria for poverty (monetary poverty) indicated by INSEE (National Institute of Statistics and Economic Studies), we see that half of these artists declare income below the poverty line. We find among the artists affiliated with the Maison des Artistes the same structure, in more acute form, that we have observed for the job market of intermittents. In line with a "widespread characteristic among arts professionals," income appears very concentrated: half of the artists share a little more than 10% of allocated revenues; conversely, 10% of artists enjoying the highest incomes share around 45% of total allocated revenues." Looking at the same study, in which the Ministry of Culture examines the changes in income of "creators" affiliated with AGESSA (the "association responsible for managing the social security regime of artists") in the three years 1993, 2000, and 2005, we see "a significant increase, in every category, in the number of artists whose incomes are below the threshold for membership." 30% of photographers, 28% of software designers, and 30% of playwrights do not meet the threshold for membership. Département des Études, de la Prospective et des Statistiques (DEPS), "Peintres, graphistes, sculpteurs… les artistes auteurs affiliés à la Maison des artistes en 2005," *Culture Chiffres, activité, emploi, travail* (2007–6), www2.culture.gouv.fr/deps. We should also note that the Maison des Artistes does not only bring together artists in the fine arts but also a whole series of new professions, which attests, in its way, to the changes in the figure of the artist and creator: painters, graphic designers, sculptors, illustrators, cartoonists, textile designers, engravers, ceramists, stained-glass artists, decorative painters, interior designers, etc.

14. Menger, who boasts of his studying the field for thirty years, nonetheless systematically and blithely confuses work and employment. Throughout his analysis and recommendations, he limits himself exclusively to employment without ever taking work into account.

15. CERC, "La sécurité de l'emploi face aux défis des transformations économiques" (Job security and the challenges of economic change) (Paris: La Documentation française, 2005), http://www.ladocumentationfrancaise.fr/var/storage/rapports-publics/054000141/0000.pdf.

16. Ibid., 38.

17. UNEDIC, the State national union for employment.

18. Michel de Certeau, *The Practice of Everyday Life*, trans. Steven Rendell (Berkeley: University of California Press, 1984), 185–186.

19. Ibid., 186.

20. "The social sciences consistently claim for themselves the unearthly power of reestablishing meaning they fearlessly assert is hidden and that it is precisely their mission to uncover. Psychologists, who are on the front lines in this, manage to silence no one: to accomplish that objective would require armies of policemen, judges, and social workers. They make do with changing the origin of speech, attributing it to irrational fears that must be explained, not in view of making a decision about those fears but of accepting them." Michel Callon, Pierre Lascumes, and Yannick Barthe, *Agir dans un monde incertain. Essai sur la démocratie technique* (Paris: Seuil, 2001), 158.

21. Gilles Deleuze, "Five Propositions on Psychoanalysis," trans. Alexander Hickox, *Desert Islands and Other Texts* (Los Angeles: Semiotext(e), 2004), 275–276. Translation modified.

22. Gilles Deleuze and Félix Guattari, *Kafka: Toward a Minor Literature* (Minneapolis: University of Minnesota Press, 1986), 83. Translation modified.

23. According to Deleuze, these apparatuses of speech production are a "strange invention" that actualizes the "cogito" in a different way every time (psychoanalysis, communications, marketing), constituting and splitting subjects, "as if in one form the doubled subject were the *cause of* the statements of which, in its other form, it itself is a part." Gilles Deleuze, Félix Guattari, *A Thousand Plateaus*, trans. Brian Massumi (Minneapolis: University of Minnesota Press, 1987), 130. The two subjects correspond to and presuppose one another. The *cogito*, or the doubling of the subject, represents the invention of a mode of signification and subjectivation that has no need for a transcendent power in order to function. One is subordinated not because one obeys an outside authority but because one obeys oneself. The power of subjection, of subordination, is thus an immanent power coming from the subject himself.

24. Reality shows use these same techniques but on another scale (in the mass auditions that take place throughout the country and in front of a public who follows

the making of "stars" as it happens). It really is a formatting of gestures, facial expressions, the voice, the way of singing, carried out by "instructors" (dance, singing, etc.) who must mold the individual's expression to the model of the "star" produced by the culture industry.

25. Gilles Deleuze, *Desert Islands and Other Texts*, trans. Michael Taormina (Los Angeles: Semiotext(e), 2004), 274.

26. Félix Guattari, *Schizoanalytic Cartographies*, trans. Andrew Goffey (New York: Bloomsbury, 2013), 43–44.

27. Michel de Certeau, *Culture in the Plural*, op. cit., 137.

28. But these dynamics are far from unilateral. "The public *is no longer there*; it is no longer circulating in these images or caught in their traps; it is elsewhere, in the background, assuming the position of an amused, interested, or bored receiver. […] For the purpose of obtaining an inkling of what the receivers of serialized messages may be, what they think, or what they desire, polls begin to multiply. Market research of this kind only yields answers by respondents who 'play' with the questions; from the polls are extracted only fragments of the theatricalization in which it is playing a role; the polls no longer affect the people who slip away and disappear into unknown realms behind the 'reactions' of a 'public' that is now and again called upon to walk onto the stage of a national commedia dell'arte." Ibid., 136–137.

29. The complicity between the social sciences and media also occurs at a less direct, less immediate, level than what we have described with regard to intermittent workers. The social sciences have invented a whole series of techniques which the media have appropriated and reconfigured. They have experimented with "methods of posing the 'right' questions allowing them to obtain the 'right' answers in opinion polls, through their phrasing of questionnaires, or in ethnographic studies of native populations. What is awe-inspiring in the social sciences is that they are sufficiently diverse and varied to be able to both stop people from speaking and make them speak." Michel Callon, Pierre Lascumes, and Yannick Barthe, *Agir dans un monde incertain. Essai sur la démocratie technique*, op. cit., 158.

30. Michel Foucault, *The Birth of Biopolitics*, trans. Graham Burchell (New York: Palgrave Macmillan, 2008), 67.

31 Ibid., 64.

32. Gilles Deleuze, "Five Propositions on Psychoanalysis," op. cit., 276.

5. "Scum" and the Critique of Performatives

1. The word "scum" translates the French *racaille*, which former French President Nicolas Sarkozy, while still interior minister, used to describe youth from impoverished Parisian suburbs during the riots that erupted there and elsewhere in France in 2005 following the death of two suburban teenagers. Recorded live, the insult was well-covered by French media and a cause of much controversy. Translator's note.

2. Paolo Virno, *Quando il verbo si fa carne: linguaggio e natura umana* (Torino: Bollati Boringhieri, 2003).

3. Christian Marazzi, *Capital and Language*, trans. Gregory Conti (Los Angeles: Semiotext(e), 2008.

4. Michael Hardt and Antonio Negri, *Multitude* (New York: The Penguin Press, 2004).

5. See J. L. Austin, *How to Do Things with Words* (Oxford: Oxford University Press, 1976).

6. François Recanati, *Meaning and Force* (New York: Cambridge University Press, 1987), 9.

7. "Thus the utterance 'I speak to you' is not a performative, although its enunciation entails that one speak." Oswald Ducrot, "De Saussure à la philosophie du langage" (introduction to the French edition of John Searle's *Speech Acts*), *Les actes de langage* (Paris: Hermann, 1972), 12.

8. Michel Foucault, *The Government of Self and Others*, trans. Graham Burchell (New York: Palgrave Macmillan, 2010), 61.

9. Ibid., 63, 62.

10. Ibid., 64–65.

11. Ibid., 68.

12. Ibid., 68.

13. "The subject of linguistics is only the material, only the means of speech communication, and not speech communication itself, not utterances in their essence and not the relationships among them (dialogic), not the forms of speech communication, and not speech genres. Linguistics studies only the relationships among elements within the language system, not the relationships among utterances and not the relations of utterances to reality and to the speaker, nor between the utterances and past and future utterances." Mikhail Bakhtin, Bakhtin, *Speech Genres and Other Late Essays*, trans. Vern W. McGee (Austin, Texas: University of Texas Press, 1986), 118.

14. Ibid., 68, 127.

15. "Instead of obliterating the possibility of response, paralyzing the addressee with fear, the threat may well be countered by a different kind of performative act [...]." Judith Butler, *Excitable Speech: A Politics of the Performative* (New York: Routledge, 1997), 12.

16. Mikhail Bakhtin, *Speech Genres and Other Late Essays*, op. cit., 76.

17. Ibid.

18. Oswald Ducrot's definition of the performative's force is in reality the force of every enunciation, every speech act, once the latter is understood as a dialogic

relation. The dialogic sphere opens the possibility for generating an event and strategy among speakers. "In this way, for the person to whom the enunciation is addressed, the field of possible actions is suddenly restructured. A new dimension emerges which brings to light a new measure of behavior. This reorganization is not an empirical fact, an accident occurring because of the utterance." Oswald Ducrot, "De Saussure à la philosophie du langage," op. cit., 22.

19. "In reality, practical intercourse is constantly generating, although slowly and in a narrow sphere. The interrelationships between speakers are always changing, even if the degree of change is hardly noticeable. In the process of this generation, the content being generated also generates. Practical interchange carries the nature of an event, and the most insignificant philological exchange participates in this incessant generation of the event." Mikhail Bakhtin, Pavel Medvedev, *The Formal Method in Literary Scholarship*, trans. Albert J. Wehrle (Cambridge: Harvard University Press, 1985), 95.

20. For there to be a power relationship (and not simply violence), it is necessary that "'the other' (the one over whom power is exercised) be thoroughly recognized and maintained to the very end as a person who acts; and that, faced with a relationship of power, a whole field of responses, reactions, results, and possible inventions may open up." Michel Foucault, "The Subject and Power," in Hubert Dreyfus and Paul Rabinow, *Beyond Structuralism and Hermeneutics* (Chicago: The University of Chicago Press, 1983), 220.

21. "This is first of all because discourse is a weapon of power, control, subjection, qualification, and disqualification. Battle discourse and not reflective discourse [...]. Discourse—the mere fact of speaking, of employing words, of using the words of others (even if it means turning them around), words that others understand and accept (and possibly turn around themselves)—this very fact is a force. Discourse is, with respect to the relation of forces, not only a surface of inscription but itself operates effects." Michel Foucault, *Dits et écrits*, vol. 3 (Paris: Gallimard, 1994), 124.

22. Bakhtin, *Speech Genres and Other Late Essays*, op. cit., 95–96. Dialogism can be understood quite well in the terms Foucault uses to describe action: "[T]he way in which a partner in a certain game acts with regard to what he thinks should be the action of the others and what he considers the others think to be his own; it is the way in which one seeks to have the advantage over others." Michel Foucault, "The Subject and Power," op. cit., 224. "Games" in Foucault are of a whole different kind than those we find in Wittgenstein.

23. V. N. Vološinov (Voloshinov), "Discourse in Life and Discourse in Art (Concerning Sociological Poetics)," trans. I. R. Titunik, *Freudianism: a Marxist Critique* (New York: Academic Press, 1976), 102, 106.

24. Ibid., 104.

25. Voloshinov quoted in Tzvetan Todorov, *Mikhail Bakhtin: The Dialogical Principle*, trans. Wlad Godzich (Minneapolis: University of Minnesota Press, 1984), 46.

26. Voloshinov, op. cit. 104.

27. Ibid.

28. Ibid., 107.

29. For Rancière the 2005 riots were not political because the "youth" failed to institute a space for interlocution.

30. "[A] certain performative force results from the rehearsal of the conventional formulae in non-conventional ways. [...] [A] formula can break with its originary context, assuming meanings and functions for which it was never intended." Judith Butler, *Excitable Speech*, op. cit., 147. Derrida identifies the "force" of the performative with a structural feature of the sign, every sign being obliged to break with the context in which it is used in order to conserve its "iterability." Here, the social conventions do not constitute the "force" of the performative, as in Austin, but rather the structural status of the sign-mark.

31. The speech act also requires a repetition but an ontological one which must be distinguished from linguistic repetition. Thus the function of repetition in Guattari's existential pragmatics.

32. Mikhail Bakhtin, *Art and Answerability*, trans. Vadim Liapunov (Austin, Texas: University of Texas Press, 1990), 308–309. See Guattari's commentary in *Chaosmosis*, trans. Paul Bains and Julian Pefanis (Bloomington, Indiana: Indiana University Press, 1995), 15–18.

33. Mikhail Bakhtin, *Art and Answerability*, op. cit.

34. Mikhail Bakhtin, *Speech Genres and Other Late Essays*, op. cit., 159.

35. Ibid., 69.

36. Ibid., 91.

37. Oswald Ducrot, "De Saussure à la philosophie du langage," 34.

38. Linguistics distinguishes between the "locutionary act," corresponding to phonetic (articulation of certain sounds according to certain rules), grammatical, and semantic activity; the "illocutionary act," defined by the "rules of discourse" (when someone asks a question, gives an order, threatens, warns, and so on, one also engages an obligation of certain discursive behavior which restructures the other's possibilities for discursive action); and the "perlocutionary act," which goes beyond discourse and is defined by the "effects" it has on the listener (it affects his feelings, thoughts, and actions). Among linguists, the last act is non-linguistic, for effects are solely the secondary, psychological, and sociological consequences supplementing the enunciation. Only Bakhtin and Guattari challenge these linguistic principles. The theorist considered the founder of semiotics follows the same path: "With Peirce, the perlocutionary effects (the fact of influencing or shaping the other's conduct), far from supplementing the act of enunciation, are an essential part of it. [...] In sum, Peirce arrives at a theory of language in

a more rigorous sense than Searle's." Christiane Chauviré, *Peirce et la signification* (Paris: Presses Universitaires de France, 1995), 148.

39. The formulation is Butler's in *Excitable Speech*, op. cit., 28.

40. Mikhail Bakhtin, *Speech Genres and Other Late Essays*, op. cit., 120.

41. Ibid. As early as 1928 Bakhtin, using the same arguments, criticized the static model of communication. "This scheme is radically incorrect. In real fact, the relationship between A and R is constantly changing and generating, and itself changes in the communicative process. And there is no ready-made communication X. It is generated in the process of intercourse between A and R. Furthermore, X is not transmitted from one to the other, but is constructed between them as a kind of ideological bridge, is built in the process of their interaction." *The Formal Method in Literary Scholarship*, op. cit., 152. Since the performative's rediscovery by critical thought, in particular in the US, a current of "performative studies" has developed which identifies performative and performance whereas their dynamics are diametrically opposed.

42. "Therefore, the single utterance, with all its individuality and creativity, can in no way be regarded as a *completely free combination* of forms of language, as is supposed, for example, by Saussure (and by many other linguists after him), who juxtaposed the utterance (*la parole*), as a purely individual act." Mikhail Bakhtin, *Speech Genres*, op. cit., 81. There is not only a combinatory of language but also one of speech genres, of ways of speaking.

43. Ibid., 77. "There are a great many everyday and special genres (i.e., military and industrial commands and orders) in which expression, as a rule, is effected by one sentence of the appropriate type. […] But for the moment we need only note that this type of sentence knits together very stably with its generic expression, and also that it absorbs individual expression especially easily. *Such sentences have contributed much to reinforcing the illusion that the sentence is by nature expressive*" (my emphasis). Ibid., 89–90. The force and expressivity of the speech act never derives from syntactic, grammatical, etc., forms, as Benveniste believes, but only from the dialogic and evaluative relationships that support them. Command or expressivity are not given via the abstract forms of language but through the "dialogic harmonics," through the voices that traverse utterances and that alone can express the "beautiful, the just, and the true."

44. Ibid., 80.

45. Ibid., 97.

46. Judith Butler, *Excitable Speech*, op. cit., 28. In these "critical" or even "revolutionary" readings of the relationship between language and power, one can still hear the "speech genres" of the priest! Radical and originary servitude to "the Law" and to "Language" [*La Langue*] (to castration, repression, to lack, in Lacan's original fully-realized version) replaces dependence on original sin. The repression of desire is the modern iteration of the old fault before the divinity. Now it is no longer humanity's sin against the

divine order, but an "individual" sin against the patriarchal order and the law of capitalism. This Hegel-Lacanian return smacks of the sacristy!

47. Jacques Lacan, *Écrits*, trans. Bruce Fink (New York: W. W. Norton, 2006), 148. Foucault always conceived power as a "relationship of power" (whether in the form of war, battle, or government) in which acting differently is always possible. A way out of power's grip is never sought in the magical Hegel-Lacanian exchange of master and slave (if servitude to power is a necessary condition for emancipation, there is no other solution but the dialectic!), but rather in the ontology of the "relation to the self."

48. Neoteny in Lacan, just as in all the other more or less reactionary social sciences, manifests an originary "lack," a constitutive absence, an "incompleteness," and man's "delay in development," which the signifier, language, and culture cover over and sublimate. Ibid., 152.

49. Mikhail Bakhtin. *The Dialogic Imagination*, trans. Caryl Emerson and Michael Holquist (Austin, Texas: University of Texas Press, 1981), 293.

50. V. N. Voloshinov, *Marxism and the Philosophy of Language*, trans. Ladislav Matejka and I. R. Titunik (New York: Seminar Press, 1973), 126.

51. Mikhail Bakhtin, Pavel Medvedev, *The Formal Method in Literary Scholarship*, op. cit., 121.

52. Ibid. "The question arises as to whether science can deal with such absolutely unrepeatable individualities as utterances, or whether they extend beyond the bounds of generalizing scientific cognition. And the answer is, of course, it *can*." Mikhail Bakhtin, *Speech Genres*, op. cit., 108.

53. "It is much easier to study the given in what is created (for example, language, ready-made and general elements of world view, reflected phenomena of reality, and so forth) than to study what is created. Frequently the whole of scientific analysis amounts to a disclosure of everything that has been given, already at hand and ready-made before the work has existed (that which is found by the artist and not created by him)." Ibid., 120.

54. Michel Foucault, *Dits et écrits*, vol. 3, op. cit., 124.

55. Mikhail Bakhtin, *Speech Genres*, op. cit., 93.

56. Ibid., 94.

6. The Discursive and the Existential in the Production of Subjectivity

1. Félix Guattari, "A propos des Machines," *Chimères* 19 (Spring 1993): 94.

2. Félix Guattari, *Soft Subversions*, trans. Chet Wiener and Emily Wittman (Los Angeles: Semiotext(e), 2009), 299. Translation modified.

3. Félix Guattari and Olivier Zahm, "Entretien avec Olivier Zahm," *Chimères* 23 (Summer 1994): 58. Nearly all of this chapter's quotations are taken from the

transcriptions of Guattari's seminars, which can be found on the *Chimères* website (http://www.revue-chimeres.fr/drupal_chimeres/?q=taxonomy_menu/3/236). These are informal discussions that the author did not plan for publication. They offer a glimpse of his thinking as it was developing.

4. Félix Guattari, "Singularité et complexité," Seminar of January 22, 1985.

5. Badiou would do well to read more attentively what Deleuze wrote with the "non-philosopher" Guattari after *Logic of Sense* and especially what Guattari wrote alone. It would prevent him from asserting falsehoods of the type: "Deleuze's formula is irrevocable: 'The event, that is to say sense.' From the beginning of his book, he fashions what to my mind is a chimerical entity, an inconsistent portmanteau-word: the 'sense-event.' Incidentally, this brings him far closer than he would have wished to the linguistic turn and the great lineage of contemporary sophistry. To argue that the event belongs to the register of sense tips it over entirely onto the side of language." Alain Badiou, *Logics of Worlds*, trans. Alberto Toscano (New York: Continuum, 2009), 386. Not only did Guattari steer Deleuze away from psychoanalysis but from structuralism as well. Foucault's last lectures equally put the lie to Badiou's criticisms, according to which Foucault is implausibly supposed to have systematized a "linguistic anthropology." Ibid., 35.

6. Félix Guattari, "La crise de production de subjectivité," Seminar of April 3, 1984.

7. Félix Guattari, "Singularité et complexité," op. cit.

8. Félix Guattari, "Machine abstraite et champ non-discursif," Seminar of March 12, 1985.

9. Félix Guattari, *Chaosmosis*, trans. Paul Bains and Julian Pefanis (Bloomington, Indiana: Indiana University Press, 1995), 127–128.

10. Félix Guattari, "Substituer l'éconciation à l'expression," Seminar of April 25, 1984.

11. Félix Guattari, Seminar of October 1, 1985.

12. Félix Guattari, "Singularité et complexité," op. cit.

13. Félix Guattari, Seminar of October 1, 1985.

14. Félix Guattari, "Singularité et complexité," op. cit. Content and sense become double: a semantic content and a pragmatic content, a semiotic sense and an existential sense.

15. Félix Guattari, Seminar of October 1, 1985.

16. "So it is that for decades, a constellation of existential ritornellos [refrains] gave access to a 'Lenin-language' engaging specific procedures which could just as well be of a rhetorical and lexical order as of a phonological, prosodic, facial, or other order. The threshold crossing—or initiation—that legitimates a relation of full existential belonging to a group-subject depends upon a certain concatenation and becoming-consistent of

these components, which are thereby ritornellized." Félix Guattari, "Ritournellos and Existential Affects," trans. Juliana Schiesari and Georges Van Den Abbeele, *The Guattari Reader*, ed. Gary Genosko (Cambridge: Blackwell Publishers, 1996), 165.

17. Félix Guattari, Seminar of October 1, 1985.

18. "The subjectivity of the collective assemblage of enunciation is characterized by a subjective transitivism: I fall and someone else cries; [...] there is no attribution of effects and affects." Félix Guattari, "Substituer l'éconciation à l'expression," op. cit.

19. Félix Guattari, *Chaosmosis*, op. cit., 92.

20. Félix Guattari, "Machine abstraite et champ non-discursif," op. cit.

21. Félix Guattari, Seminar of October 1, 1985.

22. Félix Guattari, *Chaosmosis*, op. cit., 93.

23. Félix Guattari, "Singularité et complexité," op. cit.

24. Ibid.

25. "Freud refers to various ancient myths in these connexions, and claims that his researches have now explained how it came about that anybody should think or propound a myth of that sort. Whereas in fact Freud has done something different. He has not given a scientific explanation of the ancient myth. What he has done is to propound a new myth." Ludwig Wittgenstein, *Lectures and Conversations on Aesthetics, Psychology, and Religious Belief*, ed. Cyril Barrett (Berkeley: University of California Press, 1967), 51.

26. Félix Guattari, *Chaosmosis*, op. cit., 65.

27. Félix Guattari, "Machine abstraite et champ non-discursif," op. cit.

28. Félix Guattari, "L'acte et la singularité," Seminar of April 28, 1981.

29. "Things happen outside of representations, things that aren't the product of chance but rather are highly differentiated, involving the entire economy of subsequent choices. And the first of these things [...] is the fact of acting itself. Indeed, you have the refrain of representation, 'All right, I'm going to go now.'" And then, a moment later, you're leaving but you have no representation whatsoever [...]. The 'I'm going' somewhere got disconnected from the system of representation. And yet, it has to do with representation; these aren't the reflexes of a decerebrated frog. [...] Between representation and the act, a whole range of relationships are possible!" Ibid.

30. When "It's working" during a revolution, a struggle, a social change, etc., one is not primarily dealing with "consciousness raising" but with an assemblage of discursive and non-discursive elements which function and circulate in a diagrammatic register; one is dealing with a revolutionary "war machine."

31. Félix Guattari, Seminar of October 1, 1985.

32. Félix Guattari, "L'acte et la singularité," Seminar of April 28, 1981.

33. Félix Guattari, "Crise de production de subjectivité," Seminar of April 3, 1984.

34. Félix Guattari, "Machine abstraite et champ non-discursif," op. cit.

35. "Another category must be thought up, because there is no link, because there is no discursivity, because existential territories are blocked in a non-discursive agglomeration, a non-discursive constellation." Ibid.

36. Félix Guattari, "Crise de production de subjectivité," op. cit.

37. Ibid.

38. Félix Guattari, "Ritournelles et affects existentiels (Discussion)," Seminar of September 15, 1987.

39. Ibid.

40. This relationship between the discursive and the non-discursive is always contradictory and "inevitably contradictory. You cannot seek the ethico-aesthetic completion of an affect. In saying this, I think of Deligny: we can see that his idea of completion is, I mean, at bottom, for him, at the level of the smallest gesture; there is no room for words. At the same time, Deligny has a kind of enunciative elegance, a written elegance. The ethical dimension is obvious too. Of course, Deligny still developed formidable myths. His whole life, he wrote novels, even a kind of mythology, at a certain point, of the unrepentant delinquent, at another point, of the autistic child, because there was no other way." Ibid.

41. The politics of the event they propose is a weak and stunted one since, in reality, there is not one articulation between the existential and the discursive to examine, but three: before, during, and after the event of a struggle, a change, a revolution. The relationship between subjectivation and economic, social, institutional, and linguistic flows must be posed in a radically different way before, during, and after political rupture. This I attempted to show in my book *Expérimentations politiques* (Paris: Editions Amsterdam, 2009).

42. Enzo Rullani, "La produzione di valore a mezzo di conoscenza. Il manuale che non c'é," *Sociologia del lavoro* 115 (2009). One only has to think of the "cognitive experience" of the soccer fan mentioned in Rullani's text to see that the experience he has in mind has little to do with the cognitive.

43. Gilles Deleuze and Félix Guattari, *Anti-Oedipus*, trans. Robert Hurley, Mark Seem, and Helen R. Lane (Minneapolis: University of Minnesota Press, 1983), 235–236.

44. "Here Andre Gorz's double portrait of the 'scientific and technical worker' takes on its full meaning. Although he has mastered a flow of knowledge, information, and training, he is so absorbed in capital that the reflux of organized, axiomatized stupidity coincides with him, so that, when he goes home in the evening, he rediscovers his little desiring-machines by tinkering with a television set—O despair. Of course the scientist as such has no revolutionary potential; he is the first integrated agent of integration, a refuge for bad conscience, and the forced destroyer of his own creativity." Ibid., 236.

45. Cited by Guattari in *Schizoanalytic Cartographies*, op. cit., 274n. Mikhail Bakhtin, "The Problem of Content, Material, and Form in Verbal Art," *Art and Answerability*, op. cit., 278.

46. Félix Guattari, "La crise de production de subjectivité," op. cit.

7. Enunciation and Politics

1. Jacques Rancière, interview with Eric Alliez, "Biopolitics or Politics?" *Dissensus*, trans. Steven Corcoran (New York: Continuum, 2010), 93.

2. Michel Foucault, *Ethics*, trans. Robert Hurley (New York: The New Press, 1997), 81.

3. Michel Foucault, *The Courage of the Truth*, trans. Graham Burchell (New York: Palgrave Macmillan, 2011), 9.

4. Michel Foucault, *The Government of Self and Others*, trans. Graham Burchell (New York: Palgrave Macmillan, 2010), 156.

5. Ibid., 184.

6. Jacques Rancière, *On the Shores of Politics*, trans. Liz Heron (New York: Verso, 1995), 65. "The egalitarian logic implied by the act of speaking and the inegalitarian logic inherent in the social bond," ibid., 81

7. The English-language translator of Rancière's *The Politics of Aesthetics* defines "Police or Police Order" as follows: "As the general law that determines the distribution or parts and roles in a community as well as its forms of exclusion, the police is first and foremost an organization of 'bodies' based on a communal distribution of the sensible." Trans. Gabriel Rockhill (New York: Continuum, 2004), 89. Translator's note.

8. Jacques Rancière, *Disagreement*, trans. Julie Rose (Minneapolis: University of Minnesota Press, 1999), 51.

9. Ibid., 50.

10. Ibid., 56.

11. Michel Foucault, *The Government of Self and Others*, op. cit., 62, 63.

12. Ibid., 68.

13. Michel Foucault, *The Courage of Truth*, op. cit., 13.

14. Ibid., 11.

15. William James, *The Will to Believe*, in *William James: Writings 1878–1899*, ed. Gerald E. Myers (New York: Library of America, 1992), 458.

16. Michel Foucault, *The Courage of the Truth*, op. cit., 46.

17. Ibid., 225.

18. Ibid., 287.

19. Ibid., 283, 340n.

20. Jacques Rancière, *Disagreement*, op. cit., 116.

21. Jacques Rancière, *Hatred of Democracy*, trans. Steve Corcoran (New York: Verso, 2009), 82–83. I bought this book the day it came out (September 2005) while returning from an action organized by the Coordination des Intermittents et Précaires (Association of Intermittent and Precaious Workers; see Chapter 4). We had first stormed then occupied the room in which one of the Ministry of Culture's meetings on co-determination was taking place. The latter included government representatives, unions, and management, who refused the status of political subjects to everyone except themselves. Looking over the book that evening, I was surprised to read the passage cited here. Just because neoliberals attack the welfare state does not mean that we should restrict ourselves to a defensive position and silence critiques that came out of the political movements of the 1970s (the production of dependence on the State and the exercise of power over the body, etc.) or the critiques political movements continue to put forward (the production of inequalities, social and political exclusion, control over individuals' lives, etc.).

22. Jacques Rancière, *Disagreement*, op. cit., 9.

23. Michel Foucault, *The Courage of the Truth*, op. cit., 339.

24. Jacques Rancière, "Le Scandale démocratique," interview with Jean-Baptiste Marongiu, *Libération* (December 15, 2005).

25. Michel Foucault, *The Courage of the Truth*, op. cit., 314.

26. Ibid., 264.

27. Ibid., 90.

28. Michel Foucault, *The Government of Self and Others*, op. cit., 3.

29. Jacques Rancière, *Disagreement*, op. cit., 32.

30. The Groupe d'information sur les prisons was formed in 1971 upon the release of its manifesto signed by Foucault, Jean-Marie Domenach, and Pierre Vidal-Naquet. As the name indicates, the group sought to bring to light "one of the hidden regions of our social system," in particular, the conditions of prisoners who until then had little or no contact with the exterior during their incarceration. Translator's note.

31. Jacques Rancière, "La méthode de l'égalité," in *La philosophie déplacée: Autour de Jacques Rancière*, eds. Laurence Cornu and Patrice Vermeren (Lyon: Horlieu Editions, 2006), 514.

32. Michel Foucault, *The Courage of the Truth*, op. cit., 67.